EUGENE O'NEILL'S CENTURY

EUGENE O'NEILL'S CENTURY

Centennial Views on America's Foremost Tragic Dramatist

Edited by
Richard F. Moorton, Jr.

Contributions in Drama and Theatre Studies, Number 36

GREENWOOD PRESS
New York • Westport, Connecticut • London

Library of Congress Cataloging-in-Publication Data

Eugene O'Neill's century : centennial views on America's foremost
   tragic dramatist / edited by Richard F. Moorton, Jr.
      p. cm. — (Contributions in drama and theatre studies, ISSN
  0163-3821 ; no. 36)
   Includes bibliographical references (p.) and index.
   ISBN 0-313-26826-6 (alk. paper)
   1. O'Neill, Eugene, 1888-1953 — Criticism and interpretation.
  2. Tragedy. I. Moorton, Richard F. II. Series.
  PS3529.N5Z6377   1991
  812'.52 — dc20   90-47536

British Library Cataloguing in Publication Data is available.

Library of Congress Catalog Card Number: 90-47536
ISBN: 0-313-26826-6
ISSN: 0163-3821

First published in 1991

Greenwood Press, 88 Post Road West, Westport, CT 06881
An imprint of Greenwood Publishing Group, Inc.

Printed in the United States of America

This book is dedicated to
the Connecticut Humanities Council,
without which it would never have come to be.

Contents

Preface

Eugene O'Neill was born on October 16, 1888. His career as the virtual founder and the predominant playwright of the American theater, with an international stature reflected by his reception of the Nobel prize for literature in 1936, made the recent centennial of his birth an illustrious occasion not simply in America but all around the world. As the most far-sighted of the celebrants began to cast their centennial plans in the early 1980s, Linda Herr, professor and chair of the Theater Department at Connecticut College, and George C. White, president of the O'Neill Theatre Center, pledged their two institutions to the organization of a collaborative O'Neill centennial festival, Collaborations III, in New London, Connecticut, the young O'Neill's summer home, so that the international O'Neill centennial conferences at Stockholm, Sweden, and Nanjing, China, might be complemented by a yearlong festival of performance and scholarship commemorating New London's gifted son on the playwright's native ground. In that resolve this book was born.

This collection of essays is made up of papers presented in the Collaborations III O'Neill lecture series.[1] What sets this volume apart from other anthologies of O'Neill scholarship is the range of professional interests of its contributors. The great majority of those who write on O'Neill for the journals and critical collections are professors of English or American literature or theater. Although this book includes such contributors, it also provides a forum for authors from other fields who, though often well-established scholars, come to O'Neill with fresh perspectives inspired by their expertise in their diverse disciplines. Hence this book includes essays by two English professors, Burton L. Cooper and Richard B. Sewall; three professors of theater arts, Spencer Golub, Linda Herr, and Lowell Swortzell; two professors of psychology, Roger Brown and Jane Torrey; a German scholar, Rita Terras; two classicists, Richard F. Moorton, Jr., and S. Georgia Nugent; and a professor of philosophy, Kristin Pfefferkorn. Moreover, this collection offers the critical insights of an author who approaches O'Neill less as a literary critic than as a theater professional, Jeffrey Elliott Sands, an arts administrator at the Krannert Center for the Performing Arts at the University of Illinois in Urbana-Champaign. The result is a spectrum of critical views unusual for its variety and breadth of O'Neill scholarship.

The essays in this book are organized into an introduction and three sections devoted respectively to the nature of O'Neill's dramaturgy, the cultural and autobiographical sources for his art, and the challenges of bringing that art to the stage. The introduction briefly considers the critical problems in O'Neill criticism most relevant to this volume. The first section, "O'Neill's Tragic Art," begins appropriately with what was in fact the keynote lecture in the Collaborations III O'Neill Lecture Series, Richard Sewall's "Eugene O'Neill and the Sense of the Tragic." Sewall is the author of one of the best known studies of *Long Day's Journey into Night*—published originally as the last chapter in the revised edition of his distinguished book *A Vision of Tragedy*—in which he showed that the play presents a spectacle of a tragic family heroic not for the tragic stature of its members but because through their endurance in suffering they win through to a vision, partial and perhaps fleeting, of the positive values in life that justify undergoing the ordeal that life can all too easily become.[2] In the new essay included in this volume Sewall enriches this theme with a wealth of fresh insights on the play. His thesis is that in *Long Day's Journey* O'Neill was inspired by a non-Aristotelian conception of the task of the writer derived from another sailor-turned-writer, Joseph Conrad. In the preface to the American edition of *The Nigger of the "Narcissus,"* Conrad, unlike Aristotle, professed the object of literature to be the whole human being, and in the best traditions of humanistic scholarship Sewall shows how well Conrad's view of the writer as witness is reflected in the pages of O'Neill's masterful family tragedy, which Sewall argues is developed in a way akin to opera.

The following chapter, "O'Neill and the Poetics of Modernist Strangeness," by Spencer Golub, also considers the theory of art exemplified by *Long Day's Journey* but with assumptions and results very different from those of Sewall. Employing both semiotics and the idea of the Russian formalists that writers subject their material to a process of defamiliarization through the manipulation of the conventions and devices of genre, Golub analyzes the aesthetic achievement of *Long Day's Journey*. In this study Golub does not deny the autobiographical elements in the play but endeavors to show how the artist O'Neill transformed them into a complex and ironic modernist vision of supposedly mundane reality that becomes more and more alien the more closely it is examined.

The next two chapters explore what may be called the psychological properties of O'Neill's texts. In "Causality in O'Neill's Late Masterpieces," Roger Brown analyzes the characters in *A Moon for the Misbegotten, Long Day's Journey into Night,* and *The Iceman Cometh* in the light of the attribution theory of human psychology as "depressive" or "pessimistic" personalities who consider all their misfortunes to be caused by their own inescapable shortcomings, an attributional style that, in Brown's view, they share with their author. S. Georgia Nugent provides a feminist interpretation of O'Neill in the next chapter, "Masking Becomes Electra: O'Neill, Freud, and the Feminine." Explicitly declining what she terms the all-too-tempting opportunity to analyze *Mourning Becomes Electra* as veiled autobiography, Nugent elects instead to "psychoanalyze" the text in its various stages of development. Drawing on both Freudian theory and the theory of semiotics, she argues that the apparent theme of the trilogy, the Oedipal preoccupations of the Mannon family, serves in fact as a mask for the reluctance of the characters (and the author) to confront nonpathological heterosexual impulses in women.

The section on O'Neill's dramaturgy then concludes with chapters exploring the successes and failures with which O'Neill's work has been translated into another genre, film, and other linguistic media, the languages of Europe. In his chapter "Some Problems in Adapting O'Neill for Film," Burton L. Cooper shows that an excessive reverence for O'Neill and a failure to grasp the divergent artistic possibilities of the stage and the cinema have led moviemakers and television producers to produce film adaptations of O'Neill that almost inevitably disappoint. Finally, in her chapter "A Spokesman for America: O'Neill in Translation," Rita Terras (a skilled translator in her own right) examines the ways in which O'Neill has served as a representative of American culture to the world through the many translations of his work and the strategies through which translators have or have not solved the challenges of translating his plays.

The second part of this book, "Art and Life: The Wellsprings of Genius," studies in the influences that helped to shape O'Neill's work, begins with a chapter by Richard F. Moorton, Jr., "Eugene O'Neill's American *Eumenides*," which traces an ancient artistic debt of O'Neill by arguing in opposition to the scholarly consensus that the third part of *Mourning Becomes Electra, The Haunted,* is modeled closely on the third play in Aeschylus's *Oresteia, The Eumenides,* and that scholars have failed to notice the close parallelism between the plays because of changes in the plot O'Neill made in response to cultural divergences between ancient Greece and America. The contribution of the American spirit to O'Neill's tragedy is examined more philosophically in the next chapter, Kristin Pfefferkorn's "Searching for Home in O'Neill's America," which explores both the concept of "home" in American culture and the fruitless quests of O'Neill and Mary Tyrone for home and the belonging it implies.

The next three chapters in this section focus more closely on the generally acknowledged influence of O'Neill's personal life on his dramatic art. In "'Get My Goat': O'Neill's Attitude toward Children and Adolescents in His Life and Art," Lowell Swortzell shows how O'Neill's own atypical and troubled boyhood and his consequent bafflement with the young, including his own children, are reflected in the generally (if not inevitably, nor ultimately) unsympathetic and unrealistic representation of children in his plays. Jane Torrey's essay, "O'Neill's Psychology of Oppression in Men and Women," demonstrates that although O'Neill could portray a considerable variety of oppressed *men* both sympathetically and realistically, his more narrowly drawn female characters are projections of his own stereotypes and needs rather than distillations of his experience with real women. The autobiographical interpretation of O'Neill is even more radically applied in this section's concluding chapter, "The Author as Oedipus in *Mourning Becomes Electra* and *Long Day's Journey into Night.*" In this chapter, Richard F. Moorton, Jr., undertakes the program that Georgia Nugent in "Masking Becomes Electra" rejects, the analysis of *Mourning Becomes Electra* as veiled autobiography, a study whose conclusion—that in his trilogy O'Neill has encoded the Oedipal tensions present in his own family—is then used in an Oedipal interpretation of *Long Day's Journey.*

Jeffrey Elliott Sands begins the third part, "O'Neill Onstage," with a ground-breaking treatment of an important and strangely neglected topic in his chapter "O'Neill's Stage Directions and the Actor." He argues that O'Neill's extensive stage directions were intended to ensure that his dramatic conceptions should dominate the interpretative impulses of directors and actors staging his plays and thus be realized in the performance itself. In the next and concluding chapter, "Theater and the Critics," Linda Herr explores in the context of O'Neill's dramaturgy the contributions that scholars and theater practitioners are able to make to one another's ultimately kindred pursuits.

It is not customary to dedicate a collection, but with the consent of the contributors I have in this case made an exception by beginning this volume with a dedication to the Connecticut Humanities Council, which funded the Collaborations III lecture series with a generous grant, though the opinions expressed in this volume do not necessarily represent the views of the council. A particular vote of thanks is due to Bruce Fraser, the director of the council, and Jane Christie Smith, the associate director, for their unfailing professional counsel and support. I would also like to thank Marilyn Brownstein, the senior humanities editor of the Greenwood Press, for her expertise and understanding. The contributors to this volume have my gratitude for their chapters and their cooperation in the editorial process: I have learned much from them in my own work on O'Neill.

The O'Neill lecture series could never have flourished as it has without the support of Oakes Ames, the former president of Connecticut College; Claire Gaudiani, the current president of the college; and Jane Bredeson, the secretary of the college. Dorothy James, the provost and dean of the faculty at Connecticut College, most generously made a Faculty Development Grant to help defray the expense of publication.

Collaborations III was the brainchild of Linda Herr and George C. White. For its smooth operation we are all indebted to the skill and indefatigability of the project administrator, Peggy Middleton. Other members of the administrative team include our publicists, Julie Quinn, the director of college relations at Connecticut College, and Steven Tunnell, arts intern. Those who helped to organize the lecture series and evaluate abstracts include my colleagues Michael Burlingame, Robley Evans, Camille Hanlon (who also helped, most graciously, in countless other ways), Nelly Murstein, Lester Reiss, Janis Solomon, Gerda Taranow, Rita Terras, and Jane Torrey. Dirk tom Dieck Held, my chairman in classics, cheerfully subsidized the photocopying expenses for the project through the departmental budget for years. My other departmental colleague, Joann Silverberg, provided sensitive readings of two of my essays, which appear in this volume, and much-appreciated moral support. I am also grateful to Professor Jordon Pecile of the United States Coast Guard Academy for his invaluable advice in the writing of the grant proposal and his generous help with the countless other tasks that the centennial festival entailed. Sally Pavetti and Lois McDonald, the curator and associate curator, respectively, of the Monte Cristo Cottage, also provided technical advice, facilities for lectures, and sympathetic support for our undertaking. Rae Frechette helped to manage the logistics of the lecture series, and Audrey Goldstein typed some of the manuscripts in this collection. Brian Rogers, the head librarian at Connecticut College, volunteered to edit the proofs for this book, a chore that he performed with great discernment and knowledge. Kristin Pfefferkorn also shared in this task, to which she brought so much unstinting goodwill and editorial and scholarly expertise as to function, at times, as a collaborating editor. Also assisting with professional legerdemain in the copyediting of the proofs for this book was my wife, Jeanne Moorton, who lightened the labor in many other ways. James MacDonald, the head reference librarian at Connecticut College, helped me with many bibliographical problems. I also owe thanks to Charles Luce, Jr., the associate director of college relations, and Gregg TeHennepe and Reed Berkowitz, computer technicians at Connecticut College, for their assistance in transferring electronically stored manuscripts onto disks compatible with my word processing equipment. Carmelina Kanzler, the mayor of New London during O'Neill's centennial, provided official support and recognition to Collaborations III. Our centennial festival owes a special debt to the encouragement, counsel, and other services of the eminent O'Neill biographers Barbara Gelb and Louis Sheaffer. Finally, I would like to thank Lowell Swortzell for his help in securing the publication of this collection and Mary Posner both for introducing us and for many other helpful suggestions.

It is the hope of all who helped to bring this book into being that the reader will find it an interesting and useful addition to our understanding of Eugene O'Neill.

NOTES

1. The one exception is the concluding essay, "Theater and the Critics," by Professor Linda Herr, the director of Collaborations III, who offers this postcentennial view of the subtle kinship between scholars and people of the theater as a fitting conclusion to a centennial year in which both practiced their arts in a common cause, honoring Eugene O'Neill.

2. Richard B. Sewall, *"Long Day's Journey into Night,"* in *A Vision of Tragedy,* new ed., enlarged (New Haven: Yale University Press, 1980), 161–74.

Introduction

Eugene O'Neill is one of those uncommon artists whose centennials have been thought worthy of worldwide celebration. The sheer impact of O'Neill on world culture is a measure of his importance as America's foremost playwright, an importance that American critics recognize. But there is often in their acknowledgment qualification, embarrassment, and even pain. Thus while admitting that O'Neill is the principal American author for the stage, and a dramatist of genius, Harold Bloom in his introduction to an important anthology of O'Neill scholarship returned again and again to O'Neill's alleged poverty of ideas, lack of tragic dignity, and "sheer bad writing."[1] Yet it is clear from the outpouring of acclaim accorded to him around the world in his Centennial year that O'Neill has triumphed over whatever defects his dramaturgy embodies and the damnation of faint praise they have called forth in some of his readers. It is only natural to ask how.

O'Neill's success was rooted in his professional singleness of purpose. The man lived for his art. Thus his erotic life was relatively uneventful. He was married three times, but the first marriage, to Kathleen Jenkins, was brief, and he left his second marriage, to Agnes Boulton, for the woman who would become his third wife, Carlotta Monterey, because Carlotta nurtured his creative life more single-mindedly than Agnes had. Louis Sheaffer has told us that before Carlotta he was faithful to Agnes less because of conviction than because the turbulence of adultery would have interfered with his career.[2] When the time came to choose between his alcoholism and his writing, he abandoned the bottle and surrendered himself entirely to his work. Because his art was his life, O'Neill was fiercely protective of his artistic integrity. He did not approve of the world of Hollywood and resisted the temptation to write for film.[3] He closely supervised productions of his plays and took a personal hand in picking their directors and actors. None of this would matter if the result had not been a memorable body of plays, but O'Neill's meticulousness and tenacity were rewarded with a growing artistic skill, which ended in mastery.

The driving force behind O'Neill's sense of purpose was his emotional intensity. Eugene O'Neill is one of the most supercharged of twentieth-century authors. The quality is visible in his earliest plays, though in some of the works of his apprenticeship—pieces such as *A Wife for a Life, Thirst,* and the inadvertently funny *Before Breakfast,* composed years before he mastered his medium—O'Neill's passion appears as no more than a gauche earnestness. It is more than this in successes of his middle period like *The Emperor Jones* and *Desire Under the Elms,* and even his failed experiments, works like *Lazarus Laughed* and *The Great God Brown* that dare greatly and, in their artistic boldness and sheer magnitude, create a deeper and more lasting impression than most small successes of the theater. With his late masterpieces O'Neill finally achieved the fusion of the intensity of vision and the mastery of form that entitles him to be counted among the world's genuinely great playwrights. This is why the world esteems him more than any other American dramatist.

In some ways O'Neill's success was a triumph of will. As he well knew, he did not have the great poetic gifts of, say, Aeschylus or Marlowe. His greatest assets were an implacable tenacity and an almost unparalleled grounding in the theater, his patrimony as an actor's son who grew up in the wings. O'Neill's greatest work came late, as the fruit of a lifetime of burning away the dross in his gift. Superb language was not part of his endowment, but through sheer force of character he made it his own.

This is not a judgment that every critic would accept. That O'Neill ended as an important dramatist is universally conceded, but many would deny that he ever overcame the deficiencies in language so evident in the early and middle plays. In fact, it sometimes seems as if there are two O'Neills: the literary O'Neill, a perpetual embarrassment to literary critics who must explain how such an allegedly clumsy wordsmith could nonetheless be a world-class author; and the theatrical O'Neill, acclaimed by fellow professionals as the creator of the American theater—a seminal influence on others and in his great plays a genius of the stage. To this day many American drama critics rate O'Neill as incontestably the best playwright among his countrymen.[4] Literary scholars often take a different view of O'Neill's accomplishments in the realm of words. George Steiner's harsh judgment is one with which many other literary critics would agree:

Language seeks vengeance on those who cripple it. A striking example occurs in O'Neill, a dramatist committed, in a somber and rather moving way, to the practice of bad writing. Interspersed in the sodden morass of *A Long Day's Journey into Night,* there are passages from Swinburne. The lines are flamboyant, romantic verbiage. They are meant to show up the adolescent inadequacies of those who recite them. But, in fact, when the play is performed, the contrary occurs. The energy and glitter of Swinburne's language burn a hole in the surrounding fabric. They elevate the action above its paltry level and instead of showing up the character show up the playwright. Modern authors rarely quote their betters with impunity.[5]

The "sodden morass" derided here is widely considered to be the greatest play ever written by an American. Nonetheless, Steiner criticized *Long Day's Journey into Night* as an example of the paucity of modern literary language. Without doubt he gets some things right. O'Neill is not here writing grand dramatic dialogue. He had recognized years before that he could not compete rhetorically with the great Greek and Elizabethan dramatists. What he gives us in *Long Day's Journey* is not for the most part magnificent recitative that draws attention to itself, but the transparent language of conversation. This is the way Americans talk. But it is wrong to conclude that this dramatic language is not artful.[6] In a way that is only beginning to be understood, O'Neill's unobtrusive dialogue complexly and richly contrives the drama's mounting tension and in so doing prepares the way for the devastating epiphany that concludes the play.[7]

In this quietly lethal weave of conversations O'Neill strategically inserts literary quotes—not just from Swinburne but also from Wilde, Shakespeare, Rossetti, and others—that interact with their contexts in complex and powerful ways.[8] A series of telling examples occurs in the fourth act. To the discomfort of his father, Edmund recites two poems about decadent hedonism, Symons's translation of Baudelaire's "Epilogue" and Dowson's "Cynara" (133–34), which the mischievous son specifically applies to Jamie.[9] Edmund's recitation of poems glamorizing prostitution is an ironic anticipation, in part conscious, of the coarse lover that Jamie has found this night, Fat Vi. Thus Edmund describes Jamie's predilection for sleazy love with a "fat tart—he likes them fat"—to whom Jamie is pictured as reciting Dowson's poem about a man who makes love to a prostitute though he loves another, with its melancholy refrain: "I have been faithful to thee, Cynara! in my fashion." Edmund sneers at the idea of Jamie's being faithful to anyone, but in fact his elder brother is indeed, in Dowson's words, "desolate and sick of an old passion," his impossible love for his own mother.[10] He honors this love by denying himself the love of any other woman except for transient affairs and the prostitutes he so tellingly mocks. Edmund's two quotations thus intricately interact with each other and their dramatic context. Moreover, they thematically anticipate Jamie's own literary performances in a complexly detailed way.

Soon after a very drunk Jamie, still reeking of the whorehouse from which he has just come, quotes to his drunken brother Edmund (but not his father, who has left in disgust) lines from Oscar Wilde's "The Harlot's House" (159):

> Then, turning to my love, I said,
> "The dead are dancing with the dead,
> The dust is whirling with the dust."
>
> But she—she heard the violin,
> And left my side and entered in:
> Love passed into the house of lust.

> Then suddenly the tune went false,
> The dancers wearied of the waltz.

By quoting these lines Jamie wittingly (for "he was never stupid" [p. 87]) implies that he himself, a recent and regular customer of brothels, is one of the living dead, the dust that dances, in the house of the harlot described by Wilde's persona.[11] This is both sadly descriptive of the morbidity that already possesses Jamie's spirit and hair-raisingly prophetic, since Jamie was to die of his carousing, a fate foreshadowed in the pages of the play. For Jamie, who was incapable of a mature relationship with a woman and took his pleasure with prostitutes, love had indeed passed into the house of lust.

As Jamie breaks off the quote, he tells the story of his visit to the brothel in what is a tragicomic parody of Wilde's poem. In this New London house of lust Jamie, the reveling narrator—a caricature of Wilde's narrating persona—sees his own "comic" love, Fat Violet.[12] O'Neill's inspired choice of names for the whore implies the same coarsening of the delicate and beautiful in a house of prostitution, which Wilde dramatizes in the poem. Fat Vi, it seems, is in danger of losing her job. She is too corpulent to attract customers and her alcoholism has made her incapable of continuing to earn her keep by playing the bordello's piano, an obvious analogue of the violin in Wilde's house of the harlot.[13] In Jamie's "comic" world, as in the poem, the music and the merriment falter: "Then suddenly the tune went false / The dancers wearied of the waltz." Yet the love that has passed into the house of lust still exists there, for Jamie, out of compassion masquerading as a perverse sense of humor, pays his two dollars, goes upstairs with Fat Violet, and actually makes love to her when he sees that she will be hurt if he doesn't. It is clear that O'Neill weds the solemn lyricism of Wilde with Jamie's burlesque in a whole that is greater than the sum of its parts.

For another example of the ability of O'Neill's dialogue to stand up to his poetic quotations, consider this. Nearly everyone who has read or seen the play remembers the shattering monologue with which Mary concludes its harrowing journey. But how many of these people also recall that Jamie has just been bitterly reciting the verses from Swinburne (173–74) that Steiner finds so coruscating? Far fewer. Nonetheless we *should* remember and reflect upon these passages. They are taken from a poem that evokes the alienation of a woman by the sea from the man who loves her. With consummate artistry O'Neill sets these lines in the climax of his drama as a lyric correlative to the tragic alienation of Mary from the men of the Tyrone family in the house by the Sound. In this correlation Swinburne and O'Neill fill analogous roles: Each writer creates a work in which an artist fails to recall from a mysterious abyss the distant and elusive woman who, though supremely important to him, will not listen to his tidings of the truth about the world, at least not until he is gone and it is too late. Even the title of Swinburne's poem, "A Leave-taking," is meaningful here, for *Long Day's Journey* is also a farewell, in which O'Neill bids a final goodbye to his haunting memories of his mother and her men. But Swinburne's lines are also specifically appropriate to Jamie, the lost soul who utters them, for the unhappy love poem he quotes is a covert paradigm of the dilemma of this doomed son whose forbidden love for his mother— his fatal affliction—can never find expression or touch her unheeding mind. Thus the stanzas of Swinburne are transformed by the genius of O'Neill from "flamboyant, romantic verbiage" to the somber odes of tragedy. Such analysis shows that O'Neill's use of quotations in *Long Day's Journey* illuminates his text without overshadowing or consuming it. The process is reciprocal, for O'Neill's text infuses the quotes with a particular richness of meaning they did not have before.[14]

In the end there is nothing paltry about the language or the action in *Long Day's Journey into Night*. It is true that the magniloquent kings, queens, and warriors of Greek and Elizabethan tragedy have passed from O'Neill's stage. What is left, as Egil Törnqvist put it, is "a drama of souls," ordinary people in enormous peril facing, in another critic's phrase, "great reckonings in little rooms."[15] In O'Neill's plays we see Everyman at the crossroads. And why not? It is not the mighty alone to whom comes the misfortune to choose wrong, cross fate, and endure heartbreak and ruin. The simplicity and isolation of these characters are no obstacle to tragedy. After all, Oedipus and Lear are most tragically heroic when they have nothing left but themselves. O'Neill's materials were often ordinary, but in his period of mastery he transformed everything he touched: Mundane reality became universal symbol, and melodrama was transported beyond cliche into the domain of tragedy. Meditating on the painful memories of his own restless life after wrestling for a lifetime with the intractabilities of language, O'Neill gave the world at the end of his career a series of mature masterpieces, *A Touch of the Poet, The Iceman Cometh, A Moon for the Misbegotten,* and *Long Day's Journey into Night.* Thus we can apply to this man of the theater what Steiner said of the symbolist poets: "Only genius can elaborate a vision so intense and specific that it will come across the intervening barrier of broken syntax or private meaning."[16] Eugene O'Neill was such a genius.

In an age when postmodern criticism's audacious reduction of litera- ture to nonsignifying texts with no relationship to reality is coming into question, the incessantly autobiographical O'Neill reminds us that there is indeed an "outside" of the text and that in his case the impact of that outside on the text is pervasive and profound. O'Neill in both camouflaged and transparent ways refashions his own life's story throughout his plays so relentlessly that Harold Bloom half-mocked his dramaturgy with this echo from Robert Graves: "O'Neill doggedly tells his one story and one story only, and his story turns out to be himself."[17] What Bloom and many other like-minded critics apparently do not see is the fact that O'Neill's

autobiographical instinct is not an impediment in spite of which he created
a formidable body of work but is the very essence of his success.

Twenty-four centuries ago Aristotle described in the *Poetics* the kind
of plots that most facilitate that dread or pity proper to true tragedy:

> Now if an enemy does it [a terrible act] to an enemy, there is nothing pitiable either in the
> deed or in the intention, except so far as the actual calamity goes. Nor would there be if
> they were neither friends nor enemies. But when these calamities happen among friends [*en
> tais philiais,* "in friendships," i.e., between those bound by ties of obligation and affection,
> particularly relatives by blood], when for instance brother kills brother, or son father, or
> mother son, or son mother— either kills or intends to kill, or does something of the kind,
> that is what we must look for. (1453b, p. 51)[18]

The sensitive critic will notice that in *Long Day's Journey,* a single play in
which "brother kills brother, [and] son father, [and] mother son, [and] son
mother—either kills or intends to kill, or does something of the kind," we
have *all* of these tragic antagonisms gathered together with an intensity that
in its way goes beyond anything the ancients imagined. When Clytemnestra
struck down her husband, Agamemnon, with the double-edged sword, she
killed him once and for all. But in *Long Day's Journey,* Tyrone, his wife,
Mary, and their contentious sons, Jamie and Edmund, symbolically assassi-
nate one another time and again, first plunging in the dagger of accusation
and then withdrawing it in a paroxysm of remorse or doubt, only to strike
anew in the unending cycle of familial self-destruction. More than any
other quality of the play, it is in the empathetic horror that this fact
inspires that the terrible fascination of O'Neill's drama lies. Aristotle
understood well that because the spectacle of those who are closest to one
another turning against their own is the most tragic, the family, particularly the family in which such pitiable violence erupts, is the source of the
most intense tragedy. In so concluding he explains two millennia before the
fact why O'Neill was drawn by artistic as well as psychological reasons to a
compulsive retelling of the story of his own house: "So this is the reason
. . . why tragedies are about a few families. For in their [the tragic poets']
experiments it was from no technical knowledge but purely by chance that
they found out how to produce an effect in their stories. So they are
obliged to have recourse to those families in which such calamities befell"
(*Poetics* 1454a, pp. 53, 55). O'Neill, the genius both gifted and cursed with
the memories of a family in which such calamities befell, came back again
and again to retelling "one story and one story only" not merely because
his soul compelled him, but because great plays resulted, for reasons that
Aristotle grasped with perfect clarity in the fourth century B.C.

But it is less than just to reduce O'Neill to nothing more than the
chronicler of his own house. He was one of the most fertile and comprehensive artists of the twentieth century:

> No one ever questioned Eugene O'Neill's inborn theatrical sense or the range of his
> imaginative grasp of contemporary life. He touched in his plays at so many points the

twentieth-century American scene that he seemed for two decades a major spokesman of it, more than a rival of Sinclair Lewis in his contempt for Babbittry and a compeer of all the exposers of "suppressed desires." There was scarcely a literary current of the time that did not flow through the mind of O'Neill, and one after another he took up themes that filled the lives of other writers and often developed them better than anyone else.[19]

Anarchism, socialism, expressionism, realism, naturalism, the myth of the American frontier, technological advance, Darwinism, psychoanalysis, the collective unconscious, race relations, Nietzsche, the literary avant-garde in Europe, Greek tragedy, oriental thought—these influences and countless others irrigated O'Neill's polymorphous dramaturgy. He was the greatest theatrical experimentalist in American history and, through his daring and the authority of both his failures and successes, the father of modern American drama. Now that this legacy is securely ours, it is easy to take it for granted. But if everything O'Neill has given to us were to disappear overnight, the great wound in our culture would stand as an unimpeachable testimony to the magnitude of our debt. Fortunately, the catastrophe is merely hypothetical. Critical fashions will come and go, but O'Neill's achievement abides, a monument to one artist's courage in a world that filled him with sorrow and rage. He was a dark and unappeasable man and an artist who stood as often in the valleys as on the peaks, but for all of his disappointments and sins, this American is for the ages.[20]

NOTES

1. Harold Bloom, "Introduction," *Eugene O'Neill*, Modern Critical Views, ed. Harold Bloom (New York: Chelsea House Publishers, 1987), 1–12, esp. 5.

2. Louis Sheaffer, *O'Neill: Son and Artist* (Boston: Little, Brown and Co., 1973), 164.

3. Except for a brief and fruitless interest in scenario writing in his youth. See Louis Sheaffer, *O'Neill: Son and Playwright* (Boston: Little, Brown and Co., 1968), 311ff.

4. This is the conclusion of some of America's foremost drama critics as reported by Michael Burlingame in "O'Neill's Reputation in Drama is Secure," published in the *Day*, Wednesday, 11 October 1988, sec. F, pp. 10–12, as part of New London's observation of O'Neill's Centennial.

5. George Steiner, *Language and Silence: Essays on Language, Literature, and the Inhuman* (New York: Atheneum, 1977), 31.

6. Harold Clurman saw this years ago. In an early review of *Long Day's Journey into Night* ("The O'Neills," *Nation* 182, no. 9 [3 March 1956]), he wrote this response to Edmund's (and therefore O'Neill's) description of his best efforts at fine language as mere "stammering": "O'Neill's work is more than realism. And if it is stammering—it is still the most eloquent and significant stammer of the American theatre. We have not yet developed a cultivated speech that is either superior to it or as good" (183). American speech (and this certainly includes dramatic speech) has, if anything, degenerated since Clurman wrote those words.

7. For two recent studies of O'Neill's language in *Long Day's Journey into Night*, see Jean Chothia, *Forging a Language: A Study of the Plays of Eugene O'Neill* (Cambridge: Cambridge University Press, 1979), 143–84; and Michael Manheim, *Eugene*

O'Neill's New Language of Kinship (Syracuse: Syracuse University Press, 1982), 164–90.

8. Cf. Chothia, *Forging a Language,* 175, 178.

9. All citations from the play are taken from Eugene O'Neill, *Long Day's Journey into Night* (New Haven: Yale University Press, 1955).

10. For the identification of Mary Tyrone/Ella O'Neill with Cynara, see Sheaffer, *O'Neill: Son and Artist,* 40. Jamie's obsession with his mother in *Long Day's Journey* is most easily noticed with the help of biographical data from outside the play, but once the observation is made it tellingly illuminates the text. Consider, for example, Jamie's preference for fat women in the light of Tyrone's remark early in the play (14) that Mary has put on weight and is "a fine armful" or, as Mary ruefully puts it, "fat."

11. O'Neill makes Jamie's awareness of the morbidity of his own soul explicit when he has Jamie later refer to "the dead part of me" (166), an expression paralleled by some of his other phrases on 165–66, a part of the play crucial to a full understanding of Jamie.

12. For a convincing explanation of the semiotic function of the Fat Vi episode in the play, see Timo Tiusanen, *O'Neill's Scenic Images* (Princeton, N.J.: Princeton University Press, 1968), 299. Tiusanen remarked (without extensive analysis) that the literary quotations add to the power of the "magnificent" fourth act (297). On the use of literary quotations in *Long Day's Journey* see also John Henry Raleigh, *The Plays of Eugene O'Neill* (Carbondale: Southern Illinois University Press, 1965), 231–33; and Chothia, *Forging a Language,* 175–81 (an excellent discussion to which I am indebted). Chothia said of Jamie's quotations in general, though without detailed argument (177): "Jamie quotes self-indulgently, identifying himself with the poet's persona in justification of his wastrel life." While I agree with this appraisal to a point, it underrates the irony that I find in Jamie's use of poetry.

13. The motif of the violin in the house of whores is itself foreshadowed in Jamie's earlier description of himself as "drunk as a fiddler's bitch" (155).

14. As Chothia clearly saw, particularly in the case of Swinburne (*Forging a Language,* 178–79). Chothia responded to Steiner on the same principle as I have but only in respect to Swinburne and for the most part with different (though quite persuasive) documentation.

15. Egil Törnqvist, *A Drama of Souls: Studies in O'Neill's Super-naturalistic Technique* (New Haven: Yale University Press, 1969); Bert O. States, *Great Reckonings in Little Rooms: On the Phenomenology of the Theater* (Berkeley: University of California Press, 1985).

16. Steiner, *Language and Silence,* 28.

17. Bloom, "Introduction," 4.

18. All translations from the *Poetics* are quoted from W. Hamilton Fyfe's translation in *Aristotle: "The Poetics"; "Longinus": "On the Sublime"; Demetrius: "On Style,"* trans. W. Hamilton Fyfe and R. Rhys Roberts, Loeb Classical Library, rev. ed. (Cambridge, Mass.: Harvard University Press, 1932). Chothia (*Forging a Language,* 255 n. 4) pointed out that O'Neill owned a copy of a translation of Aristotle's *Poetics* (a 1925 edition, dated "1929" by O'Neill) whose text he extensively underlined.

19. Van Wyck Brooks, *The Confident Years, 1885–1915* (New York: E. P. Dutton and Co., 1952), 551.

20. These remarks do not necessarily reflect the views of the other contributors to this volume.

Part One

O'Neill's Tragic Art

1

Eugene O'Neill and the
Sense of the Tragic

Richard B. Sewall

Since the lecture here recorded (with a few additions and subtractions) opened the yearlong celebration of Eugene O'Neill's one hundredth birthday, I thought it fitting on that occasion to begin with some remarks on centennials in general, their purpose, and meaning. The gist was this: National events (the Revolution, the Constitution) get centennials; national heroes (Washington, Lincoln) get birthdays. The only individuals we Americans celebrate by centennials tend to be artists (by no means all Americans)—musicians, poets, playwrights—Bach, Mozart, Shakespeare, Pound, Dickinson, and now O'Neill. I found meaning here, implicit, often explicit: We revere our national past and its heroes, and we rightly honor them, but the artists speak to us differently; we take them unto ourselves. Why and how this is particularly true of O'Neill was my theme.

Let me move up on O'Neill—and my theme—by way of a book that, by his own account, meant a great deal to him in his early years, Joseph Conrad's novel *The Nigger of the "Narcissus"* (1897). The book, we are told, "sparked" his first sea voyage and thus was instrumental in opening a wide area of material that O'Neill was to draw upon the rest of his life.[1] But more than that, in a brief foreword to the American edition (1914), Conrad said some important things about writing that O'Neill, as he embarked on his literary career, could hardly have missed—notably, the need for integrity, truth, or (in Conrad's phrase) "sincerity of expression." Looking back on the novel, Conrad wrote: "It is the book by which, not as a novelist perhaps, but as an artist striving for the utmost sincerity of expression, I am willing to stand or fall. Its pages are the tribute of my unalterable and profound affection for the ships, the seamen, the winds and the great sea—the moulders of my youth, the companions of the best years of my life."[2] He added that, upon finishing the novel, "I understood that I had done with the sea, and that henceforth I had to be a writer"—a conclusion that O'Neill reached after his two years at sea and with much the same feeling. We hear echoes of it in Edmund's (the young O'Neill's) impassioned reminiscence in the fourth act of *Long Day's Journey*.

But O'Neill's major debt to Conrad (although he never said as much) may well lie in the preface to *The Nigger of the "Narcissus"* that first appeared in the American edition. It is a powerful and (again) very personal "poetics," a kind of literary "This I believe." O'Neill was first an artist, not a theorist, and Conrad's meditation on the nature of art and on his own purpose as an artist might well have strengthened, given shape to, O'Neill's thinking. Conrad wrote the preface with the feeling, the passion, the "utmost sincerity," he gave to his novel. I sense O'Neill throughout, and I venture to say that O'Neill saw himself in it too.

The preface begins with an important pronouncement: "A work that aspires, however humbly, to the condition of art should carry its justification in every line" (xi), a challenge, certainly, to the careful craftsman O'Neill was endeavoring to become. But the heart of the preface lies in a distinction Conrad makes that may help us in our problem with centennials—why they go to the artists and not to the movers and shakers, even the Washingtons and Lincolns. On the one hand, Conrad wrote, there are practical people, the scientists, the thinkers, those who "appeal to those qualities of our being that fit us best for the hazardous enterprise of living. They speak authoritatively to our common-sense, to our intelligence, to our desire of peace or to our desire of unrest; not seldom to our prejudices . . . our fears, often to our egoism . . . our ambitions . . . the perfection of the means and the glorification of our precious aims" (xi).

"It is otherwise," he continued (and how could the young O'Neill have missed this?), "with the artist":

Confronted by the same enigmatical spectacle the artist descends within himself, and in that lonely region of stress and strife, if he be deserving and fortunate, he finds the terms of his appeal. . . . His appeal is less loud, more profound, less distinct, more stirring—and sooner forgotten. Yet its effect endures forever. . . . He speaks to our capacity for delight and wonder, to the sense of mystery surrounding our lives; to our sense of pity, and beauty, and pain; to the latent feeling of fellowship with all creation—and to the subtle but invincible conviction of solidarity that knits together the loneliness of innumerable hearts, to the solidarity in dreams, in joy, in sorrow, in aspirations, in illusions, in hope, in fear, which binds men to each other, which binds together all humanity—the dead to the living and the living to the unborn. (xi–xii)

How much of O'Neill is in those sentences! His metaphor for "solidarity" was loyalty to the ship—whatever it was that made sailors take such enormous risks in moments of danger at sea, risks way beyond the call of duty—and it should be remembered that O'Neill's first ship, the *Charles Racine,* was one of the last of the square-riggers, where there was danger every time it breezed up. The "capacities" to which Conrad the artist made his appeal were precisely those that the American theater, dominated by various forms of claptrap, was, as O'Neill entered it, failing to reach. A passage a few paragraphs on in the preface might have been written by O'Neill himself addressing the jaded theatergoing public:

[The artist's] answer to those who in the fulness of a wisdom which looks for immediate profit, demand specifically to be edified, consoled, amused; who demand to be promptly improved, or encouraged, or frightened, or shocked, or charmed, must run thus:—my task which I am trying to achieve is, by the power of the written word to make you hear, to make you feel—it is, before all, to make you *see*. That—and no more, and it is everything. If I succeed, you shall find there according to your deserts: encouragement, consolation, fear, charm—all you demand—and, perhaps, also that glimpse of truth for which you have forgotten to ask. (xiii–xiv)

"To make you hear, to make you feel . . . to make you *see* "—and I take it that the word *see* is underscored to bring out its meaning of "understand." Understand what? All that Conrad described as the domain of the artist (and there's no harm in repeating the litany): delight, wonder, the sense of mystery; pity, beauty, pain; the loneliness of the heart and yet its feeling of oneness with others "in joy, in sorrow, in aspiration, in illusions, in hope, in fear"—all of them (a veritable O'Neill checklist), and more, figure largely in *Long Day's Journey*.

Let me take another route in our attempt to close in on O'Neill and *Long Day's Journey*. This route is by way of Tragedy (with a capital *T*) and the tragic theater. Even here Conrad could have helped him, as witness the somber tone of the preface—the sense of mystery, the pain, the loneliness, the glimpses (but glimpses only) of truth. I don't know how many other novels by Conrad that O'Neill read, but the tragic tone pervades almost all of them, from the death of James Wait on the "Narcissus" (it clearly foreshadows the death of Yank in *Bound East for Cardiff*) to the "mist" that veils the truth about his young hero, Lord Jim, and "the destructive element" that eventually claims him. (The fog in *Long Day's Journey* might well be a descendent of Conrad's metaphor of the mist.) Conrad brought to the novel what O'Neill, historically, brought to the American theater and by much the same route.

From his early years, O'Neill widely read other sources. Greek tragedy, Strindberg, Ibsen, the morose poets whom Edmund and Jamie quote so freely in *Long Day's Journey*—Baudelaire, Dowson, Swinburne, Schopenhauer, Nietzsche, and Dostoevski—added to the tragic set of his mind. He told one of his editors, later, that had it not been for Strindberg's *Dance of Death* and Dostoevski's *Idiot* he might never have begun writing.[3] I would add Conrad.

"The tragic set of his mind." When George Pierce Baker, a professor at Harvard, asked his young friend Eugene O'Neill why he preferred "grim and depressing" subjects for the plays he was writing for the 47 Workshop and suggested that perhaps it was something of a pose, O'Neill, then twenty-six, replied simply, "Life looked that way"—an important clue to what determined the tone and tenor of his entire canon.[4] I like to imagine that young O'Neill turned on his heel.

In my career-long fumbling with the idea of Tragedy, I have come to at least one conclusion: If the set of your mind is not tragic, you'd better not try to write a tragedy. Another young man, twenty-six years of age, tried his hand at it in a play called *The Cenci*—and never tried it again. Later, Mrs. Shelley wrote in explanation: "The bent of his mind went the other way."[5] So did Byron's and Tennyson's, although they both wrote what they called tragedies. Goethe was wisest when he said, "The mere attempt to write tragedy might be my undoing"—this in spite of the fact that there are many tragic elements in *Faust* .[6]

This leads me to a crude but useful distinction between Tragedy and "the tragic." A writer—dramatist or novelist—may have a deep and abiding sense of the tragic and yet never write a full-blown tragedy. But just what is a full-blown tragedy? There is much disagreement. There are very few plays or novels universally accepted as such—a few by the Greeks (notably Sophocles), a few by Shakespeare (even *Hamlet* has been questioned), Racine's *Phédre*. A short list indeed, so sharp are the cutting edges of critical theory. Among novelists, Hawthorne, Melville, Dostoevski, Conrad, and Faulkner approach fullness of form. But *tragedy* as a term in criticism is in danger of becoming exclusive and academic. I have found the adjective more useful. It includes most of the values, the dynamics, we're presently concerned with. Miguel de Unamuno's great title *The Tragic Sense of Life*—like O'Neill's reply, "Life looked that way"—gets to the heart of the matter.

"It looks that way" to some, then, and not to others. Temperament is surely a decisive element. Unamuno described the tragic sense of life as a kind of subphilosophy, or prephilosophy, "more or less conscious," not so much flowing from ideas as determining them.[7] O'Neill read books, imbibed attitudes and ideas, took a course under Baker; but it was the temperament he was born with that determined what he took from them. Here is Conrad on temperament (again from the preface): "Fiction—if it at all aspires to be art—appeals to temperament. And in truth it must be, like painting, like music, like all art, the appeal of one temperament to all the other innumerable temperaments whose subtle and resistless power endows passing events with their true meaning" (xiii). O'Neill spoke in much the same way twenty years after his *Cardiff* was first produced (1916), only here he used the terms *spirit* and *life-attitude:* "In it [*Cardiff*] can be seen, or felt, the germ of the spirit, life-attitude, etc., of all my more important future work."[8]

The "subtle and resistless power" of temperament may well have been the driving force, "more or less unconscious" and not at the time articulated, behind those restless years of O'Neill's early twenties that took him to sea on vessels of sail and steam and to waterfronts from New London to Buenos Aires. Like Conrad, he came back knowing he had to be a writer; and it was the same resistless power that drove him, more and more, to a life of obsessive dedication to his art—in the end, into a solitary, brooding world of his own, with Carlotta the guardian at the gate.

Consider for a moment O'Neill in the tradition of the great tragic temperaments, a tradition with which he associated himself many times.

Why did the Poet of Job redo the ancient orthodox folktale he found at hand into a protracted, agonized questioning of the central belief of his time, the belief that God was just? Why did the Greek tragedians redo Homer, that textbook on How to Be a Good Greek? What got into Shakespeare after the years of those sprightly comedies? Why *Hamlet?* *Lear? Macbeth?* (Surely more than a change in theatrical fashion.) What got into Melville that he poured so much of his lifeblood into the story of his doomed Ahab? What got into O'Neill that he set out to redo the American theater? It had treated his father well; there was a good living in it. But as with these others, he was confronted by something deeply unsatisfying. It did not square with his vision of life and with his sense of the purpose of art, and in his own way, he protested.

So the tragic temperament is not for the acquiescent, the timid, the dull of soul. Part of it is the quality O'Neill saw in Strindberg and Dostoevski—in his words, "a powerful emotional ecstasy, approaching a kind of frenzy," precisely what the flabby and derivative American theater lacked.[9] This, he said, was what he wanted to communicate to his audience.

This opens up another dimension in the O'Neill temperament. Let me get to it by way of another distinction. The qualities he responded to in *The Idiot* and *The Dance of Death*—the "ecstasy," the touch of "frenzy"—are not the qualities we usually associate with writings we are apt to call satiric, or comic, or ironic. In these cases, the stance of the author seems more removed, aloof, Olympian, like George Meredith's Comic Spirit on high, which showers down "silvery laughter" on the follies of humankind.[10] Shaw, another important author in O'Neill's development, wrote with feeling, but he prided himself on being an "artist–philosopher." The Olympian stance is clear even in his most moving plays, *Saint Joan* and *Caesar and Cleopatra.* Even Conrad impressed O'Neill as being "detached and safe in the wheelhouse of the vessel, looking down at his men on the deck and describing their activities. When I write about the sea, I want to be on the deck with the men."[11] O'Neill was wrong, I think, about Conrad, but his remark points up the sense of personal involvement in the fictions that come from writers of tragic temperament. We can only guess at the personal involvement of the Greek tragedians; as to Shakespeare, we "ask and ask," he "smiles and is still." But we know enough about the lives of Hawthorne, Melville, and Dostoevski to know that much of the tragic in their fictions is autobiographic. As for O'Neill, his whole career has been described as an effort at autobiography, the search for self identity—"Who am I?"—in play after play.[12] In the hands of the true tragedian, as it does in O'Neill, the question "Who am I?" becomes Job's question "What is man that thou shouldst visit him every morning and try him every moment?" Was something like this in O'Neill's mind when he said that his concern as a dramatist was not so much man's relation to man as man's relation to God?[13] O'Neill may have been a renegade Catholic, but in the largest sense he never ceased being religious—like that renegade Congregationalist

Emily Dickinson, who never went to church after she was thirty but was clearly the most religious person in town.

O'Neill's purpose, stated again and again, was to establish in America a theater comparable to the theater of Aeschylus, Sophocles, and Euripides—and that was a religious theater, replete with smoking altars and priests in robes. But O'Neill, to his credit, did not start by staging revivals or by imitating the grand manner. He took themes and subjects from his own experience, "grim and depressing" as they were, and "with the utmost sincerity of expression" carried them to the bitter end. The series of one-acters put on by the Provincetown Players, beginning with *Cardiff* in 1916, was a clear and effective signal of his intention. From it grew the Little Theater movement and a resurgence of activity in the drama of schools and colleges—two phenomena, incidentally, whose influence on the American theater should not be underestimated.

Suffering, as usual, from a cultural lag, the New York theater finally got the message. When, in a notable essay, Arthur Miller sized up the meaning of the first successful year of *Death of a Salesman,* he might have been quoting from O'Neill: "There is no limit," he wrote, "to the expansion of the audience's imagination. . . . They will move with you anywhere, they will believe right into the moon so long as you believe who tells them this tale."[14] Here we are back again to Conrad's "utmost sincerity," his sense of involvement, his belief in the sense of solidarity that "knits together the loneliness of innumerable hearts." These, loosely speaking, are religious matters that O'Neill transferred to the theater. More specifically, it could be said that, from the dying Yank in *Cardiff,* with his stammerings about God and judgment, to Mary Tyrone's prayers to the Blessed Virgin, O'Neill never stopped asking, at least, the ultimate religious questions. To use a term from Dickinson, he never quite *abdicated* belief. She made a poem out of it:

> The abdication of Belief
> Makes the Behavior small—
> Better an ignis fatuus
> Than no illume at all—[15]

Dickinson's "belief" was more of a search than a finding. So was O'Neill's. And there is nothing "small" about their achievements as artists. They never ceased—after their own fashions—to believe.

There is also nothing "small" about *Long Day's Journey into Night.* All the foregoing has been by way of preparing for an adequate—if that is possible—indication of its impressive proportions.[16] But first a caution: To one coming to the play with a traditional Aristotelian view of tragedy, the experience is something of a shock. The materials are unpromising. Where is the tragic hero? What about catharsis? There is pity, perhaps, but where is the terror? As to the "tragic flaw," the stage is littered with flaws, but are they tragic—dope? alcohol? miserliness? Here is a wrangling family (as it looks) of born losers seemingly with no other purpose than to chew each other up. Where is the "magnitude" that Aristotle found in true tragedy? And yet . . . and yet . . .

Dearest: I give you the original script of this play of old sorrow, written in tears and blood. A sadly inappropriate gift, it would seem, for a day celebrating happiness. But you will understand. I mean it as a tribute to your love and tenderness which gave me the faith in love that enabled me to face my dead at last and write this play—write it with deep pity and understanding and forgiveness for all the four haunted Tyrones.

These twelve years, Beloved One, have been a Journey into Light—into love. You know my gratitude. And my love![17]

Many years ago, as I was beginning to think about a book on tragedy, I heard a lecture, "What Aristotle Left Out." What the lecturer—a priest—found missing, or undeveloped, in Aristotle was precisely what O'Neill put into this birthday note to Carlotta and, as I shall try to show, into *Long Day's Journey,* the blood, the tears; love, understanding, forgiveness. Later I asked my friend the priest where and how he thought I should start my book. "I don't care where you start," he answered, "so long as you start with the man of flesh and blood."

This suggests an important point about *Long Day's Journey.* With this play, O'Neill's career comes full circle. He had started with men of flesh and blood—his shipmates, often bloody in a quite literal sense—and he had found in that riotous crew the very qualities he speaks of to Carlotta: pity, understanding, forgiveness. Then followed years of experimentation with Greek, biblical, Freudian, sociological themes; with technical devices—masks, sound effects, spectacle; with asides beyond anything Hamlet ever dreamed of. Then, in this climactic play, he comes back to where he started: the simple, direct dramatization of a life situation he knew all too well—his own. He rides no theory; there is no experimentation: He "tells this tale"—and we are left to make of it what we can.

The first two acts are mostly given to the chewing-up process. It's a depressing sight. Here is a talented family on the brink of dissolution. The father, James Tyrone, is a washed-up actor, a compulsive penny-pincher, living on the glory of past triumphs that he realizes, too late, were hollow. Mary Tyrone, his wife, has slipped back into her dope habit on this very day of the Long Journey. Jamie, the older brother, is far gone in alcohol and whores. Edmund (O'Neill himself at twenty-four), the younger brother by ten years and recently returned from two years at sea, has been trying his hand at writing for the local newspaper but so far with little success. As the play opens, he is ill and learns (again on this very day) that he has consumption.

The situation looks hopeless—the one thing they all seem to agree on. They see themselves as trapped, "walled in," "fog people" unable to see their way. They look back in hopeless nostalgia on what might have been. Worst of all, they take it out on each other in an orgy of bickering and blame-laying.

And such blame-laying! Nobody takes responsibility for anything. Tyrone blames his penny-pinching on the poverty of his childhood. Mary blames her addiction on the fact that Tyrone hired a cheap doctor who got her into the morphine habit when she was sick after Edmund's birth and then never gave her a decent home where she might have conquered her addiction. She blames Jamie's alcoholism on Tyrone's giving him spoonfuls of whisky to get him over his childhood ailments. Tyrone accuses Jamie of purposely corrupting Edmund (and ruining his health) out of jealousy of his younger and more talented brother. Mary, toward the end of Act two, slips into the ultimate evasion. Speaking to Edmund about his brother, she says, "He can't help being what the past made him. Any more than your father can. Or you. Or I" (64). In the last scene of the act, in a kind of ritual return, she says to her husband, "The things life has done to us we cannot excuse or explain" (85). Tyrone, contemplating Mary's return to drugs but, in a way, summing up the whole situation, says wearily, "There's no help for it. . . . I wish she hadn't led me to hope this time. . . . I never will again" (78).

This isn't tragic, it's pathetic. At the end of Act two when the men leave the house—Edmund (with Jamie) to make his appointment with the doctor, and Tyrone to make his appointment at his club—one wonders why they should ever want to come back. After such recrimination, how can they face each other again? Each one has said enough, it would seem, to make further communication impossible. But Mary, left alone, at least can talk to herself; and what she says, I think, marks a turning point.

(*She stares about the room with frightened, forsaken eyes and whispers to herself*) It's so lonely here. (*Then her face hardens into bitter self-contempt*) You're lying to yourself again. You wanted to get rid of them. Their contempt and disgust aren't pleasant company. You're glad they're gone. (*She gives a little despairing laugh*) Then Mother of God, why do I feel so lonely? (95)

Pathetic, surely; pitiful. But something more. Mary has faced up to some solid truth. Shortly before, she had called herself a liar; but that was to Edmund, whom she was trying to comfort. Now, after two acts of blaming all the others, and Life, for her plight—even Edmund for having been born—she admits it to herself and means it. Five hours later (Act three) in this Long Day's Journey, she completes the indictment, the first in the family to face herself squarely. (She had just been boasting to the maid, Cathleen, of her youthful romance with the great actor James Tyrone. Cathleen leaves the room; Mary is alone.)

You're a sentimental fool. What is so wonderful about that first meeting between a silly romantic schoolgirl and a matinee idol? You were much happier before you knew he existed, in the Convent when you used to pray to the Blessed Virgin. (*Longingly*) If I could only find the faith I lost, so I could pray again! (*She pauses—then begins to recite the Hail Mary in a flat, empty tone*) "Hail, Mary, full of Grace! The Lord is with Thee; blessed art Thou among women." (*Sneeringly*) You expect the Blessed Virgin to be fooled by a lying dope fiend reciting words! You can't hide from her! (*She springs to her feet.*

Her hands fly up to pat her hair distractedly) I must go upstairs. I haven't taken enough. When you start again you never know how much you need. (107)

But just then she hears the men coming back. Again she feels that strange ambivalence of wanting them to stay away, yet welcoming their return: "Why are they coming back? They don't want to. And I'd much rather be alone. (*Suddenly her whole manner changes. She becomes pathetically relieved and eager*) Oh, I'm so glad they've come! I've been so horribly lonely" (108). When Tyrone enters, she "*rises from her chair, her face lighting up lovingly—with excited eagerness.*"

Mary's confessional moment here is the first of a series, involving each of the men, that takes us in the last two acts beyond pity, beyond tears, to the awed silence (as it strikes me) of the last scene of the play. Part of the power of her confession is what Mary says about herself—that is, the truth—but perhaps as important is her ambivalent feeling about the men as they leave and as they return. She doesn't generalize—she simply *feels* what it is to want solitude and yet be lonely; what it is to want, yet not want, her family with her; what it is to love and hate, condemn and yet forgive, at one and the same time. In the final act, the men reciprocate these feelings about each other—and, my feeling is, about Mary as she has her last say.

Let's see how O'Neill builds to this conclusion. Edmund, who had been relatively docile during the first two acts while the others tore each other apart, erupts twice in the final act, and each time his outburst brings, first, his father, and then his brother to their senses. The first outburst comes when Edmund learns that his father has decided to send him to a state sanatorium. The two have started what might have been an amicable card game. But it doesn't last long.

God, Papa, . . . I've tried to be fair to you because I knew what you'd been up against as a kid. I've tried to make allowances. Christ, you have to make allowances in this damned family or go nuts! . . . I've tried to feel like Mama that you can't help being what you are where money is concerned. But God Almighty, this last stunt of yours is too much! It makes me want to puke! Not because of the rotten way you're treating me. To hell with that! I've treated you rottenly, in my way, more than once. But to think when it's a question of your son having consumption, you can show yourself up before the whole town as such a stinking old tightwad! . . . Jesus, Papa, haven't you any pride or shame? (*Bursting with rage*) And don't think I'll let you get away with it! I won't go to any damned state farm just to save you a few lousy dollars to buy more bum property with! You stinking old miser—! (*He chokes huskily, his voice trembling with rage, and then is shaken by a fit of coughing.*) (145)

This is not the first time in the play that Tyrone has been so accused by one of his sons. (Jamie led off in Act one.) Tyrone bristles for a moment ("Be quiet! Don't say that to me! You're drunk!"), but Edmund's fury gets to him and he changes his mind about the state farm: "You can go anywhere you like. I don't give a damn what it costs." They both take large drinks, the card game forgotten. "*Dully, without resentment,*" Tyrone repeats the charge: "A stinking old miser. Well, maybe you're right." Then comes his own confessional—the trials of his youth (*"He wipes tears from his eyes"*), the hollowness of his early stage triumphs and the money he made. "I've never admitted this to anyone before," he says. "What the hell was it I wanted to buy, I wonder, that was worth—well, no matter. It's a late day for regrets." Edmund is moved. There is a glimpse of the truth (but only a glimpse) between father and son, a redeeming moment, at least. Edmund *"stares at his father with understanding"* and says *"slowly"*: "I'm glad you've told me this, Papa. I know you a lot better now."

Then, after some more cards, a bit of a quarrel over Tyrone's insistence on turning off a lamp to save electricity, and more drinking, Edmund's turn comes: "You've just told me some high spots in your memories. Want to hear mine?" What follows has the qualities of an aria in an opera, dramatically and psychologically right, a moment of high emotion in which the stage is given over to a single lyric outpouring, with something of the "ecstasy, approaching a kind of frenzy" that O'Neill had found in Strindberg and Dostoevski. Here is Edmund (or the young O'Neill) bound for Buenos Aires on the square rigger, "the old hooker driving fourteen knots":

I became drunk with the beauty and singing rhythm of it, and for a moment I lost myself—actually lost my life. I was set free! I dissolved in the sea, became white sails and flying spray, became beauty and rhythm, became moonlight and the ship and the high dim-starred sky! I belonged, without past or future, within peace and unity and a wild joy, within something greater than my own life, or the life of Man, to Life itself! To God, if you want to put it that way. . . . Like a saint's vision of beatitude. Like the veil of things as they seem drawn back by an unseen hand. For a second you see—and seeing the secret, are the secret. For a second there is meaning! Then the hand lets the veil fall and you are alone, lost in the fog again, and you stumble on toward nowhere, for no good reason! (*He grins wryly*) It was a great mistake, my being born a man. I would have have been much more successful as a seagull or a fish. As it is, I will always be a stranger who never feels at home, who does not really want and is not really wanted, who can never belong, who must always be a little in love with death! (153–54)

"For a second there is meaning!"—a glimpse, but a glimpse only, of a redeeming truth, the reward of O'Neill's effort, as he told Carlotta, to "face his dead" and, by implication, to face his own past for some kind of understanding and forgiveness for "*all* the four haunted Tyrones." (The emphasis on *all* was his.) His father *"stares at him—impressed."* We are left to wonder whether Tyrone's utterly inadequate comment covers the only thing that impressed him: "Yes, there's the makings of a poet in you all right." Then, *"protesting uneasily,"* he says, "But that's a morbid craziness about not being wanted and loving death." Edmund denies nothing but the "makings of a poet" in him: "I just stammered. That's the best I'll ever do. I mean, if I live. Well, it will be faithful realism, at least. Stammering is the native eloquence of us fog people."

At this point brother Jamie stumbles in, well gone in whiskey. In the long alcoholic talk that follows between the brothers, the subject veers from Jamie's sex life to their dope-addicted mother. Edmund, again, is driven to fury, this time violently; but again the result is salutary. For a redeeming moment, Jamie comes out of the "fog" into the clear. "What's the use coming home," he says, "to get the blues over what can't be helped. All over—finished now—not a hope!"

(*He stops, his head nodding drunkenly, his eyes closing—then suddenly he looks up, his face hard, and quotes jeeringly*)
"If I were hanged on the highest hill,
Mother o' mine, O mother o' mine!
I know whose love would follow me still . . . "
EDMUND. (*violently*) Shut up!
JAMIE. (*in a cruel, sneering tone with hatred in it*) Where's the hophead? Gone to sleep? (*Edmund jerks as if he'd been struck. There is a tense silence. Edmund's face looks stricken and sick. Then in a burst of rage he springs from his chair*)
EDMUND. You dirty bastard! (*He punches his brother in the face . . . For a second Jamie reacts pugnaciously and half rises from his chair to do battle, but suddenly he seems to sober up to a shocked realization of what he has said and he sinks back limply*)
JAMIE. Thanks, Kid. I certainly had that coming. . . . My dirty tongue. Like to cut it out. (161–62)

Then comes Jamie's confession, centering on his relations with Edmund. Again (as with Mary) comes the recognition of ambivalence—how he loved Edmund, yet hated him, how he tried to ruin him to save himself from being the only failure in the house. It is moving, passionate—and true. Finally, the liquor has its effect: "(*very drunkenly, his head bobbing*) That's all. Feel better now. Gone to confession. Know you absolve me, don't you, Kid? You understand. You're a damned fine kid. . . . So go on and get well. Don't die on me. You're all I've got left. God bless you, Kid. (*He falls into a drunken doze.*)"

It's hard to do justice to the final scene—Mary's scene, to which all has been moving—let alone to say precisely what it means. Mary's entrance for her own little aria is beautifully prepared for. James Tyrone enters just as Jamie falls into his drunken doze. He looks down on his first-born on whom he had pinned such hope: "A waste! A wreck, a drunken hulk, done with and finished!" That's enough to wake Jamie up, to start another row with his father (he's sober enough to quote flawlessly from *Richard III* and Rossetti) until Edmund quiets them with a warning that they might disturb Mary's sleep and bring her downstairs. The two quarrelers subside. There is a detailed stage direction:

(*Edmund sits tensely. He hears something and jerks nervously forward in his chair. . . . Suddenly all five bulbs of the chandelier in the front parlor are turned on from a wall switch, and a moment later someone starts playing the piano in there—the opening of one of Chopin's simpler waltzes, done with a forgetful, stiff-fingered groping, as if an awkward schoolgirl were practicing it for the first time. Tyrone starts to wide-awakeness and sober dread, and Jamie's head jerks up and his eyes open. . . . Mary appears in the doorway. She wears a sky-blue dressing gown over her nightdress, dainty slippers with pompons on her bare feet. . . . Over one arm, carried neglectfully, trailing on the floor, as*

if she had forgotten she held it, is an old-fashioned white satin wedding gown, trimmed with duchesse lace. . . .)
JAMIE. The Mad Scene. Enter Ophelia!
(His father and brother both turn on him fiercely. Edmund is quicker. He slaps Jamie across the mouth with the back of his hand.) (170)

Mary is far away, a girl again, back in the convent. The men look on helplessly, trying to bring her back to them. Edmund grabs her impulsively and pleads with her: "Mama! It isn't a summer cold! I've got consumption!" Mary: "You must not try to touch me. You must not try to hold me. It isn't right, when I'm hoping to be a nun." Jamie is the first to give up: "Hell! What's the use? It's no good." He quotes Swinburne's poem "A Leave-taking." Tyrone: "Oh, we're fools to pay any attention. It's the damned poison. But I've never known her to drown herself in it as deep as this. Pass me that bottle, Jamie. And stop reciting that damned morbid poetry. I won't have it in my house." All three pour themselves drinks.

But, strangely enough, they *do* pay attention. Mary wins, even over the alcohol. There is an important stage direction: "*Tyrone lifts his glass and his sons follow suit mechanically, but before they can drink Mary speaks and they slowly lower their drinks to the table, forgetting them.*" Mary, dreamily, her face "*youthful and innocent,*" an "*eager, trusting smile on her lips,*" talks aloud to herself:

I had a talk with Mother Elizabeth. She is so sweet and good. A saint on earth. I love her dearly. It may be sinful of me but I love her better than my own mother. Because she always understands, even before you say a word. Her kind blue eyes always look right into your heart. You can't keep any secrets from her. You couldn't deceive her, even if you were mean enough to want to. (*She gives a little rebellious toss of her head—with girlish pique*) All the same, I don't think she was so understanding this time. I told her I wanted to be a nun. I explained how sure I was of my vocation, that I had prayed to the Blessed Virgin to make me sure, and to find me worthy. I told Mother I had had a true vision when I was praying in the shrine of Our Lady of Lourdes, on the little island in the lake. I said I knew, as surely as I knew I was kneeling there, that the Blessed Virgin had smiled and blessed me with her consent. But Mother Elizabeth told me I must be more sure than that, even, that I must prove it wasn't simply my imagination. She said, if I was so sure, then I wouldn't mind putting myself to a test by going home after I graduated, and living as other girls lived, going out to parties and dances and enjoying myself; and then if after a year or two I still felt sure, I could come back to see her and we could talk it over again. (*She tosses her head—indignantly*) I never dreamed Holy Mother would give me such advice! I was really shocked. I said, of course, I would do anything she suggested, but I knew it was simply a waste of time. After I left her, I felt all mixed up, so I went to the shrine and prayed to the Blessed Virgin and found peace again because I knew she heard my prayer and would always love me and see no harm ever came to me so long as I never lost my faith in her. (*She pauses and a look of growing uneasiness comes over her face. She passes a hand over her forehead as if brushing cobwebs from her brain—vaguely*) That was in the winter of senior year. Then in the spring something happened to me. Yes, I remember. I fell in love with James Tyrone and was so happy for a time. (*She stares before her in a sad dream. Tyrone stirs in his chair. Edmund and Jamie remain motionless.*) (175–76)

What to make of it? It's one of those endings that leave you, as I suggested earlier, in "awed silence"—like Jamie and Edmund, "motionless." Tyrone "*stirs in his chair*"—to signify what? O'Neill does not tell; he simply presents. There is no summation as at Hamlet's death: "For he was likely, had he been put on, / To have prov'd most royally." There is nothing like Kent's agonized "Break heart; I prithee, break" as he sees Lear die. O'Neill had given each of the men his little "aria." Now he gives Mary hers—and leaves us to our own thoughts.

How variously this last scene—and the whole play—can be read is strikingly illustrated by a New York production in 1986. Its *New Yorker* reviewer, Brendan Gill, praised it for at last facing up to what he considered O'Neill's real theme, "that women are murderously destructive by nature and men are in constant peril of not surviving their machinations." In this reading, Mary is seen as imposing, through her "ineradicable, maudlin narcissism," a tyrannical hold on her "hapless husband and sons," driving them, literally, to drink. Her final words fall upon James Tyrone "like a sentence of death." This is why he "stirs in his chair." The 1986 director had him "utter a groan."[18]

My own thoughts, as should be clear by now, go in a different direction. They go back to the letter to Carlotta, to the "deep pity and understanding and forgiveness" that O'Neill had come to in this grappling with his past and that he had found, in varying degrees, in each of the "haunted Tyrones." I think of the tiny epiphanies that illuminate the last two acts. I find it useless to ask "Will they last? What about tomorrow? Have we witnessed redemption?" No. We have witnessed what we have witnessed, seen what we have seen. Disturbing ambiguities remain, of course. O'Neill does not resolve them, either in bitterness or in soothing sentiment. The point is, he had found a way of living with them. He once described tragedy as ennobling in art "man's hopeless hopes"—the hopes, I take it, that transcend the hopelessness of the here and now. So, nearly half a century later, he "ennobled" the seeming hopelessness of his one-time family situation by finding in it the possibility of pity, understanding, and forgiveness. Thus he could present the play to Carlotta in gratitude for their "twelve-year Journey into Light—into love."

NOTES

1. Arthur Gelb and Barbara Gelb, *O'Neill* (New York: Harper and Row, 1962), 146.
2. Joseph Conrad, *The Nigger of the "Narcissus,"* Concord Edition (Garden City, N.Y.: Doubleday and Co., 1914), ix.
3. Gelb and Gelb, *O'Neill*, 233.
4. Ibid., 604.
5. "Note on *The Cenci* by the Editor," in *The Poetical Works of Percy Bysshe Shelley*, vol. 1, ed. Mary Shelley (Boston: Houghton, Mifflin and Co., 1865), 281.

6. Johann Wolfgang von Goethe, letter to Schiller, 9 December 1797, as quoted in Erich Heller, *The Disinherited Mind* (Cambridge, Eng.: Bowes and Bowes, 1952), 31.

7. Miguel de Unamuno, *The Tragic Sense of Life in Men and in Peoples,* trans. J. E. Crawford Flitch (London: Macmillian and Co., 1921), 17.

8. Gelb and Gelb, *O'Neill,* 260.

9. Ibid., 233.

10. George Meredith, *An Essay on Comedy and the Uses of the Comic Spirit,* ed. Lane Cooper (Ithaca, N.Y.: Cornell University Press, 1956), 142.

11. Gelb and Gelb, *O'Neill,* 146.

12. Travis Bogard, *Contour in Time: The Plays of Eugene O'Neill* (New York: Oxford University Press, 1971), xii.

13. Eugene O'Neill, "On Man and God," in *O'Neill and His Plays: Four Decades of Criticism,* ed. Oscar Cargill, N. Bryllion Fagin, and William J. Fisher (New York: New York University Press, 1961), 115.

14. Arthur Miller, "The *Salesman* has a Birthday," in *The Theater Essays of Arthur Miller,* ed. Robert A. Martin (New York: Viking Press, 1978), 14.

15. Emily Dickinson, Poem no. 1551, *The Poems of Emily Dickinson,* ed. Thomas H. Johnson, vol. 3 (Cambridge, Mass.: Belknap Press of Harvard University Press, 1955), 1069.

16. See also Richard B. Sewall, *"Long Day's Journey into Night, "* in *The Vision of Tragedy,* new ed., enlarged (New Haven: Yale University Press, 1980), 161–74.

17. Eugene O'Neill, *Long Day's Journey into Night* (New Haven: Yale University Press, 1955), 7.

18. Brendan Gill, "Unhappy Tyrones," *New Yorker,* 12 May 1986, 93–94.

2

O'Neill and the Poetics
of Modernist Strangeness

Spencer Golub

FAMILY/FAMILIAR/"DEFAMILIARIZATION"

When one sets out to discuss the family, Tolstoy's famous dictum from the opening of *Anna Karenina* comes to mind: "All happy families are like one another; each unhappy family is unhappy in its own way."[1] "Revenge," wrote family man Eugene O'Neill, "is the subconscious motive for the individual's behavior with the rest of society."[2] The Other often bears the face of the family, meaning that "the rest of society" begins and ends with the family.

There is nothing more familiar than family. There is also nothing so ripe for "defamiliarization." It is the Ur-text of both life and art, the mother and father of us all. As such, it is the perfect body on which to experiment with perspective, style, and technique. It is a traditional and sacred construct carrying within it the possibilities of desacralization and deconstruction. Families may either be seen as coming together or falling apart. Either action, however, is at least shadowed by the image of wholeness, which gives the family its definition. The line between happy and unhappy families is not all that clear, no clearer, in fact, than the borders between the familiar and the strange and between reality and illusion.

To reinvent the family is to rewrite the text of life, to recreate life and make it more creative. The Russian formalist critic Victor Shklovsky wrote: "Art exists that one may recover the sensation of life; it exists to make one feel things, to make the stone *stony*. . . . After we see an object several times, we begin to recognize it. The object is in front of us and we know about it, but we do not see it." The object and its artistic image suffer from what Bert O. States, in reference to Shklovsky, called "the curse of familiarity." They "gravitate toward invisibility."[3] What art must accomplish, then, is to make the object unfamiliar. This process is what Shklovsky called "defamiliarization" or "making strange." Modernist writers have accomplished this by envisioning the family as a performing and performable reality. They have treated this well-made text, with its hierarchy of roles, its causal relationships, its linear storyline, and its three-act structure of beginning, middle, and end as being open, multilingual, and "polyperspectival."

The family is like the human body, which Henri Bergson suggested is "an ever advancing boundary between the future and the past."[4] Family occasions and the family itself, like theater and performance, are holding actions imbued with that "irreducible dualism, of our knowledge of death at the origin of life." This absence within presence, according to the postmodern critic Herbert Blau, "dooms us to repetition."[5]

It is common knowledge that O'Neill effected a balancing act in his drama as regards the family. In *Ah, Wilderness!* he presented a dreamlike vision of the family he wished had been his, while in *Long Day's Journey into Night,* he confessed to being of the family that was, allowing for poetic license, his. The Tyrones are not simply the O'Neills transposed or translated, but defamiliarized. *Long Day's Journey* is not O'Neill's most unabashedly modernist play, in that he here shuns the borrowed avant-garde devices of his earlier work. As in the case of Ibsen, the absorption of a modernist perspective and consciousness into what playwright Mac Wellman has conceived of as the Euclidean world of the well-made play (i.e., the "American well-made play" with its geometrically well-rounded "Euclidean Character") proves O'Neill's mature mastery of the medium. O'Neill did not here dispense with theatricality, as some have suggested. Rather, he redefined it. Nor did he succumb to proffering "a theoretical view of life" devoid of mystery, deceit, interest, and "effective inwardness," as Wellman—who classed O'Neill with the Euclidean realists—suggests.[6]

Long Day's Journey is, among other things, an ironic parody of the Irish family play. The sainted mother, whose level-headed pragmatism and enduring faith in God and the Holy Virgin solidifies and sustains the family, is transformed by O'Neill into an embittered dreamer, addicted to drugs, the past, and the self-delusion that she is the Virgin Mary. The ineffectual but endearingly dreamy father of the Irish family tradition is here not a poet but a ham actor and a pragmatic tightwad, whose self-delusion has turned to self-pity. Both father and mother in O'Neill's tale are inveterate play actors and amateur playwrights. The tragi-farce that they play in and have fashioned, "The Happy Family," is literally killing their audience, their sons, and themselves.

Judith E. Barlow reported that in reworking the early drafts of *Long Day's Journey* into its final version, O'Neill toned down the harshness of his attitude toward Mary and Mary's attitude toward the theater.[7] Yet there remains in the final version the taint of theater-in-life that has been passed on from parents to children like disease and hypocrisy in Ibsen. O'Neill's intention in writing the play is not to assign blame but, as he suggests in his dedication, to find peace for himself and his family ghosts. His parents are responsible for and yet not guilty of the destructive theatricalization here depicted, because it takes the playwright, like the historian, to quote George Kubler, to communicate "a pattern which was invisible to his subjects when they lived it."[8] For O'Neill's extended family, his audience, to perceive this pattern, we must be willing to recast the familiar images and interpretations of the play in an unfamiliar light. We must, to begin with, discover the play's pattern rather than simply pursuing its story. This is the "spatial form" of which Joseph Frank spoke in his seminal critical text *The Widening Gyre*.[9] We must come to dwell in a new, unfamiliar family abode, with many entrances and no prescribed address.

POSSESSION/DISPOSSESSION/REPOSSESSION

In *The Actor's Freedom,* Michael Goldman wrote that "the effort to possess one's past is perhaps a natural American theme, and it takes the form, in the greatest American plays, of an attempt to possess one's own family." He added that "American dramatists have tended to locate the awareness of lost or contradictory identity in the contradictions of American society and the American family."[10] These themes of possession and self-possession of the past and of one's identity, respectively, come home to roost in *Long Day's Journey*.

O'Neill wrote *Long Day's Journey,* along with *The Iceman Cometh,* as interruptions in a much more prolonged process of working on an eleven-play cycle entitled *A Tale of Possessors Self-Dispossessed.* This cycle projected America's century-long betrayal of its ideals through a particular family's history. This idea owed much to the naturalist Émile Zola, as well as to the father of the naturalist Alexandre Dumas, fils. Alexandre Dumas, père's, novel *The Count of Monte Cristo,* well-known to the O'Neill household, spanned time and bracketed history and fiction together in a sort of involuntary dialogue. Although O'Neill's cycle was never completed, his "interruption," *Long Day's Journey,* was. In it the two dialogues between history and fiction and romanticism (Dumas, père) and modernism (Dumas, fils) were embodied in the characters of James Tyrone, Sr., and his younger son, Edmund.

For Edmund, a house is not a womb. Mary, whose house is not a home, seeks to make a womb of Time. She, and to a lesser extent all of the Tyrones, is one of O'Neill's spatially dispossessed, his beached sea people in waterfront properties, who seek redress in bloated or stopped time. Time, however, as O'Neill illustrated in *The Emperor Jones* and again in *Long Day's Journey,* cannot be possessed and does not release Man but rather runs him aground. Since Time represents the ethereal nature of reality and consciousness, which cannot be captured, other O'Neill characters seek to possess things of a more elemental nature. Tyrone tells Edmund: "The more property you own, the safer you think you are. That may not be logical, but it's the way I have to feel. Banks fail, and your money's gone, but you think you can keep land beneath your feet."[11] Edmund has sought his fortune in another way; he has invested his faith, his very being in the sea. His epiphanic ode to the sea in Act four is literally drenched in moonlight, linking him to the feminine principle and to his mother: "I was set free! I dissolved in the sea, became white sails and flying spray, became beauty and rhythm, became moonlight and the ship and the high dim-starred sky! I belonged, without past or future, within peace and unity and a wild joy, within something greater than my own life, or the life of Man, to Life itself! To God, if you want to put it that way" (153).

In this momentary illusion of escape/belonging, Edmund feels empowered with what Kierkegaard called "the limitless self." His consciousness is everywhere and everything's. By losing himself, he "recovers the sensation of life." O'Neill's stake in all of this, in the posing of this problem in art, was, like James Joyce's, "to repossess the density of being, of which all events conspired to dispossess him."[12]

Edmund is the true child of Mary's estrangement. His penchant for what Tyrone considers to be atheistic, nihilistic, decadent poetry and philosophy reflects this predisposition. His spirit has not been broken by the absence of God. Instead, he sought the absence of God to validate his feeling of aloneness, of estrangement. Like his mother and his brother, he has suffered the abstraction of life by performance.

The self-consciously mechanical rhythm of the placement of scenes and behavior of characters in *Long Day's Journey* bespeaks and embodies the condition of feeling dispossessed, therefore estranged and desirous of repossession. The play, plied with alcoholic and drugged perceptions, lurches from one awkwardly introduced epiphanic moment to another. Characters mechanically attack one another, and then immediately and as mechanically retract their accusations. This pattern echoes the psychological, emotional, and linguistic configuration that we find in O'Neill's correspondence with his own family—his wife and children.[13] It also imitates, probably as unconsciously as the first example, what Robert Heilman has identified as being "a standard manifestation of the melodramatic spirit: the discharging of blame and indignation at others."[14] O'Neill has made his life into a stage melodrama built on a pattern of shifting villains and victims, with the victims defining their status in their retreat/escape into illusion. It is this revisionist shift that signals the presence of the modernist impulse.

In *Long Day's Journey*, empathic and recriminatory responses are continually flipped like a coin in the air. As in Tom Stoppard's *Rosencrantz and Guildenstern Are Dead,* one hears the participants calling out and tallying how many times the coin has come up tails and how often heads. This mechanical quality derives, in part, from a "dissociation of sensibility." Here is an example. When Mary Tyrone reenters the stage in Act four for what Jamie ungraciously entitles "Ophelia's Mad Scene," the room she encounters is familiar. It is, in fact, the same room she has inhabited and that we have watched her inhabit for the entire duration of the play. Mary is aware of and accepts everything and everyone in this room as objects that naturally belong there but that she is too preoccupied to notice. That is, everything is, in this moment, familiar yet strangely distanced. Her condition has defamiliarized them. These objects, like the white halo of hair that constantly threatens to fly away from her head, no longer seem to belong to her. Then there are her crippled hands, which seem now to be so far away. "I see them," she says, "but the pain has gone" (104). Her physical and emotional response to them, in fact to her entire environment and to someone's family—not quite her own—who lives there, has become mechanical. Her verbal response is similarly mechanical. The pain, her words say, is not just no longer there. It has been abstracted from her.

If Mary can retreat in Time (the play's original title was *A Long Day's Retreat*), she can insulate herself from both the present and from the present tenseness of things and of perception. Mary's "illness," however, is also O'Neill's invitation to us to repossess the play by objectifying our perspective in this moment and throughout the text. We recognize ourselves both in the Mary who sleepwalks her way through the text of her life and in the Mary who defamiliarizes this text in order to make it more dreamlike, more artistic, more her own. In a sense, Mary's condition, her illness, is our own, as is her journey. It is a therapeutic journey of repossession.

THE JOURNEYS

The characters in *Long Day's Journey* are embarked upon a journey that continually brings them home unfulfilled. Although their actual journey through time has been brief (historic time is very short), they are trapped in an eternal return. Like the denizens of Harry Hope's saloon in *The Iceman Cometh,* they are awake inside a nightmare, unable to sleep, except during the waking moments of the day, when drunk (Mary cannot sleep at all). They are, to paraphrase Joyce's Stephen Dedalus, struggling to awake from the nightmare that is history, their history or story. They are sailors beached on the shoals of endless time, unable to escape. This point is made again and again in the play by Tyrone, Edmund, and Jamie, with Jamie even using Edmund's sea imagery to do so. He says that he has "had enough [whiskey] to sink a ship, but can't sink" (156). Mary embodies the ghost's sleepless reality, and it is her return that gives the play its shape.

A play is, certainly in the premodernist sense, a celebration of the unique occasion of something that has not happened before, happening over and over again. This sense of uniqueness is shaped by scenes of exposition, as in Ibsen, or by expository elements braided into the present tense of the play, as in Chekhov.

In *Long Day's Journey,* O'Neill posits the past as present in the form of performable epiphany. Tyrone's remembering of what could have been had he followed in Edwin Booth's footsteps as a Shakespearean actor and Edmund's remembering of what it's like to be lost in the fog or at sea are replayed and embodied in Mary's actual return to the unique moment in her life, her moment of decision. Her decision to marry an actor rather than to become a nun is discussed, rehearsed (the story she tells Cathleen [Act three, scene one]), and finally performed with wedding dress in hand at play's end. Here "the Mad Ophelia," who dies a virgin when her beloved actor Hamlet rejects her, reenacts/reexperiences the bartering of her virgin marriage to Christ for a corporeal marriage to an actor in which children have issued and are the issue.

Although the story of this decision and of this marriage is told and retold in the play, it is the reenactment of this moment of choice to which the more important pattern of rehearsal leads. Mary is a would-be nun and (from what she tells Cathleen) a would-not-be actress. A nun renounces the world, which Mary has ironically done, but through drugs. Renunciation implies escape, true and total dissociation, freedom from the burden of earthly reality. Tyrone the actor states quite accurately (although he does so for his own motives) that Mary "was never made to renounce the world" (138). Indeed, she has not. More pointedly, she has not renounced acting, the mode of being and perception she claims to despise. Mary continues to perform the past as present. Each time she takes her drugs, the innocent schoolgirl is reborn. Each time she remarries her would-be Shakespearean actor, the drowned Ophelia, a ghost, reclaims her Hamlet, whose pursuit of a ghost redefined the path of his life. They have had three sons. One, Jamie, named after his father, is a successful drunk and a failed actor. The second, Eugene, is dead; the third, Edmund, the would-be writer in the play, the real writer of the play, and the real Eugene, is named after the fictional character Edmond Dantès to whom the father gave his career and his dream.

The Eugene/Edmund transposition frees the theme of identity from one context to another. This, too, is a journey of sorts. It disrupts the closed text of biography, that is, personal history. It mixes genre and modes of consciousness (Russian theorist Mikhail Bakhtin equates the two). In doing so, it textures the character's way of "seeing and conceptualizing reality" (Bakhtin). One could argue that in killing Eugene and reinventing Edmund as the incipient modernist poet–playwright, O'Neill is, in a sense, transposing the genre of both his art (melodrama into modernism) and his life. Transposition also involves the reappropriation of space. The character Edmund is born into the space left vacant by the dead Eugene and sees life through the eyes of the dead child whom he has replaced. This ghostly perception of the world is by definition estranged and feels at home only in fog and at sea. By giving the dead Eugene his name, O'Neill likewise counts himself among the ghosts. He reappropriates what is past as present. This is Mary's action in the play. "The past is the present, isn't it?" she asks rhetorically; "It's the future, too" (87).

George Kubler reminded us that "any work of art is actually . . . an emanation of past time," like the old light of distant, even dead stars, which reaches us in the present.[15] Edmund Husserl stated that our experience of the past is future oriented: "Every act of memory contains intentions of expectation whose fulfillment leads to the present."[16] The enactment of the reappropriation of the past by the present, of the past bodying forth as the present, is also what we mean by the "theatrical."

Finally, the Eugene/Edmund transposition is, like the play's title, a frank admission of a basic truth of art and especially theatrical art. The writer is always a near relation of his characters, of their family and yet not of their family. Flaubert was not Madame Bovary, and Tennessee Williams was not Blanche Dubois, despite their statements to the contrary. Pirandello was the father of but not father to his six characters. Somehow the relationship between author and character is more open than a true family relation and yet is as ripe for the possibility of betrayal.

In writing *Long Day's Journey,* O'Neill is seeking to exorcise not only the family demons that haunt him but also those melodramatic conventions defined by plays such as *The Count of Monte Cristo,* which killed his father's dream and haunt the son. O'Neill will, like Prince Hamlet, avenge his father, but he will do so in a play that kills melodrama where it lies, in the bosom of the family. To kill it in a less open and honest fashion would be akin to dispatching Claudius while he prays, to release a soul rather than laying it to rest, to create yet another ghost to dog one's life. O'Neill must kill these sleepers while they are awake and so writes them into a play in which they cannot sleep. He must kill the dream of romantic fiction, of melodrama-realism, which is, in some way, the furthest sounding of romanticism. He must free his walking dead not only of the burden of their lives but of the burden of their genre, their performance. *Long Day's Journey* is the dramaturgical equivalent of the ghost, the disappeared man. Apparently all of a piece, even overly present in language and as object, it rehearses and yearns for its own true disappearance.

Ghosts are ghosts because they have not embarked upon or have not completed the journey(s) of their lives. In this sense, Chekhov's characters are perhaps the most famous ghosts in dramatic literature. They are, as are so many modern men and women, too busy dreaming their lives to live them. Mary's journey in the play subsumes, incorporates, and embodies the nonjourneys of her entire family. She is the mother of the disappeared.

The "journey" of the play's title incorporates several other significant ideas or journeys. The "long day's journey into night" suggests the inevitable movement toward natural closure, death, as well as the artificial recycling and intensification of this in the Liebestod of romantic fiction and theater. It suggests the journey into dream time, a journey that, because it ends at night in sleep but with the promise of the next morning's renewal, is like a river that flows in two opposite directions. Therefore, dream and reality are inseparable and indistinguishable. In this regard, all closure is only apparent, life is a dream, an open text. Modern theater, which has embraced the dream as its signatory metaphor (Strindberg and others), presents reality as the interiorization of experience. At the same time, the theater's conflation of time, place, and action into a "long day" extends beyond the neoclassical unities into realism and even modernism.

The play's "chronotope" or time–space matrix, to again borrow from Bakhtin, is not defined by external dimension but rather by consciousness, both the characters' and the reader/spectator's, who are willing to let this "long day's journey" transpire within some four hours stage time. *Long Day's Journey* not only allows for what playwright Mac Wellman called "effective inwardness" (although he would deny that it does), it depends on it for its very existence.[17]

Umberto Eco defined *semiotics* as "the discipline studying everything which can be used in order to lie."[18] One of the journeys that O'Neill traces in *Long Day's Journey* is the journey of the lie that is the presentation of theater as life. The primary signifier here is the meal that is eaten and not eaten, the staple of happy families, as well as of well-made plays and playwrights. *Long Day's Journey* begins with the entire family entering the stage, having just completed breakfast and with the entire day laid out before them. Act two begins at lunchtime, but lunch is late because Tyrone, Sr., has not yet arrived. Act three is set at dinnertime, but there will be no food consumed, only drink. This act ends with Tyrone, Sr., going off to dine alone. Act four begins around midnight, long after meals have been completed and at the exact border between night and day. Father and sons sit nearly motionless at play's end with their drink before them.

O'Neill's structuring of his play according to meals is as purposeful as Chekhov's structural device of arrivals and departures, of seasons and guests. However, it has just the opposite effect. Chekhov employs the natural cycle of things to create an ironic perspective on his characters' lives and, at the same time, a sense of continuity and well-being in his audience by introducing the presence of Nature. O'Neill illustrates the subjugation of this natural cycle, made possible by a world that features neither seasons nor arrivals and departures. Chekhov's plays are open to the world, whereas O'Neill's are closed and define the world from the limited, artificial perspective of their existence. The closed-in boundaries of their world symbolize the "disastrous separation from a larger world of possibility."[19] As in Ibsen, meals in O'Neill's plays draw our attention back to the conventions of the play world itself. Ibsen's characters retire offstage to consume and digest heavy meals in the length of time reserved for a scene shift or an intermission. These unseen meals then serve as signifiers of compressed theatrical time.

O'Neill's meals inform our understanding of the journeys that his characters take alone and together. Their meals degenerate, as marked by the movement from food to drink as day moves into night and the past becomes the present. O'Neill neatly combines these ideas at lunchtime. Mary, who has returned to drugs, is berating her husband for the indignities he has made her suffer in the past, leaving her to fend for herself in dingy hotel rooms while he caroused with his friends in barrooms. Edmund intervenes with the suggestion that they all go in to lunch. At that moment, Mary, in the process of encouraging the consumptive Edmund to eat more, espies a whiskey glass. This action confirms in her mind both the validity of her previous complaint and the certainty of Edmund's demise. Externally, it serves notice that the family habit will help to define the journey of day into night. As with so much else that involves this family, however, the drink is not a true signifier. The level of whiskey in the bottle, which stands ever present upon the table, does not fall consistent with the actual amount of whiskey consumed as the day progresses. Jamie, Edmund, and even Mary cheat the level up with water to cover the amount of whiskey they have drunk. The bottle is emptying, the characters are getting drunk, and yet the bottle is not emptied. It is tempting to view this as being symbolic of the play's overall retarding action, the obsessive spiraling back of talk and memory as the day completes its linear progression toward night. Time does not order experience. People do.[20] In *Long Day's Journey,* it seems that people order Time as well. But only seems.

Bert States suggested that a (realistic) play "imitates the timely in order to remove it from time, to give time a shape." States argued that the role of Fate in the modern theater is played not, as is often thought, by Time but rather by Space. "Space," he said, "is destiny, the visual proof that order lurks in human affairs." Milieu recurs. "The dialogue says, in effect, 'We are here only temporarily. We are free to go elsewhere'; the setting says, in effect, 'It will all end here.' "[21]

One of the many journeys we here embark upon takes us to the point of recognizing not only the spatial pattern of the play but the "spacefulness" of all things, including Time.

READING AND PERFORMING

The Tyrones are a bookish clan. They have the Irish gift of gab and the actor's love of the spoken word. Their frequent literary allusions, true to the characters' upbringing and personalities, serve as well the intentions and ambitions of their playwright–creator. His characters' penchant for recitation allowed O'Neill to get more composition (in a musical sense) into the inner structure of his play. It also allowed him to bulk up his plays so that they resembled novels in scale, referential scope, and levels of perception. This was part of the modernist ambition to bring greater solidity to an expanded consciousness while building an edifice of classical proportions.

One way in which O'Neill increases the density of his composition is by writing lengthy narrative sections into his dramatic text in the form of stage directions. In his hands, as in G. B. Shaw's, the stage direction becomes an alternative language block that rivals and at times threatens to consume the space and function normally reserved for dialogue. O'Neill's stage directions are brethren to the lengthy monologues and the general narrative tone that fill the play. The absurdist bias for white space on the page and on the stage is not shared by all modernist and postmodernist writers. The filled space is as eloquent and effective an acknowledgment by the artist of the theater of the mind, of theater as an informed act of reading.

Let us examine the semiotics of the Tyrones' reading and performing and from there consider what and how they read and perform and how their performance of literature may be defined. First, there are the book-cases in the parlor. They contain histories of tribes, nations, and empires, by implication the story of family and genealogy and by direct reference (there are several histories of Ireland) a context within which to set the history/story of this particular family. It seems to be an almost Tolstoyan author's ploy. Then there is the literature and philosophy—classic, romantic, and modern—topped literally and figuratively by Shakespeare, whose works fill three volumes in a glassed-in bookcase and whose picture looks down upon a small bookcase containing the moderns, among them the playwrights Zola, Ibsen, Shaw, Strindberg, and Wilde. Most of these were acknowledged by O'Neill to have influenced his thinking and his work and here appropriately reflect the tastes of the younger Tyrones.

Sharing with Shakespeare the place of honor in the glassed-in bookcase are the official family texts as determined by the patriarch James Tyrone, Sr. They include the aforementioned histories of Rome, England, and, of course, Ireland, romantic texts by Dumas, Hugo, and Charles Lever. The elder Tyrone would certainly number Shakespeare's plays among these romantic texts. They, along with a miscellany of old plays and poetry, "*have the look of having been read and reread*"(11). They have been dogeared by an actor looking for likely roles and looking to validate the role he is already playing. Their contents, in particular the Shakespeare, no doubt have been committed to memory, out of love, frustration, and simply in order to work the actor's muscle so that it would not atrophy.

The moderns are consigned to "*a dark, windowless back parlor, never used except as a passage from living room to dining room*" (11). There they are watched over by the sacred shade of Shakespeare, lest the decadent atheists, whoremongers, and absinthe drinkers (Schopenhauer, Nietzsche, Swinburne, Rossetti, Wilde, and Dowson) misbehave in the dark and the political radicals (Marx, Engels, Kropotkin) foment a revolution. (Perhaps the self-involvement and endless capacity for talk of those named, along with the presence of such social do-gooders as Ibsen and Shaw, will maintain a semblance of order.) The father's books live in the best of both worlds. They are given a window-view of the grounds in back of the house but are protected by glass from the elements and, one supposes, from cross-pollination by radical texts as well.

The overall picture signifies a veritable battleground between Old and New, as well as the struggle between history and belles lettres for the custodianship of Truth and Beauty. The fact that the family contains not only serious readers but serious rereaders, initiates—before the spoken text of the play has even begun—the theme of return. This functions as both a pattern and as a behavioral paradigm in the play. There are innumerable returns: Edmund and Jamie have come home, and the family has returned to the Monte Cristo cottage, their summer home, their *only* home; Mary appears for a while to have come home from her morphine addiction, but it is soon revealed that she has, in fact, returned not from but *to* there; the fog has returned, signaling Mary's relapse, and with it the family's growing suspicions, distrust, and Mary's paranoia; Mary's father has visited his consumption through his daughter upon his grandson (an Ibsenite note), one of many ways in which the past has gnawed into the present; O'Neill has returned to his past and adapted it to suit his present need, which is, as he writes in his dedication, to exorcise his dead and to validate the new family that has made this exorcism necessary and possible, his wife, Carlotta. We know from studying the text of O'Neill's life that what he sought in his marriage to Carlotta, a wife–mother, and what he achieved, an endless cycle of mutual recrimination, marked yet another return. Then there is the play *Long Day's Journey* itself, which is O'Neill's attempt to "recover the sensation of life."

The behavioral returns in the play are the far more significant. People go back upon their words, go back to their former selves or to performable masks of themselves. They return in their minds nominally to rediscover some happiness that has been lost but, in essence, to nurse some past grief—either a wrong committed by another or one's own guilty actions. As serious and tireless readers and *re*readers, the characters in the play can tolerate these old griefs and sins, as if rereading favorite passages from a book that they have long since committed to memory (Mary Tyrone has folded over the corner of one particular page).

The light by which people read also plays a major role in O'Neill's opening stage directions and thereafter throughout the play. Beginning with the play's title, much will be made of daylight dwindling into evening and night. We think and dream, live and perform, in light. Light gives expression to perspective, and perspective informs and, depending upon your philosophical disposition, defines reality. "There are as many realities as points of view," as many spaces in reality as there are perspectives on it, wrote Ortega y Gasset.[22] Although the journey of *Long Day's Journey* is, in one sense, linear, it is, in another, diffused according to the light through which it is filtered and which is shined upon it. We witness not just the dying of the light of day representing the extinguishing of hope in the present. We experience, as did Oedipus, the inexorable movement toward the blinding light of truth.

Thus as Act four of *Long Day's Journey* begins, it is midnight, and Tyrone, Sr., is seated in near darkness. He is drunk; his eyes have a "*misty, oily look.*" He, like the house and the other characters, is entirely fogged in, in this act. The lights in his eyes are not lit. His first line to Edmund, who is entering the room, is "Turn that light out before you come in" (126). Tyrone's eyes are at this moment sensitive to the light, as is his wallet to the cost of the light, as he likes to remind his sons. When Edmund complains that he cannot see well enough to move, his father answers: "The light from here shows in the hall. You could see your way well enough if you were sober" (126). It is the "well enough . . . if . . . " construction that is of interest. What constitutes seeing "well enough" at this point in the play? What necessary adjustment or suppression of consciousness, of perspective, is necessary to make the conditional "if" operate effectively for the person seeing/not seeing? Tyrone's fear of the house being set "ablaze with electricity" (126), proclaimed at the beginning of the act, is made a self-fulfilling prophecy by the action at play's end. "*Suddenly all five bulbs of the chandelier in the front parlor are turned on from a wall switch*" (169), and Mary enters as the Mad Ophelia or, if you will, the Past. Suddenly and inevitably, Tyrone is confronted with the dreaded truth/reality, with a moment of true illumination, a spotlight that the actor has not sought and cannot control.

In this final scene, Mary speaks of having lost something and, indeed, seems fully lost at midnight. But in the romantic sense, she is here fully found, most like herself, at home. Tyrone would call this perception "morbid" and "decadent," and yet in a real sense, he accepts it as being true. He dissolves into hopelessness. He tells Jamie gruffly to pass him the bottle of whiskey and calls for him to "stop reciting that damned morbid poetry" (175). Yet he has become an audience for, even a coparticipant in, the "damned morbid poetry" embodied/enacted by his wife. His own performance is that of the disillusioned and powerless sufferer.

Before we accept his performance as the real thing, we should, however, reread the text. Everywhere Tyrone is accused of having had the power to effect change in the lives of his family and of himself but has feigned powerlessness. This defines the throughline of his wife's and sons' response to him both in the past—their transient life, the start of Mary's addiction, his sons' general lack of direction, Jamie's alcoholism—and in the present—Edmund's consumption, the return of Mary's addiction, and the general persistence of the past in the present. The actor's subtext is his admission of this culpability. His career as a matinee idol rather than a Shakespearean actor, like the rest of his life, has been a matter of choice enacted as the absence of choice. He has played himself and his family cheap in ways that are more profound than the merely financial.

Tyrone and Mary both enact the persistence of illusion into so-called reality. This theme recurs in the plays of Edward Albee and Jean Genet. In Genet's *The Balcony* this theme is even projected via the same image of light. Madame Irma, proprietress of a brothel in which illusion is performed, extinguishes the lights at the very border between the end of the play and its performance and the beginning of the audience's reality. Her complaint sounds not unlike Tyrone's and manages to say what he cannot bring himself to say:

It took so much light . . . two pounds' worth of electricity a day! Thirty-eight studios! Every one of them gilded, and all of them rigged with machinery so as to be able to fit into and combine with each other. . . . And all of these performances so that I can remain alone, mistress and assistant mistress of this house and of myself. . . . In a little while, I'll have to start all over again . . . Distribute roles again . . . assume my own.

She ends by speaking of the journey yet to come, embedding within her statement the memory of the journey that has gone before: "You must now go home, where everything—you can be quite sure—will be falser than here. . . . You must go now. . . . (*She extinguishes the last light.*) It's morning already."[23] George and Martha's journey in Albee's *Who's Afraid of Virginia Woolf?* apparently ends at daybreak on a dubious note of linguistic affirmation, Martha's "I am [afraid]," suggesting conditional reality. This ending and that of *Long Day's Journey,* Mary's "I fell in love with James Tyrone and was so happy for a time," may be read as variations on Molly Bloom's "Yes" at the conclusion of Joyce's *Ulysses.*

We have made a long day's journey into night and are now on the point of continuing back into day without a break in illusion. We leave the Tyrones in a suspended state, but as in memory and as performable characters in a play, we can be certain that they will reenact illusion continually. Cast in this light, "the long day's journey into night" is not a linear movement at all but only a point on a circle.

Upon the lit stage, an island exposed on three sides in a sea of darkness (placing us, the audience, at least physically on the side of the dreamers seeking narcosis as well as the Ideal), is another, smaller stage. This stage is a round table, its shape conducive to family equity and harmony. This table stage is lit by a green shaded reading lamp, its cord *"plugged in one of the four sockets in the chandelier above."* One socket to accommodate each of four family members, whose membership in this exclusive book club is reinforced by the four chairs that are placed around the table *"within reading-light range." "Three of them* [are]*wicker armchairs."* They belong to Mary and her two sons. The fourth, *"a varnished oak rocker with leather bottom,"* is obviously the patriarchal chair (12). The father, being an actor of the old school, no doubt views his chair as being something other than a point on the periphery of a closed circle. Instead, it marks the only break in the circle, with his supporting players/family members describing an arc that reinforces his dominant presence. As if to dramatize his pride of place, no sooner does the patriarch/leading man sit in his chair than he lights up a cigar, and this just after breakfast at 8:30 A.M.

This stage-upon-a-stage will be the center of virtually all of the play's meaningful activities and exchanges. It is where social intercourse and solitary action take place, with the borderline between the two components— which take the form of drinking, talking, arguing, card playing, and reading—being purposely obscured. The family will begin and end their long day's journey here. In the morning, Tyrone, Sr., in his *"remarkably fine, resonant and flexible"* actor's voice will perform the role of the happy family patriarch. His—and the play's—first line, "You're a fine armful now, Mary, with those twenty pounds you've gained," reassures all concerned that they have returned to a state of well-being to which they never really belonged (14). The emptiness of this line reading is soon revealed. But then James Tyrone is full of such empty line readings. His profession has taught him how to lie effectively. Only his immediate family can see through him and are not fooled. They can read him. In introducing him, O'Neill writes: *"The actor shows in all his unconscious habits of speech, movement and gesture. These have the quality of belonging to a studied technique"* (13).

If Tyrone is willing to accept the morphine addict's performance of good health as reality, this is a matter not only of conditioning but of self-protection. To unmask Mary is to risk unmasking the tenuous reality that they have created and performed together. It would demand that he become truly and fully involved with the problem that is family life. It is a problem he has never bothered to learn to solve and so now finds insoluble. He and Mary conspire to avoid discussion of the problems and substitute the performance of its solution. What is missing is the investigation of its reality from which a real process of healing might develop.

The artificial glow of Mary's and the family's good health in the play's first scene at the table will transform into an unabashed mask, *"a marble mask of girlish innocence,"* in the last scene (170). Mary's "madness" stands fully revealed in this last scene. Although this does not come as a complete surprise to the family or the audience, it compels us to reread all that we have heard, seen, and been told up to this point. O'Neill has already allowed, in fact set the stage for, this eventuality in his stage directions for the fourth and final act. The only light on stage at the beginning of the act emanates from the single reading lamp on the table.

In 1914 Russian symbolist author Dmitry Merezhkovsky wrote the following:

Ibsen's *Nora* [the Russian title for *A Doll's House*] contains . . . a detail in a moment between two characters which is important to the entire drama. A servant–girl enters the stage carrying a lamp. Immediately, the conversational tone becomes changed in the lit room. A feature worthy of a psychologist–naturalist. The change from physical darkness to light works upon our internal world. Underneath the realistic detail we find hidden an artistic symbol.[24]

O'Neill owed more than a little to Ibsen's fatalistic ghost stories, enacted in closed rooms on heavily misted landscapes. Both authors' works feature the biological passage of death-in-life from parent to child, the action of what William James called the persistence of the past, as well as the defamiliarization of the present by the past. What Merezhkovsky highlighted, however, is the modernist tendency to discover symbol below surface, pattern beneath story, via the performance of a particular part or detail, in this case, a lamp.

LANGUAGE

The structure of the unconscious, wrote Jacques Lacan, is analogous to the structure of language. Whatever resides in the unconscious must be verbalized before we accept its existence.[25] The characters in *Long Day's Journey* live in a house whose walls are lined with bookshelves. More than this, they live in a house built of language. Their unconscious, which Baudelaire might have called the self "laid bare," is exposed as/by language.[26] Their existence, defined in words, is solipsistic. There is no real world outside of this house. The family is the world. The Word is the world, Nietzsche's "prison-house of language."[27] The play's structure is epiphanic. The play's action jumps from one self-consciously revelatory moment to another. Each character has at least one clear view of what life could have been or, in the case of the play's chief protagonist, Edmund, of what it is. James Joyce used the epiphanic moment to cast his protagonist outside of history. The modernist replaces history with story. *Long Day's Journey* represents this process as does Mary's mythic approach to the past within the play. The actor, who is the paradigm for O'Neill's characters in *Long Day's Journey,* is a storyteller whose story is himself. The epiphanic nature of these stories denotes the atomization of experience that embodies the modern condition. The play's goal, which is the reintegration of the estranged self to the world via the enactment of consciousness, is at the top of the modernist agenda.

In modernist literature, language sought to become consciousness itself, and consciousness took the place of God as both the final mystery and the arbiter of that mystery. Much has been written about O'Neill's long-windedness, repetitiveness, about the self-consciousness and ineffectiveness of his language. But in his plays, especially *Long Day's Journey* and *The Iceman Cometh,* language is consciousness, and consciousness is infinite in its fluid variation. O'Neill's language seems often to be stolid, because it is so totally present, so complete a materialization of internal states, a complete world defined by inner experience.

O'Neill's infamous repetition of language and argument may also be read as an exercise in defamiliarization. Victor Shklovsky repudiated the principle of artistic economy. To quote fellow formalist Boris Eichen-baum:

He saw art as increasing the difficulty and span of perception, "because the process of perception is an aesthetic end in itself and must be prolonged"; he saw art as a means of destroying the automatism of perception; the purpose of the image is not to present the ap-proximate meaning of its object to our understanding, but to create a special perception of the object—the creation of its "vision" and not the "recognition" of its meaning. Hence, the image is usually connected with the process of defamiliarization.[28]

The function of O'Neill's language is consistent with this formalist definition. It is meant to create a visual and sound image of perception, which is its own end and not simply a means of arriving at some external meaning. "He [O'Neill] didn't feel that the fact that we live largely by illu-sion is sad," observed Dudley Nichols. "The important thing, is to see that we do," that is, live by consciousness and perception, but not necessarily understanding.[29] "For," as Nietzsche has written, "both art and life depend wholly on the laws of optics, on perspective and illusion; both, to be blunt, depend on the necessity of error."[30] The canvas of *Long Day's Journey* is word-painted to its very edges and yet aspires to the pure whiteness of ineffable consciousness.

Peter Steiner observed that for Shklovsky, "artistic prose renders extraliterary reality strange [i.e., defamiliarizes it] in the process of its verbal representation."[31] One might point not only to the Tyrones' quota-tion of literary sources but to their own self-conscious statements of authorship as examples of such defamiliarization. The clearest example of how these two variants function together is Edmund's famous Act four fog speech. Jean Chothia accurately pointed out that "whereas Jamie adopts the role implied by the poetry, Edmund uses it to seek out and comprehend his own experience of the world."[32] O'Neill frames the fog speech with Ed-mund's recitation of an Ernest Dowson poem and with Tyrone, Sr.'s, eval-uation of his son as being something of a poet. O'Neill is here "laying bare the device," that is, frankly drawing attention to his poeticizing of the text and tracing the impulse to his surrogate self in the play, Edmund Tyrone. This is what semioticians call "linguistic foregrounding." It represents both an attempt to create spatial consciousness or a virtual theater in the mind of the reader/spectator and to recast writing as performance, as what Pirandello called a "speech act."[33] The text proclaims its own theatricality, its autonomy from the stage. Just as stage space can, in States's estimation, be synonymous with the stage event, so can stage language.[34]

O'Neill was very fond of masks and experimented with them as both external and internal realities in many of his plays. "People do recognize from their knowledge of the new psychology," he remarked, "that every-one wears a mask—I don't mean only one but thousands of them."[35] It is his characters' acknowledgment of this fact, along with the ambiguousness of motive and identity it denotes, that carries within it the modernist tendency of defamiliarization.

Such a moment is the drunken "confession" of the would-be filicide, Jamie Tyrone, to his brother Edmund in the last act of *Long Day's Journey*. Jamie tells Edmund that his "hail-fellow-well-met" demeanor (like Hickey's in *The Iceman Cometh*) is no more than an insidious role he has been playing to get his younger brother to share in his self-destructiveness. Jamie communicates the core of his plan in the compressed, slurred language of the drunk and by so doing embodies its message at the same time: "Made whores fascinating vampires instead of poor, stupid, diseased slobs they really are. Made fun of work as sucker's game. Never wanted you succeed and make me look even worse by comparison. Wanted you to fail. Always jealous of you. Mama's baby, Papa's pet" (165). Since alcohol is itself a deforming/defamiliarizing device and since the drink seems to be speaking through Jamie, our perception of whom Jamie is and what he wants is likewise clouded. The alcohol causes Jamie, like the rest of his family, to overact.

One is tempted to say that drunkenness in the play serves as a metaphor for overacting, for the exaggeration of emotion into emotional posturing. Unsurprisingly, then, it is Tyrone, the sons' role model, who most cogently voices this uncertainty, despite the fact that he appears to have given up on his elder son. He tells Edmund: "I heard the last part of his [Jamie's] talk. It's what I've warned you. I hope you'll heed the warning, now it comes from his own mouth. . . . But don't take it too much to heart, lad. He loves to exaggerate the worst of himself when he's drunk. He's devoted to you. It's the one good thing left in him" (167). Tyrone's role as unsympathetic audience to Jamie's performance in the play serves to make his comments here validate our confusion vis-à-vis Jamie all the more. This is characteristic of one of the central deforming/defamiliarizing devices in the play, the constant turning over of the truth, and the interpenetration of reality and illusion. This mirrors the acceptances/denials, retreats/attacks, guilt/recrimination, and the fleeing to and from sobriety and narcosis (drink and drugs) that pattern and animate the play.

What appears on the surface to be a frank and wordy autobiographical text becomes more spectral, more absent, the more closely it is examined. As has already been suggested, one of the central oppositions between texts, written and spoken, in *Long Day's Journey* pits Shakespeare against the moderns. This opposition, however, like so much else in the play, is only the appearance of reality and not real. It is, in fact, meant to be ironic. Tyrone, Sr., blames his sons' estrangement on their poor taste in literature and philosophy, on their decision to read the "decadents" instead of Shakespeare.

The fact is that his sons *have* read Shakespeare. Edmund even memorized the entire role of Macbeth in a week to win a bet with his father. What did Tyrone's sons read in Shakespeare and how did they read, that is, understand it? What they undoubtedly encountered was the image of a play-world; (concerns over) the inauthenticity of language, art, identity, life, history-writing, and historical process; rumor, rebellion; counterfeit and player kings; regicides, patricides, filicides; people who refuse to conform to accepted codes of behavior and characters who refuse to enact accepted modes of performance; in general, the deformation/defamiliarization of nearly everything that was/is thought to be "real." They certainly would have discovered numerous instances of sons rebelling against their parents. In fact, Jamie has for a time been "educating" Edmund in an irresponsible manner akin to Falstaff's education of Prince Hal. Both Jamie and Falstaff are rather rough actors, and Jamie's "education" of his brother may or may not constitute attempted filicide. Edmund, who will grow up to be the author of this text, is his father's true heir. O'Neill, much like the upstart Hal trying on the crown of his recumbent father the king (*Henry IV,* part 2, act 4, scene 5), stated that some day his actor–father would be remembered solely as having sired his playwright–son.

There is only an apparent, not a true, opposition between Shakespeare and the moderns in *Long Day's Journey.* Being moderns has enabled the sons to read Shakespeare more closely and to enact their findings better than their father, steeped in the romantic, melodramatic, rhetorical posturings of the previous century, ever could. What would the old ham actor hope to see in Shakespeare but a series of potential starring roles? Jamie calls his father "old Gaspard." He does so first to suggest Tyrone's miserliness. Gaspard was, according to Jamie, a character in the nineteenth-century melodrama *The Bells.* "Old Gaspard," however, does not, in fact, appear in Leopold Lewis's *Bells.* Yet the name seems instantly familiar to us as belonging to the world of melodrama. The suggestion is that melodramatic roles (and the acting that brings them to life) are somehow more generic, more interchangeable, than others. This is one-half of the meaning of Jamie's conflation of a character name and an inappropriate play. The other is the play and the celebrated actor who performed in it. Sir Henry Irving played the role of the old burgomaster–innkeeper Mathias in *The Bells.* This character is haunted by his sense of sin and remorse for the murder forty years before of an old Polish Jew for his bag of gold. Mathias kills for profit. In a metaphorical sense, so did Tyrone. He killed his dream for profit and has been haunted by this action ever since. Tyrone does not, like Mathias, hear accusatory bells. It is the ghostly image of his wife and the recriminations of his family that keep his guilt alive.

To finalize the link between Irving and James O'Neill/Tyrone, consider this quotation from George Rowell's *Theatre in the Age of Irving* documenting the failure of the marriage of Henry and Florence Irving fomented by his role in *The Bells:*

Irving's triumph on the first night . . . [has] become part of theatre history, rendered all the more haunting by the knowledge that this triumph coincided with the irrevocable breakdown of his marriage. As they drove home past Hyde Park Corner, the wife who *had never fully accepted her translation from Surgeon-General's daughter to actor's wife* [my emphasis] and now saw that fate sealed by the evening's outcome, exclaimed: "Are you going on making a fool of yourself like this all your life?" Her husband stopped the carriage, got out and turned his back on her for good.[36]

The Bells was the vehicle that made Irving famous, but it did not make him great. "Gaspard" is Jamie's coded reminder to his father that he chose not to become the next Edwin Booth, the great Shakespearean actor of his day. In fact, Jamie's linkage of "old Gaspard" and *The Bells* suggests an ironic and meaningful paraphrase of Tyrone's Edwin Booth story, in which he says: "I played Cassius to his Brutus one night, Brutus to his Cassius the next. Othello to his Iago, and so on" (150). Jamie's purposeful "mistake" suggests that it would be closer to the truth to speak of Tyrone playing "old Gaspard" to Irving's Mathias, but even this isn't possible because the two characters and their interpreters do not belong in the same play. Neither, perhaps, do James Tyrone and Edwin Booth belong on the same stage. In 1881 Henry Irving and Edwin Booth alternated in the roles of Othello and Iago on the London stage.

In making his career choice, Tyrone not only compromised his credentials as a professional actor, he transposed his thwarted acting ambition to his life. There the play he enacts is a typical melodrama of the son of a poor immigrant family, constantly threatened with foreclosure, starvation and the poorhouse. The hero of this tale, this play is the actor/author himself, James Tyrone, Sr., who grew up, bettered himself, and saved his own wife and children from the poorhouse. This he did by turning his back on his beloved Shakespeare and becoming "the Count of Monte Cristo" on stage and "old Gaspard" on the stage of his life. Poverty for the heroic actor and author of the text of his life was not, as he claims it was for his younger son, "a game of romance and adventure . . . play" (147). Surely, he implies, it was no more than this for the opium eaters whom his younger son emulates.

Furthermore, by saving his family from knowing the poverty he has known, Tyrone has kept the starring role for himself. "You said you realized what I'd been up against as a boy," he tells his son in *"a scornfully superior"* tone. "The hell you do! How could you?" (146). James Tyrone, Sr., will be damned if he will let another's life experience upstage his own. Tyrone's behavior throughout the play resembles that of an actor who knows that he is losing his audience but is powerless to prevent it. His family tunes him out, figuratively walks out on his performance. His best audience, the person whom he once truly inspired, is his wife. She is now not only lost to him, she has become his competition. A modern behavioral actress to his romantic, rhetorical actor, she is willing to be, cannot help but become, totally immersed in her role. Tyrone is forced into becoming her audience.

Tyrone and his wife, and not their rebellious, cynical sons, are the codissolvers of the myth of the happy family. Tyrone, the ham actor and romantic storyteller, has theatricalized his family's existence. He continues to narrate his role within the developing family saga, a distancing action that his sons resent. He performs his loss as it transpires, thus making it inevitable and cynically removing himself from its effect. His performance of sincere concern over the health of Mary and Edmund strikes his family, and especially the sensitive Edmund, as being cruelly parodic.

The fact that the Tyrones so emulate Shakespearean figures in the patterns of their actions reminds us and Tyrone's sons, who are the modern readers within the text, how far outside of Shakespeare's realm they dwell. Jamie and especially Edmund, who already possesses an author's eye, refuse to accept Shakespeare as a tonic, the textual equivalent of their father's medicinal whiskey. Shakespeare is not the closed text that Tyrone presents to his sons. To think him so casts him as a tradition, not a living reality.

Prospero's "We are such stuff / As dreams are made on, and our little life / Is rounded with a sleep," can be appreciated by Edmund, a good formalist, for its formal beauty. But when transposed from the context of Prospero's enchanted isle to the context of the Tyrone household, it becomes a cruelly ironic pronouncement. For this is a house whose inhabitants are haunted by sleeplessness and by waking dreams. The words *sleep* and *dream* recur often in the text of their lives. The last person to invoke them will be Mary, when she descends from upstairs as the Mad Ophelia. "Let me see. What did I come here to find?" she asks of no one in particular. "It's terrible, how absentminded I've become. I'm always dreaming and forgetting" (171). "What is it I'm looking for? I know it's something I lost," repeats the dreamer (172). The sad theme of Mary's "little life" is that it is not "rounded with a sleep." It is instead subsumed by a waking dream. It is a long journey, an open text, an endless return in which nothing is ever forgotten and the trace of pain is never lost.

Chekhov recreated the pain of one futile episode in his life, the senseless shooting of a woodcock, as the play *The Seagull*. In this play, a young man shoots a seagull as a frustrated tribute to the girl he loves but cannot possess. This seagull is stuffed and mounted on the young man's mantle much as the girl's life is manipulated and then preserved by the author Trigorin in his short story. The images of girl, seagull, the girl in Trigorin's short story, and, indirectly, of Chekhov's original woodcock are all captured or repossessed by Chekhov's play. The action of *Long Day's Journey* is not dissimilar. Edmund, who feels himself to be of the sea, like a fish or a seagull, is both Treplev the would-be possessor and Nina the water sprite who would be possessed. He is as well Treplev, the seeker of new artistic forms, with the paternal figure, Trigorin, the preserver of old forms, embedded within him. Both plays have at their center a mother whose absence forces the life's perspective of their son. Treplev and Edmund both seek to return to the watery womb/grave. As with Edmund, the limitless self masks the disappearance of self, the uncertainty whether a self can be differentiated from the world, the Other, the family.

There is an even more significant transposition at work in this play than that of Eugene O'Neill into Edmund Tyrone from Eugene Tyrone, which speaks to the issue of modernist strangeness. Mary Tyrone's absence in the play and her disappearance from the stage suggested by the play prefigure her reappearance and underscore her presence in the consciousness of the family and the audience, the extended family. Her reappearance renders her family inert and speechless, freezing the past and the present in a desperate clinch. Her reappearance signals the play's disappearance as text and the seeming disappearance of the theatrical illusion and the reappearance of our life reality. The end of the play like the end of illusion is, as has been previously suggested, illusory. However, this moment also marks the dawn of a new, truer perception of reality.

The play has captured for us, its audience, the family's reality, the interlocking guilt and responsibility of the individual family members, the interweaving of their perspectives and the pressures that have forced these perspectives. But for the family who lived this reality and who relived it as characters in a play, this reality has been lost. Mary, in particular, expresses and embodies this irretrievable loss. Even we lost this reality in time. Such is the unreality of the theatrical moment. Still, while the illusion persists and especially in the final image that orders our perception of this illusion as a reality, we have learned how Tolstoy's maxim must be adapted to suit O'Neill's play. The issue here is not the similarity of happy families or the dissimilarity of unhappy families. It is rather, on the evidence of O'Neill's text, how little a family resembles its image of itself, how strange is the seemingly familiar.

NOTES

1. Leo Tolstoy, *Anna Karenina,* trans. David Magarshack (New York: New American Library, 1961), 17.

2. Eugene O'Neill, as quoted in Croswell Bowen, "The Black Irishman," in *O'Neill and His Plays: Four Decades of Criticism,* ed. Oscar Cargill, N. Bryllion Fagin, and William J. Fisher (New York: New York University Press, 1961), 82.

3. Victor Shklovsky, "Art as Technique," in *Russian Formalist Criticism: Four Essays,* trans. Lee T. Lemon and Marion J. Reis (Lincoln: University of Nebraska Press, 1965), 12, 13; Bert O. States, *Great Reckonings in Little Rooms: On the Phenomenology of Theater* (Berkeley: University of California Press, 1985), 186.

4. Henri Bergson, *Time and Free Will,* as quoted in Stephen Kern, *The Culture of Time and Space, 1880–1918* (Cambridge, Mass.: Harvard University Press, 1983), 43.

5. Marvin Carlson, *Theories of the Theatre: A Historical and Critical Survey, from the Greeks to the Present* (Ithaca, N.Y.: Cornell University Press, 1984), 514.

6. Mac Wellman, "The Theatre of Good Intentions," *Performing Arts Journal* 24, vol. 8, no. 3 (1984): 60, 62, 64.

7. Judith E. Barlow, *Final Acts: The Creation of Three Late O'Neill Plays* (Athens: University of Georgia Press, 1985), 86, 91.

8. George Kubler, *The Shape of Time: Remarks on the History of Things* (New Haven: Yale University Press, 1962), 13.

9. Joseph Frank, "Spatial Form in Modern Literature," in *The Widening Gyre: Crisis and Mastery in Modern Literature* (New Brunswick, N.J.: Rutgers University Press, 1963), 3–62.

10. Michael Goldman, *The Actor's Freedom: Toward a Theory of Drama* (New York: Vintage Press, 1975), 158, 159.

11. Eugene O'Neill, *Long Day's Journey into Night* (New Haven: Yale University Press, 1955), 146.

12. See Richard Ellmann, *The Consciousness of Joyce* (New York: Oxford University Press, 1977), 50.

13. See, for example, Louis Sheaffer, *O'Neill: Son and Artist* (Boston: Little, Brown and Co., 1973), 290.

14. Robert B. Heilman, *The Iceman, the Arsonist, and the Troubled Agent: Tragedy and Melodrama on the Modern Stage* (Seattle: University of Washington Press, 1973), 109.

15. George Kubler, *The Shape of Time*, 19.

16. Edmund Husserl, *The Phenomenology of Internal Time-Consciousness*, trans. James S. Churchill, ed. Martin Heidegger (Bloomington: Indiana University Press, 1964), 76. See also 41, 43, 52, 149.

17. Wellman, "The Theatre of Good Intentions," 60.

18. Umberto Eco, *A Theory of Semiotics* (Bloomington: Indiana University Press, 1976), 7.

19. Heilman, *The Iceman, the Arsonist, and the Troubled Agent*, 106.

20. Thus I view the order of events in *Long Day's Journey* in a way similar to, but not identical with, the view Caryl Emerson takes of it in Pushkin's *Boris Godunov*. See Emerson, *Boris Godunov: Transpositions of a Russian Theme* (Bloomington: Indiana University Press, 1986), 117.

21. States, *Great Reckonings in Little Rooms*, 50, 69.

22. José Ortega y Gasset, "Adám en el Paraíso," as quoted in Kern, *The Culture of Time and Space*, 151 (see n. 4).

23. Jean Genet, *The Balcony*, rev. ed., trans. Bernard Frechtman (New York: Grove Press, 1966), 95–96.

24. Dmitry Merezhkovsky, *Polnoe sobranie sochineniy* (St. Petersburg, 1914) XVIII, 248, quoted in George Kalbouss, *The Plays of the Russian Symbolists* (East Lansing, Mich.: Russian Language Journal, 1982), 27.

25. Jacques Lacan, "The Insistence of the Letter in the Unconscious," as paraphrased in Frederick R. Karl, *Modern and Modernism: The Sovereignty of the Artist, 1885–1925* (New York: Atheneum, 1985), 100.

26. See Frederick Karl's discussion of Baudelaire's concept of the Dandy in *Modern and Modernism*, 44, 140–42. I have applied the formalist notion of "laying bare the device" to Karl's characterization of Baudelaire's concept, particularly the Dandy's implicit rejection of the rational and the conscious.

27. Nietzsche, in "On Truth and Falsehood in an Extra-moral Sense" ("Über Wahrheit und Lüge im außermoralischen Sinne"), wrote of "the prison-walls" ("Gefängnisswänden") of the false belief that language conveys "objective truth," inasmuch as both language and "truth" are, in Nietzsche's view, merely accretions of metaphor (*Nietzsche: Werke. Kritische Gesamtausgabe*, pt. 3, vol. 2, ed. Giorgio Colli and Mazzino Montinari [Berlin: Walter de Gruyter, 1973], 377). See also Ronald Hayman, *Nietzsche: A Critical Life* (New York: Oxford University Press, 1980), 165.

28. Boris Eichenbaum, "The Theory of the 'Formal Method,'" in *Russian Formalist Criticism: Four Essays*, 114 (see n. 3).

29. Dudley Nichols, as quoted by Barbara Gelb, "O'Neill's *Iceman* Sprang from the Ashes of His Youth," *New York Times*, 29 September 1985, sec. H, p. 4.

30. Friedrich Nietzsche, "A Critical Backward Glance [at *The Birth of Tragedy*]," as quoted in Herbert Blau, *Take Up the Bodies: Theater at the Vanishing Point* (Urbana: University of Illinois Press, 1982), 18–19.

31. Peter Steiner, *Russian Formalism: A Metapoetics* (Ithaca, N.Y.: Cornell University Press, 1984), 148.

32. Jean Chothia, *Forging a Language: A Study of the Plays of Eugene O'Neill* (Cambridge: Cambridge University Press, 1979), 177.

33. Pirandello, as quoted in Keir Elam, *The Semiotics of Theatre and Drama* (London: Methuen, 1980), 17, 126.

34. States, *Great Reckonings in Little Rooms,* 50.

35. Sheaffer, *O'Neill: Son and Artist,* 376.

36. George Rowell, *Theatre in the Age of Irving* (Totowa, N.J.: Rowman and Littlefield, 1981), 10.

3

Causality in O'Neill's Late Masterpieces

Roger Brown

Jim Tyrone in *A Moon for the Misbegotten* said that "there is no present or future—only the past happening over and over again."[1] This is the impression we have of the life enacted in *A Moon for the Misbegotten* and also in *Long Day's Journey into Night* and *The Iceman Cometh*. We have this impression because the stage is filled with repetitions, repetitions that are not just unwilled or involuntary but are actually willed against. The thing repeated, the past that happens over and over again, could not be some strong action that comes to consummation; it is simply speaking—speaking things that are unspeakable.

When O'Neill was composing *Mourning Becomes Electra,* he kept a work diary and in the first extract (spring 1926) he asked whether it is possible to get a "modern psychological approximation of the Greek sense of fate" into a play intended to move a modern audience that has no belief in gods or supernatural retribution.[2] He wrote the first draft of the play between September 1929 and February 1930, and when he read it over, a month later, he felt that he had failed to produce this sense of fate. To correct this, he experimented with "thought asides" and masklike makeup and a Greek chorus. He used repetition, undesired but irrepressible repetition, in *Electra* in the form of the mysterious Mannon curse that corrupts one generation after another even when, like Christine and Lavinia, they fight against it. The somewhat contrived destiny of the house is realized in a frenetic, melodramatic plot. *Mourning Becomes Electra* is all swift single-minded theatrical action whereas the late plays are slow and meditative, but it is the late plays that convey the more persuasive sense of fate.

We know that O'Neill always denied any direct Freudian influence, even for *Electra*.[3] So I am sure he would deny any connection between Freud's 1920 monograph *Beyond the Pleasure Principle* and the fact that repetition, as used in the last three masterpieces, creates a crushing sense of inevitability without introducing any gods. Probably there *was* no influence, though we do know he read the monograph and called it "interesting."[4] I think I know just what it was that interested him in *Beyond the Pleasure Principle.* It would not, I think, have been Freud's untenable "libido theory." Probably it was the "repetition compulsion."

Freud held that some people, possibly all, feel compelled to repeat actions, style of action, even total relationships that can never have given pleasure but only regret or remorse. There is the benefactor whose protégés always turn against him, the lover whose love affairs all pass through the same dismal phases. "The impression they give," and here Freud wrote a sentence that would have interested O'Neill when he was working on *Electra,* "is of being pursued by a malignant fate or pursued by some 'daemonic' power, but psychoanalysis has always taken the view that their fate is for the most part arranged by themselves and determined by early infantile experiences." Finally, there is a sentence that could go as it stands into any of the last plays: "[For such people life is] a perpetual recurrence of the same thing."[5]

Remember what Jim Tyrone says in *A Moon for the Misbegotten:* "There is no present or future—only the past happening over and over again—now. You can't get away from it" and what Mary Tyrone says in *Long Day's Journey:* "The past is the present, isn't it? It's the future too. We all try to lie out of that but life won't let us."[6]

A world in which there is no present or future but only the past happening over and over again is a world of total inevitability, without either free will or responsibility. In *All God's Chillun Got Wings* (1924), an early, somewhat autobiographical play, when Ella says: "I'm free, Jim," his weary answer is "We're never free—except to do what we have to do."[7] The more eloquent statement by a later incarnation of Ella O'Neill in *Long Day's Journey into Night* is: "None of us can help the things life had done to us. They're done before you realize it, and once they're done they make you do other things until at last everything comes between you and what you'd like to be, and you've lost your true self forever" (61).

The *assertions* O'Neill makes about inevitability and recurrence are not important for philosophy. On the general subject of free will and determinism it takes a very subtle academic mind to say anything even slightly new. What is important is his ability in the last three masterpieces to dramatize a fatalistic view so effectively as to cause people, who are far indeed from believing that the past is the present and also the future, to experience for a time both the weight and the *relief* of that view.

INVOLUNTARY REPETITION

Personality is the natural naive unit for the explanation of action, probably because the physical person is a figural unit in visual perception. Audience members' first thoughts about causality for the actions they see on the stage will be internal or characterological. For most dramas, this bias does not make a problem. It will usually exactly suit the playwright's intention. But, for the writer who wants to convey inevitability, there is a problem. The problem is that we tend to think of personalities or characters as autonomous agents, free to choose their actions, primary causes of their actions.

Long Day's Journey into Night

The general solution of the late plays is to present a spectacle of involuntary repetitions. The exact nature of these repetitions varies from one play to another. In *Long Day's Journey* we have the central fact of four principals with addictions. Morphine gets the most attention, and Mary's guilt and excuses and failed "cures" constitute the strongest example of involuntary repetition, but booze is also ubiquitous and has done much damage to them all and is at least occasionally a cause of guilt.

More overpowering for the audience than the drugs are conversational cycles in which something wounding is said, then repented, and eventually repeated—not in the exact words but in general effect. In Act four Jamie tells Edmund: "Mama and Papa are right. I've been rotten bad influence. And worst of it is, I did it on purpose. . . . Wanted you to fail. Always jealous of you. Mama's baby, Papa's pet!" (165). Then comes repentance: "But don't get wrong idea, Kid. . . . What I wanted to say is, I'd like to see you become the greatest success in the world." After repentance comes repetition. "But you'd better be on your guard. Because I'll do my damnedest to make you fail. Can't help it" (166). The cycles of repentance and repetition in *Long Day's Journey* convey very strongly the idea that volition counts for nothing.

The Iceman Cometh

The involuntary repetition in *Iceman* is exactly the same in form for the fourteen pimps, tarts, deadbeats, and derelicts, all of them drunks, who pass their time in Harry Hope's saloon. The mood is very different from *Long Day's Journey*. Travis Bogard has likened the scene in Hope's saloon to a tidal pool, "a world that barely holds to the fringes of consciousness . . . a . . . trance-like existence . . . [with] light . . . insufficient to separate day from night."[8] All the characters have pipe dreams that tomorrow will be different, but so far tomorrow has always been the same as yesterday. Everyone can see the folly of the other fellow's dream but none their own. Into this quiet harbor comes a hearty affable salesman, Theodore Hickman, known as Hickey. It is Hickey's custom to visit twice a year, always including Harry Hope's birthday—which is now, once again, imminent. Hickey's visits are very welcome because he stands drinks for everybody and is a great joker, but this time he is altogether different. He acts like some kind of preacher and says he has come to free them all from their pipe dreams as he has been freed of his own.

Hickey persuades, cajoles, or goads each one to attempt to act on the dream, to create a real tomorrow. He pretends to believe they can do so though in fact he knows they cannot. They all do make the try and they all do fail. Harry Hope, who has not stepped outside his door since the death of his wife, Bessie, twenty years ago, has always planned to take a walk around town—tomorrow. When Hickey has mercilessly analyzed away all his excuses, Hope sets forth but does not make it across the street. By night they have all failed and come back. The attempt to act has left them stuporous, near-dead, for now they realize their dreams have always been lies. They have no hope, and the magic has gone out of the booze; they can no longer pass out and find peace. Harry Hope hits on the good thought, however, that Hickey is not only changed but is insane. It follows—by a boozy sort of logic—that they have only been humoring a madman and have not really tested their dreams at all, which leaves the dreams intact. Hope for tomorrow returns, the booze works once more, and there is peace again in the "Bottom of the Sea Rathskeller."

This is not a story of repentance but of reluctant painful attempts to change that are foreordained to fail and do fail. Whereas *Long Day's Journey* compulsively repeats across multiple themes interrelating just four people, *Iceman* repeats across fourteen persons with largely unrelated dreams and very different past histories. O'Neill did not intend to suggest that only the lower depths needed pipe dreams. Hickey is the Iceman and the Iceman brings unsparing truth, a kind of death for all who accept it.

A Moon for the Misbegotten

A Moon for the Misbegotten is almost all involuntary repetition. Jim Tyrone begins his confession to Josie Hogan: "It was long ago. But it seems like tonight" (128). You feel that the story has been going through his mind ever since it happened—like the recurrent nightmares in traumatic neurosis, which Freud discusses in *Beyond The Pleasure Principle*.

About a year ago when Mama died, James brought her body back east by train and for four days he was pie-eyed in a private drawing room. A silly verse kept running through his head:

> And baby's cries can't waken her
> In the baggage car ahead. (150)

He picked up a blonde and "every night—for fifty bucks a night—" (149). Perhaps he had "some mad idea she could make [him] forget—what was in the baggage car ahead." But "[he] didn't seem to want to forget. . . . It was as if [he] wanted revenge—because [he'd] been left alone" (149–50).

When Mama died, James had been on the wagon for two years. He had stopped drinking for her sake—after Papa had died—because she hated it and she had no one else to look after her. But when she became ill on the West Coast—a brain tumor—James became frightened and got drunk and stayed drunk. Before she died she saw that he was drunk and "closed her eyes so she couldn't see, and was glad to die" (147).

Although *A Moon for the Misbegotten* is mostly compulsive drinking and hopeless love, the ending is distinctly elegiac, even prayerful. Josie Hogan, when she has heard everything, forgives everything—in her own name and also in the name of James's mother, and more surprisingly, James drops his cynicism to say that he accepts absolution and will never forget her love. The last lines—they are spoken by Josie—are: "May you have your wish and die in your sleep soon, Jim, darling. May you rest forever in forgiveness and peace" (177). These are the last words O'Neill wrote for the stage, and biographers and critics like to take them as a kind of final mellowing. Another Great Artist moves gracefully off stage humming "The September Song."

That mold will not fit Eugene O'Neill and *A Moon for the Misbegotten*. On July 22, 1952, eight years after *A Moon for the Misbegotten* was completed, O'Neill gave a copy of the play to his wife, Carlotta, with an inscription that read, in part, "a play . . . which I have come to loathe." What a fascinating remark. It is his last recorded word on the play; he died in 1953. It was not a passing distaste because in 1951 he refused permission to produce it because, as Lawrence Langner relates in a letter to Elia Kazan, September 6, 1951, "he wanted to do some rewriting on it." He never did the rewriting—he was too ill. Yet in 1943, composing the play, his work diary records "real affection for it."[9]

Why should O'Neill have turned against *A Moon for the Misbegotten?* It is a real mystery. No one knows the answer. Perhaps the prayerful ending became distasteful to him because it falsified his feeling for James or because it falsified his feeling about life. Eugene had many reasons to feel guilty about his behavior toward James. He gave excuses for not flying to the West Coast when Ella was dying, for not accompanying James on the train ride home, for not even meeting the train but letting his almost incoherent brother be deposited in a Times Square hotel. When James was dying in a sanatorium, Eugene stayed away—for the last six months of James's life.[10] He had reason to feel guilty, and we know that he felt so not just because he generally did feel guilty if there was any opportunity but because in the original typescript of *A Moon for the Misbegotten* there is a speech, later removed, in which Jim speaks bitterly of his younger brother's inability to forgive that train ride with Mama's body.[11] Eugene also had countless reasons to *hate* James. Even after the elder brother's death, Eugene O'Neill, Jr., took him as a kind of model and led the dissipated life that ended in suicide in 1950. So perhaps in 1952 the playwright did not feel elegiac and prayerful about James—or, as the terrible events of his last year would suggest, about anything.

I can make a case arguing that O'Neill finally loathed *Moon for the Misbegotten* and wanted to change it because it did not express honestly his feelings for his brother, but I do not convince myself. Arguments like that attribute too much importance to self-expression and too little to art. In spite of all the fact–fiction correspondences, the life did not write the plays. It seems most likely to me that O'Neill finally disliked *Moon for the Misbegotten* for reasons intrinsic to the structure of the play. Somehow I cannot believe that anything outside the work would make that work-obsessed man rewrite.

SPEAKING THE UNSPEAKABLE

If we compare the late three masterpieces with *Mourning Becomes Electra* (1931), *Desire Under the Elms* (1925), or *Strange Interlude* (1928), the late plays are strikingly uneventful. Think how much goes on in *Electra*. Christine poisons Ezra, Orin kills Brant, Orin kills himself. In the later masterpieces people mostly just sit around and talk. The plays are uneventful—but not tame. For most of us they are harrowing. What does O'Neill substitute for action? He causes the unspeakable to be spoken.

All God's Chillun Got Wings (1924) is an early play with a simple straightforward example. In this play a woman named Ella says to a man named Jim: "You dirty nigger!" (337). The scene as I have thus far described it, though shocking, is not an example of the unspeakable—in the sense I intend. Ella's speech is shocking in a completely general way; it is something no one should ever say or have to hear—an established obscenity. There is more than that to the unspeakable in late O'Neill.

The hearer of the shocking speech is usually established in advance as one for whom this speech from this person will be uniquely painful. Jim in *All God's Chillun* is a black man (Paul Robeson in the 1924 production) deeply in love with Ella, a white woman. He speaks of her to his sister in these terms: "I can do anything for her! I'm all she's got in the world! . . . I've got to prove worthy! I've got to prove she can be proud of me! I've got to prove I'm the whitest of the white!" (335). Now we know the speech will really hurt; it will hurt us as well as Jim, and the names we give our hurt are pity and horror.

The unspeakable in O'Neill's late plays seems usually to be foreshadowed. Typically, the audience knows in advance that what has not yet been said exists already in the inner life of the speaker-to-be. That inner life must therefore be somehow represented. Representation of inner life fascinated O'Neill throughout his career, and he experimented with various techniques (masks in *The Great God Brown* [1926], *Lazarus Laughed* [1927], and other plays; "thought asides" in *Strange Interlude*

[1928]; expressionistic sets in *The Hairy Ape, The Emperor Jones,* and, to some degree, every play). In *All God's Chillun* the device is old and honorable. Ella delivers a soliloquy. She stands alone on the stage looking at a gold-framed photograph of an elderly black man in outlandish lodge regalia and speaks these words to the audience:

It's his Old Man—all dolled up like a circus horse! Well, they can't help it. It's in the blood, I suppose. They're ignorant, that's all there is to it. . . . *(She goes to the window and looks down at the street* . . .) . . . Why it's Shorty! *(She throws the window open and calls)* Shorty! Shorty! Hello, Shorty! . . . He doesn't want to know you any more. . . . He's afraid it'd get him in wrong with the old gang. Why? You know well enough! Because you married a– a– a– well, I won't say it but you know without my mentioning any names! (330–31)

Now the audience knows roughly what is to come and both dreads it and looks forward to it. Inner life advance notices function in O'Neill's late plays very much like the prophecies and curses of Greek drama. In *Oedipus Rex* the oracle at Delphi has prophesied, and Apollo has decreed that Oedipus shall kill his father, Laius, and marry his mother, Jocasta. The audience knows that this has already happened, and dreads Oedipus's recognition.

Parenthetically, I disagree with Freud's view that the power of Sophocles' play is to be explained by its content or theme.[12] The Oedipus Complex and incest generally are so very familiar today that they shock few, but I saw the play recently and it is as gripping as ever. I think the fascination is primarily intellectual rather than emotional. It is the immense cunning with which Sophocles progressively discloses information that grips us. O'Neill has shown a cunning almost as great in spacing the clues that Mary is once again using morphine in *Long Day's Journey,* and he has done it again in *Iceman* in revealing that Hickey has murdered his wife and Parritt betrayed his mother.

The unspeakable spoken in O'Neill has two usual components. The hearer-to-be is established as one who will suffer keenly from what is to be spoken, and the speaker-to-be is revealed to the audience to have the knowledge or feeling in mind before, usually well before, speaking it. In short, there is an exposed heart and a camouflaged but aimed arrow. We dread what is coming and feel pity when it happens.

THE REPRESENTATION OF INNER LIFE

O'Neill's interest in the representation of inner life was so great that a few notes on this large subject are not a serious digression. Inner life, which I take to be the same as William James's "stream of thought," is not representable at all for two reasons James gave.[13] Consciousness is always sensibly continuous without breach or interruption. Even when there are time gaps, the thought before feels as if it belongs with the thought after.

Each consciousness is personal and perfectly insulated from each other; there is no mutual awareness or interaction.

Now take the case of O'Neill's most interesting experiment, the "thought aside" of *Strange Interlude*. The technique of speaking thoughts aloud directly to the audience was an old one, but in *Strange Interlude* the asides constitute a third of what the audience hears. There was a lot of discussion at the time of production about how to differentiate inner speech from speech to others, whether by stage area, tone of voice, special lighting, or freezing the action.[14] There seems to have been no discussion of the fact that speech could not really represent thought because it could not be simultaneously continuous for all, and in fact, characters took turns as if conversing. Nor could speech be insulated as thought is because although characters in the play could pretend not to hear one another, the audience has to hear. Since the goal is to make the private public, the contradiction is inescapable. "Thought asides" have to be thought samples, acceptable as such only because of acquiescence in certain conventions.

The "thought asides" of *Strange Interlude* are interesting to study. Nina Leeds, bitterly regretting that she did not make love with the ineffable Gordon Shaw before he went off to war and got killed, will at the end of the act attack her father for interfering between them. Before she does so, however, her thought asides build tension with lines such as: "I must keep calm . . . I mustn't let go or I'll tell him everything . . . and I mustn't tell him . . . he's my father."[15]

The surprising thing about these "thoughts" is that they not only keep Nina's secret from her father; they keep it also from herself. How could anyone possibly worry about telling someone something without thinking what it was that might be told? The same thing happens in Act two when Mrs. Evans keeps from herself the fact that the thing she must not reveal is the existence in her family of hereditary insanity. It's like something out of Gilbert and Sullivan. The point is to keep these disclosures from the audience so as not to weaken their impact when finally spoken. O'Neill had too strong a theatrical sense to do that.

There is a larger point. When you see *Strange Interlude* you do not notice the confusions of point of view. If the "thought asides" irritate, it is because they are often redundant, stating explicitly what we have already inferred from speech and action. The convention itself is easily acceptable as are asides and soliloquies generally. In opera, the audience listening to a number of simultaneous voices seldom notices which are supposed to be thoughts and which are supposed to be speech. Being accustomed to the conventions must be one reason, but I think there is another.

Probably, we always feel that we are in contact with the minds of others and not just their speech and action. The infinitely subtle business of interpreting nonverbal behavior and drawing many kinds of inference and implication from language has only come into human awareness in recent times as a result of the labors of the communication sciences, but it has all always been there, operating smoothly and swiftly, and experienced as mind-to-mind contact.

In the late plays O'Neill dropped all his special techniques for representing inner life, and yet the minds in those plays are in such close contact as to be rubbed raw. How has he done it? By the ordinary means of real life. In *Long Day's Journey,* for instance, all possible dyads, triads, and tetrads have scenes to themselves. (I was interested to read that O'Neill had to make notes to keep track of who had spoken to whom about what.)[16] What is spoken in one scene can be assumed to belong to inner life in another. Having heard Mary say to Edmund and Tyrone in Act three that Jamie will never be content until he makes Edmund a hopeless failure, we confidently furnish both Edmund and Jamie with this thought when the two talk together in Act four before the thought is spoken.

What else? Inference. Mary ate very little breakfast this day, and last night she slept in the spare room. These are nonverbal clues to the resumption of morphine use. They are not the only indicators. Mary keeps fussing with her hair, and she talks on and on in a foolish way, and, a terrible moment, Jamie notices her eyes in Act two, scene one—more signs that she is using morphine. What else? Body types. Edmund, like O'Neill himself, is an ectomorph, and both the Jameses are mesomorphs. Truly or falsely, body types suggest temperament types. However, mistakes are made when characters read one another's inner life or when audiences do, but mistakes occur outside the theater also. The point is that the processes are all normal, and the contact between minds is no less intimate, probably more so, than when special techniques are used.

THE EXPOSED HEART AND THE UNSPEAKABLE SPOKEN

I have claimed that in the late plays O'Neill replaces terrible events with terrible words spoken to the one who will suffer most from them but have not given many examples. Here are some.

Long Day's Journey into Night

In *Long Day's Journey* Mary has said that she loves Edmund most, and so her heart is exposed to maximal anguish when he calls her a "dope fiend" (120). And Edmund's devotion to Mary has been established long before she says: "I never knew what rheumatism was before you were born" (116). *Rheumatism* is Mary's word for morphine. All three men, the father and two sons, have spoken in Act one of their happiness and pride at seeing Mama her old self once again. This makes her lapse in Act two very painful for them and also for us.

The Iceman Cometh

In *Iceman* (1940), it is useful to distinguish, as Travis Bogard did, between the fourteen characters suspended in the aqueous atmosphere of Hope's saloon—who constitute a kind of Greek *choros*—and the three principals.[17] In *Iceman* the most painful speeches are those that attack each life-sustaining pipe dream. From the start there are many lines making fun of the pipe dreams, some for each speaker, some applying to each listener, but with one significant omission. None speaks such lines to himself or to herself. These self-acknowledgments, the most painful speeches in the play, do not come until late in Act three and in Act four when the failure to act has forced the realization that tomorrow will not be different and so all hope is gone. Cora says: "Jees, imagine me kiddin' myself I wanted to marry a drunken pimp."[18] Harry Hope remembers that his late wife, dear old Bessie, whose death caused his twenty-year seclusion, had always been a "nagging bitch" (692). Larry Slade confesses that his professed impatience for death had been just another pipe dream (689). Most poignant to me is Jimmy Tomorrow's "Yes. Quite right. It was all a stupid lie—my nonsense about tomorrow" (707).

The play gives us good reason to anticipate the self-acknowledgments that come near the end. After all the boozy foolishness of the first act, the characters can only grow in insight. Although I think we can prophesy what will happen, I do not think we can be said to dread it. The poor fish in the "No Chance Saloon" are too distant from us. The mood of the play is very different from *Long Day's Journey*. *Iceman* drifts along and finally you are surprised how warmly you feel toward everyone in "Bedrock Bar" and how relieved you are when the booze starts to work again.

A Moon for the Misbegotten

The most painful thing in this play is Jim Tyrone's story of his train ride. It caused the first production to be closed for obscenity in Detroit and labeled a slander on American motherhood.[19] For whom should this story be *most* painful? Not the one who hears it—Josie Hogan—but Mama, who is dead. Jim Tyrone in important ways is like Hickey and like Don Parritt, two of the principals of *Iceman*. All three are without hope and ready to die. But whereas Hickey and Parritt seek punishment, Jim Tyrone seeks to confess and has chosen Josie Hogan to hear his confession. She is a suitable surrogate for his mother because she is fine and beautiful and warmhearted and a virgin (always a desirable attribute for the mother of such a son).

A DEPRESSIVE ATTRIBUTION STYLE

Let me close with a difficult question. Is it true, this view of causality in human life that O'Neill asserts and dramatizes in the late plays? Is it true, as Jim Tyrone says, that "there is no present or future—only the past happening over and over again." Of course it is not. Of course it is.

Long Day's Journey into Night is set in 1912, and the past happening over and over again is what the play seems to promise. But what happened in fact? Edmund recovered completely from tuberculosis in May 1913. In 1914 Ella went to a convent for a short time to make one final attempt to overcome her "curse," and she succeeded.[20] In 1920 Jamie quit drinking cold.[21] These are three futures very different from the yesterday of 1912, three bright tomorrows realized. As we know from Louis Sheaffer and *A Moon for the Misbegotten,* however, in 1922 Ella died and Jamie went back to his dissipation. As for Edmund, he won the Nobel prize and four Pulitzer prizes, but remember, he is the one who wrote in his last play: "There is only yesterday happening over and over again." Eugene, Jr.'s death was something like Jamie's; son Shane's addiction something like Ella's; and Eugene shouted at last: "I knew it, I knew it! Born in a goddamn hotel room and dying in a hotel room!"[22] The facts of life allow for more than one causal interpretation, and interpretations may even be largely independent of any facts, including personal fortune, and determined largely by genetic and/or early life experience factors. I know a wise psychiatrist who whenever he hears a litany of disaster says: "I know, but that's no reason to be depressed."

In social psychology the principles of perceived causality are called attribution theory with *attribution* used in the sense of "to what or whom do you attribute something?" Research on attribution has included individual differences, and one stable style has been identified and studied for about ten years by Martin Seligman of the University of Pennsylvania and his associates.[23] It is a cognitive style, a way of construing causality in one's own life, and is called either the "depressive" or the "pessimistic" attributional style. It is related to clinical depression but characterizes many people who have never been psychiatric patients. The style can be identified either by coding spontaneously produced verbal materials or from answers to a standardized questionnaire.

A person with a depressive attributional style takes the darkest possible view of any unhappy outcome in his life. He considers it to be internally caused—his own failing. He construes the failure in global terms—not just a little failing but a very general one. He believes that the failing is stable, it is always going to be this way. If I get a disappointing grade on a particular exam and I think in the depressive way, my conclusion might be that I am unintelligent, not in one field but very generally, and, furthermore, will always be so. If I have a more cheerful and self-protective style, I will probably conclude that it was a stupid exam.

I don't think we need a completed questionnaire to diagnose O'Neill's style. I am sure he would have refused to fill out any such damn fool thing. But in reading Louis Sheaffer's biography, I have noticed how many quotations over O'Neill's full life span meet all criteria—internal, global and stable. How about this one: "It seems as if we manage things in the exact way to make everything turn out all wrong." Or this one: "Something in me is so utterly dead that I don't care about anything anymore." However, there is a last phrase on that one: "—except doing my work."[24]

José Quintero, the director of the first successful productions of *Iceman* and *Long Day's Journey,* has recently published an account of the period in which he was rehearsing *Journey.* Many things were going on at once. The play caused Quintero and the actors to recollect their own early years and replay, in memory, conversations eerily close sometimes to scenes in the play. Everyone had a father who turned out light bulbs to cut down on the electric bill and several had fathers who had squandered their young talents not on *The Count of Monte Cristo* but on other unworthy projects. Some days Quintero had Monterey cocktails and luncheon with Carlotta O'Neill who had released *Long Day's Journey* to him because she liked him. These conversations, as he reports them, drift between past and present, one family and another, the life and the play.

The waiter brought my lamb chops and Mrs. O'Neill her Monterey. "Are they all right?" she asked.

"Yes, delicious. But I feel awful eating while you're having nothing."

"It's wonderful talking to you. Everything you say and do shows that you were brought up properly in a lovely home, I'm sure. Do you know how many homes I made for O'Neill? Oh, they were such beautiful homes. I selected everything myself, to the last piece of furniture. He didn't help me, wouldn't put himself out the least bit. *He didn't know how to act in a home. He never really wanted one . . . never, since the day we were married.* Yet he kept saying how much he hated hotel rooms."

* * * * * * *

"Aren't these Montereys delicious?"

"Yes. Did you teach them how to make them?"

"I certainly did. As a matter of fact, I'm going to be a tiny bit naughty and have another."

* * * * * * *

"When I married O'Neill, I began to live the life of a recluse. We hardly saw anyone. And during the day, he would lock himself in his study and I was left alone with the servants for company. It got worse after the war. It became impossible to get help. But it wasn't always like that. *At the convent,* I told you that my mother had sent me to a convent in Europe to be educated there, so in a way I was raised a Catholic, *at the convent I had so many friends. Girls whose families lived in lovely homes. I used to visit them and they'd visit me in my father's home. But naturally after I married . . ."*

* * * * * * *

"I'm sorry, Mrs. O'Neill, but I have to be going. I just had to come and tell you how well things are going. I don't want you to worry because I like you very much."

"Bless you," she said and took my hand, which she held for a little while. "Long fingers held together by such a delicate wrist. Just like his."

"This afternoon we begin working with the boys."

"You mean Jamie?"

"Yes. And Edmund, too. You know, the scene where they . . ."

"Be merciless with Jamie," she interrupted in a voice almost distorted by an old anger which had never stopped growing, "He almost destroyed Gene . . . *he deliberately ruined his health . . . . Even before that when he was in prep school, Gene began dissipating and playing the Broadway sport to imitate him, when he knew he never had his constitution to stand it.*" She drank half of the Monterey and motioning me to come closer to her, she whispered, "And the worst of it was that . . . *he did it on purpose.*"[25]

The sections Quintero has italicized in this conversation are virtual quotations of statements in *Long Day's Journey* by Mary Tyrone—the stage version of O'Neill's own mother, Mary Ella Quinlan O'Neill—grieving over the loss of the happiness she knew as a girl in a convent school and her husband's unwillingness to give her a real home, and of other complaints by both Mary and James Tyrone about the malice of their older son Jamie toward his younger siblings, Edmund and Eugene, both alter egos of the playwright himself.[26] Carlotta herself once declared that O'Neill was seeking a mother in her.[27] It is evident from her comments to Quintero that she played the part, and even became the part, by identifying with O'Neill's stage portrait of his real mother to the extent of appropriating her very words.

That is the past happening over and over again—even across generations and jumping the gap between life and art.

NOTES

1. Eugene O'Neill, *A Moon for the Misbegotten* (New York: Random House, Inc., 1952), 128.

2. Eugene O'Neill, "Working Notes and Extracts from a Fragmentary Work Diary," *The Unknown O'Neill: Unpublished or Unfamiliar Writings of Eugene O'Neill,* ed. Travis Bogard (New Haven: Yale University Press, 1988), 394.

3. Louis Sheaffer, *O'Neill: Son and Artist* (Boston: Brown, Little and Co., 1973), 382.

4. Ibid., 174.

5. Sigmund Freud, *Beyond the Pleasure Principle,* in *The Standard Edition of the Complete Psychological Works of Sigmund Freud,* ed. and trans. James Strachey (with Anna Freud, Alix Strachey, and Alan Tyson), vol. 18 (1920–1922), *"Beyond the Pleasure Principle," "Group Psychology," and Other Works* (London: Hogarth Press and the Institute of Psycho-Analysis, 1955), 21, 22.

6. Eugene O'Neill, *Long Day's Journey into Night* (New Haven: Yale University Press, 1955), 87.

7. Eugene O'Neill, *All God's Chillun Got Wings* in *The Plays of Eugene O'Neill,* vol. 2 (New York: Random House, Inc., Modern Library, 1982), 315.

8. Travis Bogard, *Contour in Time: The Plays of Eugene O'Neill* (New York: Oxford University Press, 1972), 414.

9. Judith E. Barlow, *Final Acts: The Creation of Three Late O'Neill Plays* (Athens: University of Georgia Press, 1985), 116, 118, 120.

10. Sheaffer, *O'Neill: Son and Artist,* 116.

11. Barlow, *Final Acts,* 132.

12. Freud, *The Development of the Libido and the Sexual Organizations,* in *The Standard Edition of the Complete Psychological Works of Sigmund Freud,* ed. and trans. James Strachey (with Anna Freud, Alix Strachey, and Alan Tyson), vol. 16 (1916–1917), *Introductory Lectures on Psycho-Analysis (Part III)* (London: Hogarth Press and the Institute of Psycho-Analysis, 1963), 330–31.

13. William James, "The Stream of Thought," Chapter 9 in *The Principles of Psychology,* vol. 1 (New York: Henry Holt and Co., 1890), 224–90, esp. 225–29, 237–48.

14. Sheaffer, *O'Neill: Son and Artist,* 274–75.

15. Eugene O'Neill, *Strange Interlude* in *The Plays of Eugene O'Neill,* vol. 3 (New York: Random House, Inc., Modern Library, 1982), 17.

16. Saxe Commins wrote about these notes in a passage in *"Love and Admiration and Respect": The O'Neill-Commins Correspondence,* ed. Dorothy Commins (Durham: Duke University Press, 1986), 29.

17. Bogard, *Contour in Time,* 410.

18. Eugene O'Neill, *The Iceman Cometh* in *The Plays of Eugene O'Neill,* vol. 1 (New York: Random House, Inc., Modern Library, 1982), 700.

19. Sheaffer, *O'Neill: Son and Artist,* 595–96.

20. Louis Sheaffer, *O'Neill: Son and Playwright* (Boston: Little, Brown and Co., 1968), 257, 280–81.

21. Sheaffer, *O'Neill: Son and Artist,* 40.

22. Ibid., 83–88, 563, 615, 616, 624, 631, 670.

23. See, for example, M. E. Seligson, L. V. Abramson, A. Semmel, and C. von Baeyer, "Depressive Attributional Style," *Journal of Abnormal Psychology* 88 (1979): 242–47.

24. Sheaffer, *O'Neill: Son and Artist,* 261, 278.

25. José Quintero, *If You Don't Dance They Beat You* (Boston: Little, Brown and Co., 1974), 229–35, 236–38.

26. See *Long Day's Journey* 34, 44, 61, 67, 72, 86, 87. Also compare with Carlotta's last sentence Jamie's comment about his corruption of Eugene on 165: "And worst of it is, I did it on purpose." In my text I have abridged Quintero's account of the conversation, which contains even more italicized paraphrases of *Long Day's Journey* by Carlotta than appear in my excerpts.

27. Sheaffer, *O'Neill: Son and Artist,* 669–70.

4

Masking Becomes Electra: O'Neill, Freud, and the Feminine

S. Georgia Nugent

O'Neill's detailed stage set for *Mourning Becomes Electra* features the Mannon mansion with its Greek *"temple portico . . . like an incongruous white mask fixed on the house to hide its somber gray ugliness."*[1] We might characterize the trilogy itself with a reversal of this image: O'Neill's work affixes a projecting facade of Freudian concepts to an underlying structure derived from Greek tragedy. Freudian theory would seem to offer the playwright a means of illumining the psyche of the Electra figure. Instead, O'Neill uses Freud not to reveal but to mask a darkness, specifically "the dark continent" of feminine sexuality. Overtly, *Mourning Becomes Electra* seems to be about unresolved Oedipal attachments. They are *so* overt, however, as to lack Freudian resistance and repression altogether. Something else, however, is systematically repressed in the trilogy— namely, non-Oedipal sexual relations and particularly feminine desire and sexual activity.

I shall argue here that O'Neill, in the process of writing and rewriting the play, consistently cut passages revealing feminine desire or sexual activity and replaced them with passages that displace and conceal that activity, and, moreover, that *suppressed* sexuality (we will discover) is displaced onto the author's own writing. An analysis of the trilogy clearly demonstrates O'Neill's fear of confronting or portraying desire, but the playwright's own commentary on the trilogy reveals a consistent system of sexual metaphor involving both male adequacy of performance and female parturition. The eroticism displaced from the play's narrative is transferred to the act of writing like a Freudian "return of the repressed." Within the work itself, O'Neill's eroticization of writing is translated into epistolary terms with the result that in *Mourning Becomes Electra* a refusal to write signals a refusal of sexuality, whereas the choice to write signals an aggressive and dangerous entry into sexuality.

FROM FATE TO FREUD

Most obviously, by his naming of the trilogy (and by the use of the trilogic structure itself) O'Neill designates that his work is to be understood in the context of Greek tragic theater and, most especially, as a modernization of Aeschylus's *Oresteia,* the only complete Greek trilogy extant. Each major narrative element of the Greek drama finds its counterpart here. The war hero (Agamemnon/Ezra Mannon), returning home, is treacherously murdered by his unfaithful wife (Clytemnestra/ Christine) with the aid of her lover (Aegisthus/Adam Brant), also a dispossessed heir of the household. Subsequently, the children (Electra/Lavinia, Orestes/Orin) take their vengeance upon both lover and mother and, in the final play, must come to terms with their own part in the family's history of crime and punishment. In other details as well, from providing a narrative background of lust and betrayal in the previous generation to experimenting with the formal use of a "chorus" of townspeople to introduce the plays, O'Neill attempts to transfer Greek tragedy to the American stage.

In addition to specific narrative and formal elements of the *Oresteia,* what O'Neill has carried over into his modern version is the powerful force of a family curse working its way through generations. Whereas others have seen economic determinism as the modern equivalent for the ancient concept of tragic fate, O'Neill sees in its place psychological complexes.[2] He insists that "fate from within the family is modern psychological approximation of the Greek conception of fate from without, from the supernatural."[3]

Although O'Neill's debt to classical tragedy is undisputed, the extent of his familiarity with and exposure to psychoanalytic theory remains a topic of some debate.[4] The playwright himself demurs when the question of his psychologizing in *Mourning Becomes Electra* is raised.[5] Yet his working notes for the trilogy clearly indicate from the beginning his desire to experiment with the possibility of introducing psychological compulsion in the place of Greek tragedy's motivating Fate.

If one of O'Neill's major motives in writing the trilogy was to explore the psychological translation of the Greek notion of fate, another was his desire to explore the Electra figure herself. We know from his working notebooks that as early as 1926 he had read versions of the Electra story and conceived the idea of transferring the Greek tragic plot to a modern setting.[6] O'Neill speaks of Electra as "the most interesting of all women in drama."[7] Electra is indeed the only figure for whom we have a full, extant treatment by each of the great Greek tragedians (Aeschylus's *Choephoroi,* Sophocles' and Euripides' respective *Electras*). Despite this considerable attention in ancient drama, however, O'Neill is right in identifying a curious gap in the treatment of her tale. "Why," he asks, "did the chain of fated crime and retribution ignore her mother's murderess?—a weakness in what remains to us of Greek tragedy that there is no play about Electra's life after murder of Clytemnestra."[8] The modern dramatist seeks to redress the balance by focusing on this female protagonist rather than on the Orestes figure as had the Greek tragedians.

In theory, O'Neill's decision to wed psychoanalytic theory to the Greek mythic material seems well motivated. Freud himself frequently appealed to Greek mythic material and especially to the Oedipal tragedy in naming what he called "the central phenomenon of the sexual period in early childhood."[9] In practice, however, O'Neill's choice of classical Freudian theory to explore the female psyche via Greek tragedy makes strange bedfellows indeed. The Greek tragic stage was capable of creating female figures of remarkable power and complexity and of exploring feminine interiority with extraordinary insight.[10] Freudian theorizing of the feminine, on the other hand, has been an area of psychoanalytic theory repeatedly challenged and contested (first in the 1930s and recently by a new generation of feminists) as inadequate or misconceived.[11] The weaknesses of the Freudian imagination in this regard work directly counter to O'Neill's desire to trace and illumine the character of Electra. Freudian theory, however, may have served O'Neill very well as a way to mask his own fears and inadequacies in the portrayal of the feminine psyche.

One key to understanding O'Neill's superimposition of Vienna on Greece is his fascination with the mask, which, as we shall see, provides a bridge for him between Greek dramatic convention and psychoanalytic theory. In the stage directions of *Mourning Becomes Electra,* the mask is a constantly recurring feature. All of the Mannons are said to possess masklike faces, and one of O'Neill's "choral" figures makes this explicit for the audience early on. Although O'Neill had already experimented with the use of masks (notably in *The Great God Brown,* produced in 1926), he eventually chose not to use actual masks in this production. Yet his concept of the mask is central to his particular fusion of the classical and the psychoanalytical.

An essay by O'Neill that is contemporary with the trilogy expresses his endorsement of masking as a theatrical convention: "The mask *is* dramatic in itself." But more importantly, the essay documents for us how theater and psychology met for O'Neill in the concept of the mask. Consider the following passages:

The use of masks will be discovered eventually to be the freest solution of the modern dramatist's problem as to how . . . he can express those profound hidden conflicts of the mind which the probings of psychology continue to disclose to us.

Dogma for the new masked drama. One's outer life passes in a solitude *haunted* by the masks of others; one's inner life passes in a solitude *hounded* by the masks of oneself. [I have italicized *haunted* and *hounded;* cf. the titles of the trilogy's plays, *The Hunted* and *The Haunted,* as well as Orin's comment on Lavinia in the latter play: "You'll have to haunt and hound her for a lifetime!"]

For what, at bottom, is the new psychological insight into human cause and effect but a study in masks, an exercise in unmasking?[12]

In terms of the theater, then, O'Neill sees the mask as a way of directing the audience's attention inward, to the characters' interior states, rather than dissipating it on the superficial (for example, as he notes, on a "star" performance). In terms of psychoanalysis, however, O'Neill sees the journey to the interior as an *un*masking. Yet the psyche itself, it seems, is constituted of masks. In other words, although O'Neill speaks of analysis as an unmasking, that process itself can yield only the discovery of more masks. On this view, O'Neill seems to constitute the self as structured like an onion. Mask after mask might be removed, but underneath would lie only other masks and, ultimately: nothing, *horror vacui*.

If masks are so deeply implicated in O'Neill's conceptions both of the theater and of the self, the first thing that might strike us about *Mourning Becomes Electra* is the *absence* of masks. On the most obvious level, O'Neill decided to eschew the use of actual masks in favor of stage directions repetitively characterizing the Mannons as having masklike faces. Those faces, however, reveal much more than they conceal. In O'Neill's explicit directions, virtually every flicker of emotion is registered melodramatically on the faces of his protagonists. More significant than these aspects of the staging, however, is the fact that the psyche itself in this trilogy requires no unmasking, no psychoanalysis. "An exercise in unmasking" is *not* what O'Neill's trilogy provides. Oddly, the truth seems always there, right before the audience and (more curious still) evident to the protagonists as well. With the single exception of Vinnie's strong attraction to Brant (to which we shall return), O'Neill's characters are remarkably *un*deceived about their passions, fantasies, and motives. Indeed a number of lines are almost embarrassingly direct in voicing these:

VINNIE [to her father]. . . . You're the only man I'll ever love! (*Homecoming,* act 3, p. 51)
EZRA [to his daughter]. . . . I want you to remain my little girl. (*Homecoming,* act 3, p. 51)
ORIN [to his mother]. . . . You're my only girl! (*Hunted,* act 2, p. 90)
CHRISTINE [to her son]. . . . We had a secret little world of our own in the old days, didn't we? (*Hunted,* act 2, p. 85)

These family members might have stepped out of a textbook of Freudian neuroses immediately onto the stage.

The problem seems to be that O'Neill has allowed an overdose of Freudian theory to rob his characters of life and credibility.[13] Doris Alexander, however, has pointed out that this is a misdiagnosis. In fact, O'Neill's representations of the Oedipal Complex are so explicit that they cease to be Freudian at all. She specified the nonorthodox nature of O'Neill's "Freudian" ideas: The dramatist's "peculiarly non-Freudian version of the Oedipus complex," she wrote, "lacks the most important elements of Freud's, ambivalence and unconsciousness."[14] More than simply diagnosing the heterodoxy of O'Neill's apparent Freudianism, however,

Alexander's important article offers a convincingly documented explanation for its origin.

She showed that O'Neill's nonorthodox version of Freudian theory was highly influenced by a book published in 1929 by his friend and correspondent Kenneth Macgowan.[15] The book, entitled *What Is Wrong with Marriage?* was in turn a popularization of an academic psychoanalytic study, *A Research in Marriage,* completed by Dr. G. V. Hamilton, based on his analysis of two hundred married men and women. Among the research subjects was O'Neill himself, who participated in the study in exchange for Hamilton's services in treating his drinking problem. O'Neill's peculiar form of the Oedipal Complex—in which intricate, subtle, and unconscious affinities (as Freud theorized them) are replaced by straightforward attractions, voiced without hesitation and based on obvious physical resemblance—can be seen to have a clear parallel in Macgowan's book. Both literalize and reify concepts that, in Freud, may exist on a level of *relations* rather than objects and be *metaphorical* rather than literal.

What Alexander carefully and convincingly documents in a scholarly analysis has been expressed in a satiric vein but nonetheless accurately by Eric Bentley:

O'Neill has boasted his ignorance of Freud but such ignorance is not enough. He should be ignorant also of the watered-down Freudianism of Sardi's and the Algonquin, the Freudianism of all those who are ignorant of Freud, the Freudianism of the subintelligentsia. . . . Now, what is it that your subintellectual knows about Freud? That he "put everything down to sex." Precisely; and that is what O'Neill does with the [Electra] myth. . . . *Mourning Becomes Electra* is all sex talk. Sex *talk*— not sex lived and embodied but sex talked of and fingered. . . . O'Neill is an acute case of what D. H. Lawrence called "sex in the head." Sex is almost the only idea he has—has insistently—and it is for him *only* an idea.[16]

My contention here will be that Bentley is fundamentally correct. However arch his criticism may sound, he has hit upon the basic problem of *Mourning Becomes Electra.* That problem does not have to do with the pathologically intense Oedipal relations so insistently displayed before us on the stage. They are merely a screen. Indeed, the very reason they are so openly presented and voiced is that they are not what is psychologically at stake in the trilogy. In fact, all is not openly voiced and displayed. The plays still circle about a center of darkness and the unknown. It is the origin of all subsequent action, and it remains almost entirely obscure. What is really at issue is confrontation of the female as a sexual being. Thus "sex talk"—via a popularized version of Freud—serves as a way for the playwright to mask "sex lived and embodied" and to displace it from his treatment of the Electra tragedy.

REPRESSION

Despite O'Neill's explicit claim to investigate the Electra figure, in practice he has rigorously and systematically repressed feminine sexuality, initiation, and satisfaction. For this purpose, the vagaries of Freudian theory on the feminine are perfectly well suited. "O'Neill always had a problem depicting women," noted one scholar.[17] Surely, that is an understatement. In O'Neill's canon, women seem capable of occupying only two positions; childlike or domineering, they remain in either case secretive, manipulative, dangerous, and incomprehensible.[18] Freudian psychology does not illumine these characters; it merely provides new masks.

In *Mourning Becomes Electra,* several crucial moments that motivate the action and yet are never directly confronted can be identified: all concern feminine sexuality, its awakening, and its threatening quality. This is true through three generations. Not only Christine's wedding night but also Marie Brantôme's attraction for the Mannon brothers and Vinnie's attraction to Brant (as well as, subsequently, to the native Avahanni) remain (as Freud says of feminine sexuality) "shadowy and incomplete." The female's sexual desire or activity is consistently and systematically repressed in the play, yet is actually the motive of the action. In terms of plot, the apparently pathological relations within the family are of second-order importance. The first order, the prime sources of narrative, are two non-Oedipal, nonaberrant sexual moments—the sexual relations of David Mannon with Marie Brantôme and of Ezra Mannon with his wife, Christine.[19]

Given the seething passions supposedly lurking at the heart of the action, the trilogy itself is remarkably reticent in touching upon those passions. In the first generation, the original attraction between the governess, Marie Brantôme, and one (both?) of the Mannon brothers is almost as completely suppressed in the drama as it is in the family history. Despite multiple allusions to the tale (by the chorus, Seth, and Brant) the narrative remains obscure, both because of its compressed complexity and because of the very different points of view of the narrators. Since its informants' views are diametrically opposed and equally highly prejudiced, the audience acquires an unclear and fragmented knowledge of the affair.

In the subsequent generation, the wedding night between Ezra and Christine, for all its centrality to the play, is more radically suppressed. Concerning this nuptial moment, O'Neill never reveals more than that the experience was "disgusting." This adjective recurs several times in the trilogy, all but once in the context of feminine sexuality and initiation:

CHRISTINE. . . . I loved him once—before I married him. . . . He was silent and mysterious and romantic! But marriage soon turned his romance into—disgust! (*Homecoming,* act 2, p. 31)
LAVINIA. So I was born of your disgust! (*Homecoming,* act 2, p. 31)

CHRISTINE. . . . . I loved you when I married you! I wanted to give myself! But you made me so I couldn't give! You filled me with disgust! (*Homecoming*, act 4, p. 61)
ORIN. . . . . The naked women [of the Islands] disgusted me. . . . (*Haunted*, act 1, scene 2, p. 145)
LAVINIA. Orin! Don't be disgusting! [At the suggestion that she fell in love with the Islanders.] (*Haunted*, act 1, scene 2, p. 145)
LAVINIA. How can you make up such disgusting fibs? [In the same context as the preceding reference] (*Haunted*, act 1, scene 2, p. 145)

The playwright's refusal to confront the nuptial scene directly—which makes of this moment the unfathomable origin of what transpires onstage—may be a counterpart to Freudian notions of "the primal scene," the coupling of parents that the child barely glimpses (or merely imagines) and yet realizes is fraught with meaning.[20] In Freudian theory, the "primal scene" plays a crucial role in the generation of subsequent neurosis, as Christine's "disgusting" wedding night generates the subsequent aberrance in the family. Only in his notes does O'Neill comment on the source of the problem in the Mannon marriage: "Reason for Clytemnestra's hatred for Agamemnon sexual frustration by his Puritan sense of guilt turning love to lust."[21] This explanation bears comparison with O'Neill's earlier outline of the play's characters. Of "Clementina" (who will later become "Christine"), he remarks: "Her passionate, full-blooded femaleness had never found sex-satisfaction in his repressed morally-constrained, disapproving sex-frigidity."[22] It is worth remarking the reversal of typical gender stereotypes here, with the female seeking "satisfaction," the male afflicted by "frigidity."

If Christine's initiation into marital "duty" is hidden under the designation "disgusting," her second initiation, into fulfilling sexuality with Brant, is also displaced by O'Neill as far as possible: removed, mediated, and downplayed. The illicit couple's rendezvous are remote from the Mannon home, staged in distant New York. Our knowledge of them comes, via hearsay, from Vinnie's detective mission to the city. She reports the results of her spying, which significantly culminates in what she has *heard* outside of Brant's room, and what she has heard is "kissing." O'Neill's choice to represent the lovers' affair in this way departs substantially from his initial scenario. Originally, the lovers' passion was verified by the written evidence of love letters exchanged between the two—letters that spoke explicitly, for example, of Christine's white body in her paramour's arms. In addition, the couple were to embrace passionately onstage and verbally recall moments of their affair.[23] Though *The Hunted* does include a scene of embrace between the two, at the time their passion is unquestionably subordinated to fear. Thus the erotic relations between the lovers have been suppressed in the final text.

Not only Christine's erotic nature but also Vinnie's figures in the trilogy. But it is a nature well hidden. Perhaps the only truly repressed and unspoken Oedipal desire in the drama is that of Lavinia for Adam Brant. Before Lavinia's final "Freudian slip" (when, in a passionate embrace with Peter, she cries out, "Want me! Take me, Adam!" [177]), only unreliable intimations indicate the extent to which a thwarted passion for her mother's lover motivates her single-minded vengeance. Although Christine and Orin both charge Vinnie with a jealous passion for Brant, the jealousy of the accusers themselves leads us substantially to discount their accusations. O'Neill's documentation of his writing shows, however, that the recognition of Lavinia's love for Brant was explicit in the early scenario and in fact was excised from the final text at the last moment. In the original scenario, the "Vinnie" character (called "Elena" at this point) feels "a strange conflict is going on within her, she cannot help being fascinated by the idea of being his [i.e., Brant's] wife, in bed with him."[24] Later, Elena, having discovered the correspondence between the lovers, is repulsed—but attracted by the love letters she has read. "She would make him forget her mother in her arms!"[25] In fact, Lavinia, until the last of the play's six revisions, explicitly acknowledged her love for Brant in the dialogue. A small journal, kept while traveling in the Canary Islands and dedicated to his wife, Carlotta, indicates that not until March 8, 1931 (i.e., three weeks before deciding he had truly completed the five-year writing process), did O'Neill cut the "one passage" that "reveals what is only implied in the published text—that Lavinia loves her mother's lover."[26]

As with Christine's second sexual initiation, so Lavinia's second erotic attraction is remarkably displaced in the text. This concerns her mysterious relation to the "native," Avahanni. Again, the association, whatever we are to make of it, is distanced geographically, this time not merely from New England to New York but much further to "the Islands," which function as a mythologized landscape throughout the plays. Again, all that we know initially of the relation we learn through hearsay, this time through Orin rather than Lavinia. Whereas Lavinia had, however, at least heard *something* (however slight, however mediated), Orin's evidence of Lavinia's alleged sexual attraction is even more attenuated. He accuses Lavinia of an unspecified incident at which he was not present either to see or to hear. Rather, he infers her guilt from looking at her face—and projects it into the future as well with his claim that "if we'd stayed another month, I know I'd have found her some moonlight night dancing under the palm trees—as naked as the rest!" (145) To this Vinnie twice objects that Orin is being "disgusting." She herself, however, will later complicate the picture by the now familiar strategy of concealing/revealing. Her thoroughly romantic and sensual evocation of the Islands to Peter seems to confirm Orin's thinly attested accusation. Subsequently, she will twice claim sexual intimacy with the native Avahanni—and each time, immediately withdraw and repudiate that claim. In this case, then, not only is the representation of the woman's sexual satisfaction or initiation displaced and suppressed; it is in fact completely unclear whether there has even been such a scene of initiation.

What is represented on the stage is the relation between Vinnie and Peter, her would-be fiancé. Here, it is clear that the woman has been transformed by her voyage to "the Islands." In this case, O'Neill registers ambivalent messages about the female's assumption and open expression of sexual desire in the stage directions rather than directly in the dialogue. Thus we learn that, when Lavinia impulsively embraces and kisses Peter passionately, *"He returns it, aroused and at the same time a little shocked by her boldness"* (147). Later, he will be *"shocked and repelled by her display of passion"* (177). Finally, when he believes that Lavinia had "lusted" with Avahanni, Peter *"stares at her with a stricken look of horrified repulsion"* (177). But Peter has no inkling of Vinnie's role as accessory in the deaths of Brant, Christine, and Orin. But, for him, her entry into sexual relations takes on the dimensions of a criminal offense. In horror at the thought that Vinnie has been initiated into sexuality, he cries, "you are bad at heart—no wonder Orin killed himself—God, I—I hope you'll be punished" (177). He then runs offstage. Thus O'Neill effects an important transposition, which manages to equate or replace criminal activity with sexual activity. The punishment that might indeed be meted out to the woman on the grounds of her implication in multiple deaths is here seen as merited on the grounds of her participation in sexual relations.

Each of the trilogy's encounters with female desire remains "shadowy and incomplete." Each, however, is a source of anxiety, to be displaced, mediated, and replaced by various textual strategies. O'Neill has exfoliated a series of complexities, like a series of masks, around a central problem—confronting female desire, initiation, and satisfaction. This is what is systematically repressed throughout the plays. Even more striking is the fact that this repression—which takes the particular form of revealing too much of the inessential (Oedipal neurosis) in order to hide and deflect attention from the essential (feminine desire) is replicated in O'Neill's writing of the trilogy itself. If O'Neill has effectively resisted the representation of female desire by displacing it from the final text of the trilogy, sexuality does surface elsewhere—namely, in O'Neill's own relation to the drama and its writing. His documentation of that process reveals the return of the repressed.

THE RETURN OF THE REPRESSED—IN WRITING

It is at this point that we must psychoanalyze the plays themselves, as it were. The autobiographical elements that pervade O'Neill's work are well known. In a very real sense, the plays *are* the man, and more than one critic has remarked that O'Neill's theater is in fact an unmediated presentation of self, that the dramatist's audience is often less engaged with the characters of O'Neill than with the man himself.[27] It is all too tempting, therefore, to launch into a reading of O'Neill's psychosexual history, as it is (irrepressibly) represented in his drama. What I shall attempt here is not a psychobiography but rather a psychoanalysis (if that is not too grand a term) of the trilogy itself and O'Neill's writing of the trilogy as displaying a coherent set of symptoms or strategies. When we examine the playwright's notes—and other documentation relevant to the writing of the trilogy—we find a pattern of metaphor emphasizing exposure/concealment and a strikingly sexual relation to the writing.

O'Neill's production of the Electra trilogy entails a peculiar pattern of hiding and exposing. (We might compare Ezra's confession to Christine: "Something queer in me keeps me mum about the things I'd like most to say—keeps me hiding the things I'd like to show" [55].) On the one hand, O'Neill was uncharacteristically secretive about the work.[28] In contrast to his usual practice, he did not reveal his material to friends; in a letter to Benjamin de Casseres of April 20, 1930, he noted only that the work is a "psychological drama of lust" but that this description is sent "*in strictest confidence.*"[29] Oddly, however, while he was anomalously tight lipped to others concerning the project, he was also anomalously complete in his private record of the work.[30] Then, uniquely, O'Neill agreed to introduce these private notes into the public sector by publishing them—not once, but twice![31] Curiously, however, the notes themselves insist, by their overdetermined title ("Working Notes and Extracts from a Fragmentary Work Diary"), upon their incompleteness, as if something were still hidden and inaccessible. The publication manages, therefore, both to reveal and conceal at the same time.[32] Something of the same may be said of O'Neill's drama itself. Having completed his first draft, he exclaims that "reading this first draft I get the feeling that more of my idea was left out of play than there is in it!"[33] In an article on *Mourning Becomes Electra,* Barrett Clark made a strikingly similar observation: "What appeals to me most strongly in those of [O'Neill's] plays I most respect and like is this uneasy undertone that hints at something not completely expressed."[34] Indeed, something very similar is what I claim—that the completed text symptomatically "leaves out" or represses disturbing sexual material and that this project leaves its traces in the process of the writing itself.

At the same time that female sexuality is being edited out of the work, O'Neill's set of metaphors for the creation of the play consistently refers to adequacy/inadequacy of male sexual performance. Very early in his "Working Notes," O'Neill states his objective: to give Electra a tragic ending worthy of her, since in Greek versions she merely "peters out into an undramatic married banality."[35] After his first attempt, O'Neill alludes to his "scrawny" first draft. Having completed his second draft, however, he "feel[s] drained out." Rereading this draft a week later, he is heartened but finds that his technique "cause[s] action to halt and limp."[36]

Particularly intriguing is his "solution" to the problem of writing—an insistent, monotonous rhythm, a breakthrough so appealing that he insists on describing it three times. It should not escape us that this is the prose model selected to represent a tragedy significantly motivated by the sexual inadequacies of Ezra Mannon as a cold, unimaginative, and unsatisfying lover. (Relevant here as well is Orin's discussion of his father's nickname in the army, "Old Stick": "Father was no good on an offensive but . . . [he'd] stick in the mud and hold a position until hell froze over!" [94].) The day after expressing the fear that his drama is "limp," O'Neill exhorts himself to "try for prose with simple forceful repeating accent and rhythm which will express driving insistent compulsion of passions."[37] So pleased is he with this "new conception" that he describes it yet again the next day: "Think I have hit on right rhythm of prose—monotonous, simple words driving insistence."[38] Upon reading his third draft two months later, he is still obsessed with rhythm—which now expresses itself more openly in sexual terms, in his instructions to himself: "Get all this in naturally in straight dialogue—as simple and direct and dynamic as possible . . . stop doing things to these characters—let them reveal themselves—in spite of (or because of!) their long locked-up passions, I feel them burning to do just this!"[39]

Through three more rewritings, however, the drama continues to be recalcitrant. George Jean Nathan recalled that the writing of this work was uniquely difficult for O'Neill, who wrote to him at one point, "I'm beginning to hate it and curse the day I ever conceived such an idea."[40] Later, however, when the work was finally completed, he wrote again to Nathan: "I have a feeling of there being real size in it, quite apart from its length."[41]

Despite O'Neill's difficulties in writing the trilogy, as documented in his letters and notes, upon completion of the drama he was enthusiastic about the work accomplished. In a letter to Nathan (April 7, 1931) he wrote, "It has been one hell of a job! Let's hope the result in some measure justifies the labor I've put in." The most striking document, however, is the inscription with which he dedicated the script to his newly married third wife, Carlotta Monterey. As Croswell Bowen recorded, "Mrs. O'Neill sent 50 copies of the inscription to friends with the following printed note: 'Fifty copies of Eugene O'Neill's inscription to the final longhand manuscript of *Mourning Becomes Electra* have been reproduced in facsimile. This copy is No. _____ .' "[42]

In stark contrast to this public dissemination of the inscription text is the intimacy of the terms in which O'Neill describes therein the production of the trilogy. He begins with "the impenetrable days of pain in which you privately suffered in silence that this trilogy might be born." Oddly, although he alludes to the work as "this trilogy of the damned!" he immediately continues: "These scripts are like us and my presenting them is a gift which, already, is half yours." He speaks of "the travail we have gone through for its sake" and concludes with the remarkable closing: "Oh, mother and wife and mistress and friend!—And collaborator! I love you."

That the dedicatee chose to commercialize this document by circulating it to fifty of her closest friends is a topic we shall not broach here. What is relevant to our inquiry, however, is the curious birthing process of the trilogy that O'Neill's metaphors describe. Consistently, the language associated with the completion of the work is that of midwifery. But the mother in question vacillates between being O'Neill's wife and himself.

Michael Manheim has called attention to a kind of gender-free identification in O'Neill's plays—that is, that "a character's sex has little to do with the figure he or she represents in O'Neill's mind."[43] Such a bisexuality seems to inform O'Neill's view of his relation to the Electra trilogy. On the one hand, the "Working Notes" employ a metaphorics of male performance and adequacy. On the other hand, the author's dedication of the work casts him as its mother, with the writing presented, as a child, to the spouse (Carlotta). We could, however, view this in Freudian terms (as the negative Oedipal Complex of the male child, who wishes to present a baby to the father).

REINSCRIPTION

Rather than turning to theory external to the trilogy, however, let us consider O'Neill's relation to his own writing by examining his characterization of writing within the plays. In O'Neill's original scenario, an exchange of letters between Christine Mannon and her lover, Adam Brant, played an important, revelatory role. In the reworking of the trilogy, this correspondence has disappeared altogether. Yet the act of writing has by no means disappeared from the published drama. On the contrary, the epistolary genre recurs intermittently, retaining erotic associations throughout, and other acts of writing as well prove crucial in the narrative.

The association of writing and eros is established very early in the trilogy when Peter confides to Vinnie: "Hazel feels bad about Orin not writing. Do you think he really—loves her?" (14) From this point on, the absence rather than the presence of epistolary exchange often is significant. The next unanswered letter of which we learn is that of Adam's mother to Ezra Mannon—a letter prompting Adam's charge that because "he never answered her," Ezra is "as guilty of murder as anyone he ever sent to the rope when he was a judge!" (26–27) From Seth's exposition of the Mannon past, we know that Ezra too, like his father and uncle, was attracted to Marie Brantôme: "He was only a boy then, but he was crazy about her." Confronted with the knowledge of her sexual relations, however, he rejects his earlier feelings: "He hated her worse than anyone when it got found out she was his Uncle David's fancy woman" (44). This repudiation of erotic attraction is thus reenacted by his refusal to respond to her writing. In *The Hunted,* Orin rebukes his mother bitterly for her failure to write (which, as we know—and he senses—signals her transfer of erotic involvement from her son to Adam). Orin rebuts her claim of loneliness with the exclamation: "So lonely you've written me exactly two letters in the last six months!" (84) Later he complains: "Your letters got farther and farther between—and they seemed so cold! It drove me crazy!" (89)

If correspondence broken off (like coitus interruptus) is a source of frustration, yet to engage in writing itself in the trilogy is consistently threatening or dangerous. The act of writing is in both of these ways distinctly eroticized in O'Neill's work. To refrain from writing is to refuse erotic involvement, but to write is to enter into an economy of life and death, as is entry into the sexual cycle. Thus acts of writing in the plays are consistently bound up with death—for oneself or another. Marie Brantôme's desperate letter to Ezra Mannon will be the prelude to her death. Ezra's own letter home from the front, describing his heart condition, will supply a pretext for his own murder. That murder will be set in motion by Christine's writing out for Adam the prescription for poison. At the same time, she recognizes that this act of writing binds Adam irrevocably to her. Having passed the note to him, she observes triumphantly, "You'll never dare leave me now, Adam" (42).

The use of writing as a threat (more specifically, as a means of coercion in the sphere of one's own erotic fantasies) seems one of the many characteristics inherited from Christine by her children, for both Vinnie and Orin engage in similar practices of coercive writing. Vinnie, by writing to her father and Orin "only enough so they'd be suspicious" (35), inserts herself between her father and mother, forces Christine into her power, and, through the threat of writing again (more completely), keeps her there. The most significant scribal act of the trilogy, however, is surely Orin's writing in the final play. Orin at first has difficulty carrying out his intention to write the family's history, for he is resistant to the realization that relations between Vinnie and himself replicate the relation between their parents ("That's the evil destiny out of the past I haven't dared predict. I'm the Mannon you're chained to!"[155]). Having completed the document, he presents it first to the would-be wife, Hazel. Soon, however, he withdraws his text from her and re-presents it to the mother/sister Lavinia, using his writing as a means to coerce her consent to incest. In this way, the act of writing is virtually fetishized, for in Orin's fantasy the completion of the text yields power to fulfill the Oedipal desires. That desire is not fulfilled, however; in the end, the completion of the text "stands in" for engagement in the sexual cycle.

Throughout the trilogy, writing maintains a consistent status, one that associates it closely with erotic activity. The refusal of epistolary intercourse is a sign of a concomitant refusal of sexual intercourse. We can see this in the cases of Orin and Hazel, Ezra and Christine (for he has evidently written to Vinnie concerning his homecoming but not to his wife), Ezra and Marie Brantôme, Christine and Orin. But daring to write bestows an almost magical potency, rendering one capable of binding others, often in the realm of sexual desires (whether explicit or implicit). Thus Vinnie writes to her father and Orin—and threatens to write more—Christine writes a formula that will bind Adam to her, and Orin writes a text intended both to bind Lavinia irrevocably and illicitly to himself as well as to sever her from Peter.

That text, the history of the Mannon family, must bear a great resemblance to the text of the trilogy itself. Orin's history, therefore, and O'Neill's trilogy invite comparison. I suggest that, with Orin's writing of the family history and his bestowal of it, O'Neill has reinscribed within the text his own textual production of the trilogy—and his presentation of it to the mother/wife, Carlotta. In this way, O'Neill has employed a strategy of displacing sexuality to textuality in such a way that the mastery of authorship becomes a means of confronting feminine desire. Underlying the surface of mere "subintelligentsia Freud," this displacement of erotic empowerment, from sexual to textual relations, is the mask behind the mask in *Mourning Becomes Electra,* the truly psychoanalytic basis of the trilogy.

NOTES

This chapter was first published in *Comparative Drama* 22, no. 1 (Spring 1988): 37–55. It is reprinted here with the permission of the editors of *Comparative Drama.* Minor changes in style and documentation have been made to enable the reprinted text to conform in format with the rest of the volume. For his always patient and perceptive readings, I thank my toughest editor, First Lieutenant Thomas J. Scherer of the U. S. Army. I would also like to thank my colleagues David Konstan and Coppélia Kahn as well as *Comparative Drama*'s anonymous referee for helpful suggestions and encouragement.

1. Eugene O'Neill, *Mourning Becomes Electra,* in *The Plays of Eugene O'Neill,* vol. 2 (New York: Random House, Inc., Modern Library, 1982), 5.
2. Cf. Doris V. Falk, *Eugene O'Neill and the Tragic Tension: An Interpretive Study of the Plays* (New Brunswick, N.J.: Rutgers University Press, 1958), 26.
3. Eugene O'Neill, "Working Notes and Extracts from a Fragmentary Work Diary," in *The Unknown O'Neill: Unpublished or Unfamiliar Writings of Eugene O'Neill,* ed. Travis Bogard (New Haven: Yale University Press, 1988), 399.
4. See Arthur H. Nethercot, "The Psychoanalyzing of Eugene O'Neill" *Modern Drama* 3, no. 3 (December 1960): 242–56; idem, "The Psychoanalyzing of Eugene O'Neill: Part Two," *Modern Drama* 3, no. 4 (February 1961): 357–72; and idem, "The Psychoanalyzing of Eugene O'Neill: Postscript," *Modern Drama* 8, no. 2 (September 1965): 150–55. The first two largely recapitulate views expressed by other critics, notably Edwin A. Engel, *The Haunted Heroes of Eugene O'Neill* (Cambridge, Mass.: Harvard University Press, 1953), and Falk, *Eugene O'Neill and the Tragic Tension.* The third draws upon the biography of Arthur Gelb and Barbara Gelb, *O'Neill* (New York: Harper and Row, 1962), to document further O'Neill's actual knowledge of what he called merely "the new psychology." For the relevant view of a practicing psychoanalyst, see Phillip Weissman, "Conscious and Unconscious Autobiographical Dramas of Eugene O'Neill," *Journal of the American Psychoanalytic Association* 5, no. 3 (July 1957): 432–60.
5. See his personal letter to Barrett H. Clark (6 June 1931, quoted in *Selected Letters of Eugene O'Neill,* ed. Travis Bogard and Jackson R. Bryer [New Haven: Yale University Press, 1988], 386): "Critics . . . read too damn much Freud into stuff that could very well have been written exactly as is before psycho-analysis was ever heard of. . . . And I am no

deep student of psycho-analysis. As far as I remember, of all the books written by Freud, Jung, etc., I have read only four [Nethercot, "The Psychoanalyzing of Eugene O'Neill: Postscript": 153, identifies these as *Totem and Taboo, Beyond the Pleasure Principle, Wit and the Unconscious*, and Jung's *Psychology of the Unconscious*], and Jung is the only one of the lot who interests me." Throughout *The Tragic Tension*, Doris Falk traced the Jungian aspects of O'Neill's work—and, indeed, his anticipation of several "neo-Freudians," notably Karen Horney.

6. Virginia Floyd, *Eugene O'Neill at Work: Newly Released Ideas for Plays* (New York: Frederick Ungar Publishing Co., 1981), 185: "While the first idea for *Mourning Becomes Electra* appears in the notebook in 1928, O'Neill's statements indicate that his decision to write the 'Greek tragedy' dates to spring 1926 after he had read Arthur Symons's translation of Hugo von Hofmannsthal's *Electra*." During June 21–26, 1929, O'Neill read Greek plays in translation (Floyd, *Eugene O'Neill at Work*, 196). The trilogy was begun in 1929 and, after six revisions, completed in 1931.

7. Eugene O'Neill, letter to Robert Sisk, 28 August 1930, as quoted in Floyd, *Eugene O'Neill at Work*, 185 (see n. 6).

8. O'Neill, "Working Notes," 394.

9. Sigmund Freud, "The Dissolution of the Oedipus Complex" (1924), in *The Standard Edition of the Complete Psychological Works of Sigmund Freud*, ed. and trans. James Strachey (with Anna Freud, Alix Strachey, and Alan Tyson), vol. 19 (1923–1925), *"The Ego and the Id" and Other Works* (London: Hogarth Press and the Institute of Psycho-Analysis, 1961), 173. Freud himself rejected the use of the Jungian term *Electra Complex;* he preferred instead to speak of the female Oedipus Complex: See "Female Sexuality" (1931), in *The Standard Edition of the Complete Psychological Works of Sigmund Freud*, vol. 21 (1927–1931), *"The Future of an Illusion," "Civilization and Its Discontents," and Other Works* (London: Hogarth Press and the Institute of Psycho-Analysis, 1961), 228–30.

10. On the apparent discrepancy between women's inferior social position in classical Athens and their powerful portrayal on the Athenian stage, see M. Shaw, "The Female Intruder: Women in Fifth-Century Drama," *Classical Philology* 70, no. 4 (October 1975): 255–66; Helene Foley, "The 'Female Intruder' Reconsidered: Women in Aristophanes' *Lysistrata* and *Ecclesiazusae*," *Classical Philology* 77, no. 1 (January 1982): 1–21; Froma I. Zeitlin, "The Dynamics of Misogyny: Myth and Myth-making in the *Oresteia*," *Arethusa* 11 (1978): 149–84; and H. Foley, "The Conception of Women in Athenian Drama," in *Reflections of Women in Antiquity*, ed. H. Foley (New York: Gordon and Breach, Science Publishers, 1981), 127–68.

11. Juliet Mitchell presented a clear summary of the so-called Jones–Freud controversy over feminine sexuality in "Freud, the Freudians, and the Psychology of Women," *Psychoanalysis and Feminism* (New York: Pantheon Books, 1974): 121–31. Critiques of the Freudian view of the feminine that remain within the psychoanalytic discourse may be found in Mitchell's book, as well as in Janine Chasseguet-Smirgel, *Sexuality and Mind: The Role of the Father and the Mother in the Psyche* (New York: New York University Press, 1986), 9–28. Another such voice, which acknowledges the authority of Freud while significantly reinterpreting the understanding of the feminine is that of Lacan. See Jacques Lacan and the école freudienne, *Feminine Sexuality*, ed. Juliet Mitchell and Jacqueline Rose (New York: Pantheon Books, 1982).

12. Eugene O'Neill, "Memoranda on Masks," in Bogard, *The Unknown O'Neill*, 406, 407 (see n. 3).

13. For such a view, see Chaman Ahuja, *Tragedy, Modern Temper, and O'Neill* (Atlantic Highlands, N.J.: Humanities Press, 1984), 96: "But O'Neill *did* indeed read Freud before he wrote *Strange Interlude*. . . . His mind seething with case-histories, he merely gave dramatic shape to such material as might have been useful for the mental clinics but was patently questionable for the theatre." Certainly, the explicitness with which the interlocking Oedipal attractions of this family are voiced violates our sense of verisimilitude. But O'Neill indicates that, rather than reality, he was striving to achieve an

"unreal realism" ("Working Notes," 401). Cf. Leonard Chabrowe, *Ritual and Pathos: The Theater of O'Neill* (Lewisburg, Pa.: Bucknell University Press, 1976), 161–62.

14. Doris M. Alexander, "Psychological Fate in *Mourning Becomes Electra*," *Publications of the Modern Language Association* 68, no. 5 (December 1953): 923–34.

15. A letter to Macgowan, dated June 14, 1929, playfully alludes to "you psychosharks!" (*"The Theatre We Worked For" : The Letters of Eugene O'Neill to Kenneth Macgowan*, ed. Jackson R. Bryer with the assistance of Ruth M. Alvarez [New Haven: Yale University Press, 1982], 190). By this term O'Neill means those who would read autobiography into his *Days Without End*.

16. Eric Bentley, "Trying to Like O'Neill," in *In Search of Theater* (New York: Alfred A. Knopf, 1953), 246.

17. Virginia Floyd, *The Plays of Eugene O'Neill: A New Assessment* (New York: Frederick Ungar Publishing Co., 1987), 405.

18. Is it mere coincidence that O'Neill, who was no stranger to Spanish-speaking regions, should give the name of "Nina,"—in Spanish, "little girl"—to the protagonist of what he called his "woman's play," *Strange Interlude?*

19. Cf. Chabrowe, who located the first "visible link in the chain" of Mannon tragedies as the marriage relationship of Ezra and Christine (*Ritual and Pathos*, 149) but also noted that "the events of the trilogy are all to be traced to Abe Mannon's one act of jealousy" and that this origin seems both overdetermined and "too arbitrary a beginning" (162).

20. Freud's most elaborate exposition of the primal scene occurs in the Wolf Man case history, "The Dream and the Primal Scene," pt. 4 of *From the History of an Infantile Neurosis* (1918), in *The Standard Edition of the Complete Psychological Works of Sigmund Freud*, ed. and trans. James Strachey (with Anna Freud, Alix Strachey, and Alan Tyson), vol. 17 (1917–1919), *"An Infantile Neurosis" and Other Works* (London: Hogarth Press and the Institute of Psycho-Analysis, 1955), 29–47. For a discussion of whether the parental coitus is actually viewed or merely imagined, (i.e., "recollected" or "constructed"), see "A Few Discussions," pt. 5 of *From the History of an Infantile Neurosis*, 48–60. Recently, the concept of the primal scene has been subjected to new scrutiny, as has the narrative of the Wolf Man itself. See A. Esman, "The Primal Scene: A Review and Reconsideration," *Psychoanalytic Study of the Child* 28 (1973): 49–81; H. Blum, "On the Concept and Consequences of the Primal Scene," *Psychoanalytical Quarterly* 48 (1979): 27–47; idem, "The Pathogenic Influence of the Primal Scene: A Re-Evaluation," in *Freud and His Patients*, ed. Mark Kanzer and Jules Glenn (New York: Jason Aronson, 1980), 367–372; and Patrick J. Mahony, *Cries of the Wolf Man*, History of Psychoanalysis, no. 1 (New York: International Universities Press, 1984).

21. O'Neill, "Working Notes," 395.

22. Eugene O'Neill, as quoted in Floyd, *Eugene O'Neill at Work*, 188 (see n. 6).

23. Floyd, *Eugene O'Neill at Work*, 193–94, 200.

24. Eugene O'Neill, as quoted by Floyd, *Eugene O'Neill at Work*, 195 (see n. 6).

25. Floyd, *Eugene O'Neill at Work*, 196.

26. Ibid., 208.

27. Francis Fergusson, "Melodramatist," in *O'Neill and His Plays: Four Decades of Criticism*, ed. Oscar Cargill, N. Bryllion Fagin, and William J. Fisher (New York: New York University Press, 1961), 271–82. See also Harold Clurman, "The O'Neills," *Nation* 182, no. 9 (3 March 1956): 182–83; and Falk, *The Tragic Tension*, 12, 119.

28. Travis Bogard, *Contour in Time: The Plays of Eugene O'Neill* (New York: Oxford University Press, 1972), 334.

29. Ibid., 335.

30. Floyd, *Eugene O'Neill at Work*, 186.

31. First in the *New York Herald Tribune* of 3 November 1931. Then, in response to a request from Barrett Clark, O'Neill suggests their republication in the book that became *European Theories of the Drama with a Supplement on the American Drama*, ed. Barrett Clark, rev. ed. (New York: Crown Publishing Co., 1947). This document has been most recently republished by the Yale University Press (see n. 3).

32. Cf. Clark's speculation on O'Neill's "own private notes" on *Mourning Becomes Electra:* "Are these notes complete?" ("Aeschylus and O'Neill," *English Journal* 21, no. 9 [November 1932]: 699). Obviously, Floyd's subsequent publication of O'Neill's notebooks (itself only partial) shows that they were not (Floyd, *Eugene O'Neill at Work,* 185–209).

33. O'Neill, "Working Notes," 397.

34. Clark, "Aeschylus," 701. Cf. also Falk, *The Tragic Tension,* 139.

35. O'Neill, "Working Notes," 394.

36. Ibid., 397, 398, 399.

37. Ibid., 399.

38. Ibid.

39. Ibid., 400.

40. George Jean Nathan, *The Intimate Notebooks of George Jean Nathan* (New York: Alfred A. Knopf, 1932), 28. See also Eugene O'Neill, letter to George Jean Nathan, 1 December 1930, in *"As Ever, Gene": The Letters of Eugene O'Neill to George Jean Nathan,* ed. Nancy L. Roberts and Arthur W. Roberts (Rutherford, N.J.: Fairleigh Dickinson University Press, 1987), 114.

41. O'Neill, letter to Nathan, 7 April 1931, in *"As Ever, Gene,"* 121 (see n. 40).

42. Croswell Bowen, "The Black Irishman," in *O'Neill and His Plays,* 76–77 (see n. 28).

43. Michael Manheim, *Eugene O'Neill's New Language of Kinship* (Syracuse: Syracuse University Press, 1982), 78.

5

Some Problems in Adapting O'Neill for Film

Burton L. Cooper

Near the end of *O'Neill on Film,* John Orlandello observed that "the process of stage-to-screen adaptation should be reciprocal—the film translation should not only shine with a light of its own, but should also help to illuminate the original work."[1]

Film adaptations of O'Neill's plays do not exactly "shine with a light of their own." People who take movies seriously, who are critically concerned with movies as works of art, cannot take these adaptations seriously. With the single exception of *The Long Voyage Home,* they contain nothing of cinematic interest. Still, they are not without value; they are useful in two ways. First, when we consider that "cinema is a 'medium' as well as an art, in the sense that it can encapsulate any of the performing arts and render it in a film transcription,"[2] we find that these films provide a useful record of O'Neill, a means by which we can hear his language spoken, see his scenes acted out. In the case of the videotape of *Hughie,* we have a transcription of an actual stage performance. Second, apart from the documentary value, these flawed films provide a means of insight into certain aspects of the plays themselves. My aim is to account for the failure of the films (both movies and television versions) and to indicate some things these adaptations reveal about the nature of O'Neill's art.

O'Neill himself admired only two film versions of his plays: the silent *Anna Christie* and *The Long Voyage Home.* For the most part, he did not pay much attention to the other films, though he was particularly disappointed (and angered) by the adaptation of *Strange Interlude.* His interest in movies varied considerably throughout the years. In 1914 and 1915 he thought he might make a lot of money by writing photoplays.[3] Six or seven years later, he was furious at Agnes Boulton's suggestion that she was going to write for the movies.[4] In the early 1920s he considered making a film of *The Emperor Jones* (but he and Robert Edmond Jones could not raise any interest in it); and, in 1927, he wrote some now lost sketches for scenarios of *The Hairy Ape* and *Desire Under the Elms.*[5] In 1921 O'Neill saw *The Cabinet of Dr. Caligari* and was impressed by the artistic possibilities it implied (probably this is what inspired the *Emperor Jones* project). In 1929 he turned down a lucrative offer to write for the movies. But then he saw *Broadway Melody* and was "most enthusiastic" about talkies, a medium, he said, that "could set me free . . . to realize a real Elizabethan treatment and get the whole meat out of a theme."[6] O'Neill may have misunderstood something of the nature of movies, but he did see their possibilities as means of achieving what he earnestly desired: breaking through the dramatic restrictions of the proscenium stage. His adapters, by and large, did not think much about that.

In 1915 D. W. Griffith remarked on the superiority of screen drama over that of the stage: "Screen drama is hampered by far fewer limitations and by reason of range and method of treatment its emotional, fictive and historical values are superior. . . . We exhibit both the *thought* and the action, while we can boast the whole world as our stage."[7] Another time Griffith observed that the task of the filmmaker is to "photograph thought."[8] Movies, then, make manifest unlimited space, both inner (thought) and outer ("the whole world"). Griffith understood this from his practice. The critic and scholar Erwin Panofsky saw that movies can project emotion and feelings directly: "[In movies] any attempt to convey thought and feeling exclusively, or even primarily, by speech leaves us with a feeling of embarrassment, boredom, or both."[9] André Bazin noted that it is the "verbal form" of a play that resists translation to the screen.[10] We have only to think of what O'Neill was trying to do in *Strange Interlude* or to consider his problems in trying to find a new dramatic language to see how rich the possibilities of film might have appeared.

O'Neill wanted to avoid the melodramatic excesses of his father's theater. He wanted to develop what he called "behind life" drama, drama that is generated by values (largely psychological, in O'Neill's case—whatever he may have called them) rather than by incident. This attempt may account for some peculiarities in his play, notably an emphasis on the metaphoric function of stage sets, inordinate length and relentless verbal repetition. Because time and space are differently available in movies, none of this is important there—unless one wants to use film only to document plays. The "behind life" quality that O'Neill admired in Strindberg's plays is best realized in Strindberg's expressionism, in distorted images rather than literary language, for example, the peasants' dance in *Miss Julie* or the appearance of the Mummy in *The Ghost Sonata*. When "behind life" is articulated rather than set out in images, it becomes static discourse. This is a real problem in *Strange Interlude* and *Mourning Becomes Electra*. Both of those plays use a kind of "international" middle-class discursive language that tends to undercut the usefulness of stage images, so an adapter has a significant challenge in finding visual equivalents. If the adapter attempts to preserve the language, he finds that it bogs him down with an emphasis on plot and so exaggerates the melodramatic elements of the plays. The size of the movie screen contributes to the sense of overwrought melodrama if there is no compensating visual distraction. In the movie of *Strange Interlude,* for instance, the very faces of the actors become obtrusive. The voice-overs of their thoughts are accompanied by close-ups presumably meant to indicate that they are thinking the thoughts we *hear.* But thinking is not action; it does not organically interact with time and space—without images it has no cinematic life. Even Ibsen, who was more given than Strindberg to discursive language, moved away from bourgeois realism to represent the moral and psychological forces behind event, behind Apollonian life, in images like the artificial forest of *The Wild Duck,* the spire on the house in *The Master Builder,* and Hedda's babbling about Thea's hair as she burns Lovborg's manuscript. O'Neill often attempts this kind of imagery to express what must be conventionally inexpressible. In *Long Day's Journey into Night,* for instance, the gradual loosening of Mary's hair does more to "explain" her situation than all the explanations that are articulated. The play works on the tensions between the articulation and the theatrical poetry of stage images that O'Neill developed. The question of articulation of a clinical sort is obviated in *The Iceman Cometh* because discourse is blocked—"behind life" is rendered mute though apprehensible—by the exigencies of pipe dreams. In effect, O'Neill has to break through the conventional language of the realistic stage, has to give substance to thought and feeling. The artistic success of the silent *Anna Christie* probably derives from its silence. John Griffith Wray, the director, had to find visual means of conveying the notions inherent in O'Neill's dialogue. Significantly, O'Neill approved of the additions, finding the movie "remarkably well acted and directed, and in spirit an absolutely faithful transcript."[11] It is likely, too, that the success of *The Long Voyage Home* derives, in part, from its basis in short plays about inarticulate, unschooled men. Language becomes suggestive rather than discursive, making cinematic images more possible than in movies drawn from other plays. O'Neill himself seems to have thought this when he observed in 1943: "Talking pictures seem to me a bastard which has inherited the lowest traits of both parents. It was the talkless part of *The Long Voyage Home*—the best picture ever made from my stuff—that impressed me the most."[12]

Sound and critical acclaim for the playwright were the undoing of O'Neill's plays as material for cinematic adaptation. Pulitzer and Nobel prizes made official what influential critics had generally proclaimed: O'Neill was a literary master. He was not just a great playwright, he was one of the ornaments of our literature. To adapters this meant that his words should take precedence over other considerations.[13] Always excepting Nichols's and Ford's version of *The Long Voyage Home,* O'Neill's adapters were not innovative. They stood in awe of the great writer and fell prey to a vulgar prejudice that a play is necessarily superior to a film. They seem to have thought that, as stage drama is "literary" and screen drama is not, movies achieve a kind of "class" if they imitate the language of the legitimate theater (the phrase itself is revealing). Sound made all this possible; in the early years of sound a movie was generally thought to be a play filmed. In 1928 a group of Russian filmmakers, Eisenstein among them, expressed the fear that "the advent of sound might engender a flood of 'highly cultured dramas' and other photographed performances of a theatrical sort."[14] Susan Sontag complained that movies are too often seen as "the democratic art, the art of mass society," but that theater, on the other hand, "smacks of aristocratic taste."[15] André Bazin remarked "that the delight we experience at the end of a play has a more uplifting, a nobler, one might perhaps say a more moral, effect than the satisfaction which follows a good film."[16] O'Neill complained that the mass audience for a "talky" was not the audience for him; he hoped for "a sort of Theatre Guild 'talky' organization that will be able to rely only on the big cities for its audiences."[17] In fact, two O'Neill movies, *Mourning Becomes Electra* and *The Iceman Cometh,* were originally released in that "Theatre Guild" way. Nearly all movies that came from O'Neill's plays were initially promoted as an attempt to bring *art* to a mass audience.

Adapters wanted to preserve O'Neill, the literary lion, and so preserved the staginess of the plays instead of using the plays as raw material for the art of cinema, in the way, according to Bela Balazs, Shakespeare used what he found in Italian novellas: "[Shakespeare] saw [an event] isolated from the story form, as raw life-material with all its dramatic possibilities . . . which Bandello could never have expressed in a *novella.*"[18] Richard Watts, Jr., praised O'Neill for writing a scenario for *The Hairy Ape* "with a magnanimity hitherto unknown among playwrights slumming in the films[. He] rewrote the play by the simple means of casting aside the stage version and regarding the work as a film."[19] Those who undertook to rework O'Neill's plays did not have his daring. Mostly, they attempted to enshrine the master through a kind of adaptation that Dudley Andrew called "intersecting," that is, intentionally leaving an "original text . . . unassimilated in adaptation."[20] At its best, this intersection permits us glimpses into corners of the original that may have at first appeared obscure, or, especially in the case of an adapted play, it provides, as the videotape of *Hughie* does, a documentary record of performance. But mostly O'Neill was preserved out of reverence. Peculiar details bear this out. The television *Emperor Jones* is called "Eugene O'Neill's great American classic." The television *Iceman Cometh* is reverentially introduced by Worthington Minor (the producer) and by Brooks Atkinson who praised "America's greatest playwright." The credit sequence of the movie version of *Ah, Wilderness!* identifies the work as "Eugene O'Neill's comedy of recollections." Furthermore, O'Neill's fame tended to prompt moviemakers to populate his films with stars, leading to a variety of confusions of style and taste. *Mourning Becomes Electra,* for instance, features Rosalind Russell as Lavinia, Katina Paxinou as Christine, Raymond Massey as Ezra, and Michael Redgrave as Orin. This casting led Pauline

Kael to observe: "It is apparent from their accents that they have only recently become a family."[21] *Desire Under the Elms* is an even more ludicrous illustration of the problem of star casting. Less ludicrous but perhaps more damaging is the casting of *Long Day's Journey into Night*. Katherine Hepburn is too mannered and too conspicuously a star to be convincing as the only member of the Tyrone family who is not theatrical.

Certain aspects of O'Neill's plays themselves encourage this literary and lionizing tendency. As early as *Beyond the Horizon* (1918) one can see a kind of elevation of literature and of literary experience over other forms, other experiences. Robert Mayo reads poetry and seeks poetry in life. He is destroyed by those, like his wife and his brother, who do not share his poetic sensibility. Robert is the precursor of many O'Neill protagonists who are sympathetically treated in their aspiration to rise above the workaday world through a transcendent literacy and literariness. We find these figures in the plays of every period. Sometimes their aspirations are tragically treated, as with Jim, for instance, in *All God's Chillun Got Wings*. Sometimes they are comically treated, like Richard in *Ah, Wilderness!* But they are always ironically treated. That irony is what O'Neill's adapters too often miss. In *Long Day's Journey into Night,* though the play concerns itself with a theatrical family, we find both Edmund's plays and his father's are contained in books to which the action draws our attention, and father and son recite a lot of poetry. But the words are stifling until Edmund can go out into the world and launch those words—those books and those poems—in theatrical enterprise. O'Neill did aim at a literary theater; he did try to transform Nietzsche, for instance, into drama, and he was unsympathetic to the theatrical contrivances of his father's tradition. But his art was "literary" only in that he sought dramatic means of communicating those matters that the poets and novelists managed in the forms available to them. He admired Greek and Elizabethan drama as living art, poetically free from the restraints and restrictions of post-Belasco Realism.

O'Neill found a new art in Strindberg not because of Strindberg's literary language but because of Strindberg's dramatic themes—which must have seemed particularly startling to someone who had listened to *The Count of Monte Cristo* as often as O'Neill had—and because Strindberg was able to break through the limitations of the realist-melodramatic theater of his time. In referring to the Elizabethans when he was discussing talking pictures, O'Neill spoke of "Elizabethan *treatment*." Poetry, in the literal sense, was only a part of that treatment. Although O'Neill's characters frequently yearn to be poets, they are not poets. They have "a touch of the poet," and this heightens the claustrophobia of his plays. Poetic words alone are not enough for his characters to break through their enclosures. In his most successful plays, O'Neill's "poetic" characters know that the larger world exists, but they cannot participate in it, so they adopt roles of some sort—*The Iceman Cometh* and *A Touch of the Poet* are particularly illuminating in this regard—making an ironic metaphor of the stage itself. Insofar as he can be thought of as a poet, O'Neill is the poet of enclosure, and the realistic theater is one of the enclosures with which he had to struggle. It is a mistake to ennoble it in adaptation, a mistake O'Neill did not himself make when he fashioned *The Iceman Cometh* out of Gorki's play. His characters dream of a world beyond the horizon; a world contained in their poetic language, in the poetic texts they recite, but their existential situation is expressionistically conveyed by the confined or static space of the stage and by the oppressive length of the dramatic action. The attenuation of the dramatic action shows us a character's repeated suffering of the same psychic trauma. O'Neill was right to insist on retaining the repetitions in *The Iceman Cometh*. It is a pity that Ingmar Bergman has not turned his hand to an O'Neill movie. His is a sensibility in tune with O'Neill's.

Still, most adapters do not want to transform; they want to retain the text—or as much of it as they can. But in film the text is not, as it is in the theater, "the essential thing."[22] Moreover, enclosure must be reseen in cinematic terms, for "drama is freed by the camera from all contingencies of time and space."[23] Panofsky wrote of "unique and specific possibilities" of film that can "be defined as *dynamization of space* and, accordingly, *spatialization of time.* . . . In a theater space is static, that is, the space represented on the stage, as well as the spatial relation of the beholder to the spectacle, is unalterably fixed." But Panofsky went on to say that language is, in a compensatory way, freed of the restrictions of space. He observed that it does not matter where Hamlet is on the stage or how visible he is; his language is what moves the audience. In movies, however, the spectator, though he "occupies a fixed seat," is not bound by the limitations of the playing area. His eye moves, as it were, with the camera. Objects in space and "space itself" move and change continually, offering possibilities "of which the stage can never dream."[24]

This shift from the static space of the theater to the fluid space of film means, among other things, an implied reality of a vast world where life goes on with or without the participation of particular characters. On stage Nina's house may stand as a metaphor for the world of the characters; in the larger and more dynamic space of the screen, the house becomes an object in a great world, Nina herself becomes the metaphor. "In the theater the drama proceeds from the actor, in the cinema it goes from the decor to man."[25] Given these facts, it would seem that those plays of O'Neill most suitable for cinematic treatment are *Ah, Wilderness!* (in which there is some irony about poetic texts and the setting is benevolent and a microcosm of an American-Edwardian world in which Richard and his family live), *The Iceman Cometh,* and *A Touch of the Poet.* Both of them, incidentally, are plays that have had reasonably successful television productions; in them, again, poetry is ironically treated, and the larger world—which does intrude on the action—retains its importance though it has been rejected by the characters: It retains a force as a place where they have lived and where others continue to do so.

But not all of O'Neill's plays treat the world in that way, and movies made of those plays rely too heavily on stage signifiers rather than discovering cinematic ones. Plays, with their divisions into acts and scenes, tend to be formal, ritualized. O'Neill, looking back to the Greeks and the Elizabethans, manifesting a literary bent, attempting to intensify the dramatic action, heightens that ritual tendency, bringing the plays again into a precarious relation with movies.

As the form that accepts narrative interruption the least, movies can include much more intense conflict and violence [than theater]. The patterns of ritual movement or the form of the proscenium stage that hold together ballet or theater are gone in film, and in their place is a sense of continuity, the invisible connections of film art that hold together the world of visible objects, whose essence seems to be unritualistic, unpatterned, and unpremeditated.[26]

The world as theater or the world as world? It is sometimes difficult to decide. Some problems in the film adaptations of *Mourning Becomes Electra* and *Long Day's Journey into Night* might be illustrative here.

The movie version of *Long Day's Journey into Night* is far too reverently developed. It is intensely serious. It recognizes the stages of the development of the journey as O'Neill planned them for the stage. But movie time is not stage time, and one keeps expecting the curtain to fall every so often. For all the sophistication of the cinematic technology, the pace is too slow, the points made are too deliberate. We should have the thrilling sense of discovering the wedding ring on Mary's hand at the end rather than the sense that it has been laid there for the camera to see. There is no sense of contingency in the movie; it cannot break out of its ritualized theatrical pattern. A little overlapping dialogue (the men are drunk in the last act, after all) would be enlivening and cinematically effective. The weather is important in the text of the play. But in the movie, where one might expect it to be a crucial element in a visual rendering of the world of the Tyrones, it remains a figure of speech. It remains inert on the screen, not forcefully effective as it is, in language, on the stage. Everybody talks about it, as the saying goes, but nobody does much with it. The play is tightly structured, and we respond to that in the intimate space of the live theater, but that tightness of structure seems too deliberate in its presentation of lives enlarged by the camera. *Citizen Kane,* for example, may seem to some too self-consciously plotted, but the sweep of activity, of surface pleasure, compensates for that; Welles makes something of the weather. A film of Ingmar Bergman's or R. W. Fassbinder's may seem deliberate, too, but expressionistic artifice works to enrich and enlarge the moral action. *Long Day's Journey into Night* remains a movie in realistic style without employing the devices of cinema to make that style meaningful; it becomes a transcription of the words of the play—useful, but not a significant work of art in itself.

Mourning Becomes Electra, a less well-shaped play than *Long Day's Journey into Night,* suffers more in its adaptations, though perhaps that is a function of the weakness of the play. *Long Day's Journey into Night* suffers less from the camera's insinuation of a "real" and spacious world outside the house because all of the significant events in that world, for the purposes of the action, are personal, and all took place before the action of the play commences. *Mourning Becomes Electra,* however, evokes the Civil War. But good as O'Neill is in dramatizing the force of American history on his characters, the Civil War really has little to do with the moral lives of these characters. It serves as an excuse to keep some characters offstage for a while. It serves plot, not moral action. In both plays a house is of central importance, and in both plays the house—by its elegance in *Mourning Becomes Electra,* by its shabbiness in *Long Day's Journey into Night*—cuts a family off from familiar intercourse with the surrounding community. A house in the enclosed space of a stage is quickly seen as metaphoric, and that is what O'Neill clearly meant these houses to be (although one, a memory of his own young life, has an existence other than metaphor). But the camera implies a larger world, and a house becomes an entity in that world. Since in neither movie is anything much done to temper the cinematic space and bring the houses into some kind of organic connection with it, we are left with an impression that the metaphor is arbitrary, that there is no force other than the plotting mind of the writer to cause Lavinia's entombment in the Mannon house. The static space of the theater, according to Bazin, restricts the play to its decor, making the scenery the universe of the dramatic action, much as a "painting exists by virtue of its frame." But movies, by their very nature, reject such restriction: "It is clear that filmed theater is basically destined to fail whenever it tends in any manner to become simply the photographing of scenic representation . . . and perhaps most of all when the camera is used to try and make us forget the footlights and the backstage area."[27] This is why John Ford was O'Neill's most successful movie director. He managed to evoke atmosphere, to make realistic elements expressionistic, to make the sea claustrophobic and dangerous.

Mourning Becomes Electra was adapted twice, once for the movies, once for television. The movie version follows O'Neill's play fairly closely. It shuts off the outside world, as the play does (except for the visit to Brant's ship). But because the space of a movie is so suggestive, we become curious about the surrounding world—even in so artificial a set as we find in this movie. We wonder, for instance, why there are no servants in this rich house. The Greek revival house itself, set apart on a large property, calls up not classical Greece but cinematic associations with southern mansions, and we wonder why the Mannon men fought on the side of the North. There is muddle here, confusion, absurdity. The television version opens out the play to a southern Connecticut community; Stonington seems to be the local train station; townspeople come to a party at the house. We see the South Sea islands that Lavinia and Orin visit. We see the family in a real geography. But the play won't accommodate that without serious revision of the text. The physical enclosure of the Mannon world is a metaphor for the mind and the emotions. Once it is made material, we wonder why Hazel and Peter, members of a real community, do not call the police.

What we need are new and freer adapters of O'Neill's plays, people who can penetrate to the dramatic intent without feeling the restraint of preserving the text as holy word. Television, with its smaller screen and more apparently mediated space, might be one solution. Certainly, it has done better by O'Neill than Hollywood has.

TELEVISION ADAPTATIONS OF O'NEILL

The Emperor Jones

Aired: 1955 by The Kraft Television Theatre on NBC
Music: Wladimir Selinsky

Cast
Brutus Jones: Ossie Davis
Smithers: Everett Sloane
Lem: Rex Ingram

Other credits are not available. The videotape is in the collection of the Museum of Broadcasting, New York. This tape is in black and white, though apparently it was originally produced live and in color.

The Iceman Cometh

Aired: 1960
Director: Sidney Lumet
Producer: Lewis Freedman
Executive Producer: Worthington Miner, who introduces the play.

Cast
Hickey: Jason Robards, Jr.
Harry Hope: Farrell Pelly
Larry Slade: Myron McCormick
Don Parritt: Robert Redford

Willie Oban: James Broderick
Rocky: Tom Pedi
The Captain: Ronald Radd
The General: Roland Winters
Jimmy Tomorrow: Harrison Dowd
Hugo: Sorrell Booke
Margie: Hilda Brawner
Pearl: Julie Bovasso
Cora: Joan Copeland

Brooks Atkinson also introduces the play, which was performed live and in two parts. The videotape is in the collection of the Museum of Broadcasting, New York.

Hughie

Aired: 1961
Director: José Quintero
Director for Television: Terry Hughes
Producers: Theodore Mann and Paul Libin (A Circle in the Square production).

Cast
Erie Smith: Jason Robards
The Night Clerk: Jack Dodson

This is a videotaped performance of an actual stage performance. The videotape is commercially available.

A Touch of the Poet

Aired: 1974 by Theatre in America on PBS
Director: Stephen Porter
Director for Television: Kirk Browning
Producer: David Griffiths

Cast
Sarah: Roberta Maxwell
Con Melody: Fritz Weaver
Nora: Nancy Marchand
Deborah Harford: Carrie Nye
Mickey Malloy: Robert Phalen
Jamie Cregin: Donald Moffat

The videotape is in the collection of the Museum of Broadcasting, New York.

A *Moon for the Misbegotten*

Aired: 1975 as a Mobil Showcase presentation of ABC Theatre
Director: José Quintero
Director for Television: Gordon Rigsby
Producer: David Susskind

Cast
Josie Hogan: Colleen Dewhurst
Jamie Tyrone: Jason Robards
Phil Hogan: Ed Flanders
Harder: John O'Leary
Michael: Edwin J. McDonough

This is apparently a filmed version of a stage performance. The videotape is in the collection of the Museum of Broadcasting, New York.

Beyond the Horizon

Aired: 1976 by the McCarter Theatre Company as part of the series Great
Performances: Theatre in America, for PBS
Director: Michael Kahn
Director for Television: Rick Hauser
Producer: Lindsay Law

Cast
Robert Mayo: Richard Backus
Andrew Mayo: Edward J. Moore
Ruth: Maria Tucci
Mr. Mayo: John Randolph
Mrs. Mayo: Kate Wilkinson
Mrs. Atkins: Geraldine Fitzgerald
Uncle Dick: James Broderick
Dr. Fawcett: John Houseman

The play is introduced by Geraldine Fitzgerald, who relates a biographical sketch of
O'Neill to a montage of stills of the O'Neill family. The videotape is in the collection of the
Museum of Broadcasting, New York.

Mourning Becomes Electra

Aired: 1978 in the series Great Performances on PBS
Director: Nick Havinga
Music: Maurice Jarre

Creative Consultant: Kenneth Cavender

Cast
Seth: Roberts Blossom
Lavinia: Roberta Maxwell
Adam: Jeffrey DeMunn
Christine: Joan Hackett
Orin: Bruce Davison
Peter: Peter Weller
Hazel: Deborah Offner
Ezra: Josef Sommer

This was presented in many episodes, each followed by an afterword by Erich Segal. The videotape is in the collection of the Museum of Broadcasting, New York.

Strange Interlude

Aired: 1988 in the series American Playhouse on PBS
Director: Herbert Wise
Producer: Philip Barry
Executive Producer: Robert Enders
Writer for Television: Robert Enders

Cast
Nina Leeds: Glenda Jackson
Charles Marsden: Edward Petherbridge
Ned Darrell: David Dukes
Sam Evans: Ken Howard
Professor Leeds: José Ferrer
Mrs. Evans: Rosemary Harris
Young Gordon: Kenneth Branagh

This was a television adaptation of a theatrical production, and was broadcast in three parts. The videotape is commercially available.

Long Day's Journey Into Night has been frequently broadcast on television; usually, these telecasts have been filmed versions of theatrical productions. The movie version, directed by Sidney Lumet, is commercially available on videotape. There was a production of *Ah, Wilderness!* by the McCarter Theatre Company in the Great Performances Series, but I have been unable to locate a tape of it. *The Hairy Ape* and *Mourning Becomes Electra* are sometimes listed as available in videotape, but I have not been able to find them either—and I've tried a number of sources. There is a television version of *The Rope,* broadcast on the Arts & Entertainment cable network, but I have been unable to collect much useful information about the production.

O'Neill himself is represented on film. Played by Jack Nicholson, he is a character in Warren Beatty's film *Reds*. O'Neill and his connection with the Provincetown Players are featured in a 1960 segment of the CBS Series *The Twentieth Century* entitled "New

York in the 1920s." *Camera 3,* a CBS Series, produced in 1962 "The Making of a Biography," a show celebrating the completion of the Gelbs' biography of O'Neill, in which the Gelbs provide a biographical summary with many interesting still photographs. O'Neill's life and work are the subject of a 1986 program in the American Masters Series on PBS entitled *O'Neill: A Glory of Ghosts.*

A videotape of James O'Neill, Sr., in scenes from *The Count of Monte Cristo* is readily available. It is rather scratchy, but does give one some faint sense of the reasons for his great popularity—and the disappointment it eventually made him feel.

NOTES

1. John Orlandello, *O'Neill on Film* (Rutherford, N.J.: Fairleigh Dickinson University Press, 1982), 166.

2. Susan Sontag, "Film and Theatre," in *Film Theory and Criticism,* 3d ed., ed. G. Mast and M. Cohen (New York: Oxford University Press, 1985), 341.

3. Louis Sheaffer, *O'Neill: Son and Playwright* (Boston: Little, Brown and Co., 1968), 311–12.

4. Louis Sheaffer, *O'Neill: Son and Artist* (Boston: Little, Brown and Co., 1973), 55.

5. Ibid., 352.

6. Eugene O'Neill in a letter to George Jean Nathan, 12 November 1929, in *"As Ever, Gene": The Letters of Eugene O'Neill to George Jean Nathan,* ed. Nancy L. Roberts and Arthur W. Roberts (Rutherford, N.J.: Fairleigh Dickinson University Press, 1987), 101.

7. Richard Schickel, *D. W. Griffith: An American Life* (New York: Simon and Schuster, 1984), 290.

8. Ibid., 536.

9. Erwin Panofsky, "Style and Medium in the Motion Pictures," in *Film Theory and Criticism,* 219 (see n. 2).

10. André Bazin, *What Is Cinema?* vol. 1, trans. Hugh Gray (Berkeley: University of California Press, 1967), 107.

11. Sheaffer, *O'Neill: Son and Artist,* 104.

12. Ibid., 546.

13. There are three exceptions to this general tendency: *The Emperor Jones, Ah, Wilderness!* and *Strange Interlude.* The last one is not a real exception. The adapters, worried about censorship, simply cut out more than half of O'Neill's play, but what words they kept were mostly O'Neill's. The drama of *The Emperor Jones* does not reside in its words and did not conform to cinematic narrative conventions of 1933, so the adapters invented a life for Jones (drawn from suggestions in O'Neill's play) before he gets to the island. Two thirds of the movie takes place before O'Neill's play begins. *Ah, Wilderness!* although remaining closer to the original, was, with the enlargement of the role of Muriel and, consequently, of a romantic plot, made to conform to a fixed state of cinematic signs, apparently in the hope of encouraging popular appeal—and making money.

14. Siegfried Kracauer, *Theory of Film: The Redemption of Physical Reality* (New York: Oxford University Press, 1960), 216. As some indication that the Russians had a point, the movie review of the *New Republic* observed of *Mourning Becomes Electra:* "No one can pretend it isn't culture" (Orlandello, *O'Neill on Film,* 105).

15. Sontag, "Film and Theatre," 342.

16. Bazin, *What Is Cinema?* 98.

17. Eugene O'Neill in a letter to George Jean Nathan, 12 November 1929, in *"As Ever, Gene,"* 102 (see n. 6).

18. Bela Balazs, "Art Form and Material," in *Film and/as Literature,* ed. John Harrington (Englewood Cliffs, N.J.: Prentice-Hall, 1977), 10.

19. Sheaffer, *O'Neill: Son and Artist,* 352.

20. Dudley Andrew, *Concepts in Film Theory* (Oxford: Oxford University Press, 1984), 99.

21. Pauline Kael, *5001 Nights at the Movies: A Guide from A to Z* (New York: Holt, Rinehart and Winston, 1982), 392.

22. Bazin, *What Is Cinema?* 111. Cf. Panofsky's statement that "the living language, which is always right . . . still speaks of a 'moving picture' or, simply, a 'picture,' instead of accepting the pretentious and fundamentally erroneous 'screenplay' " ("Style and Medium in the Motion Pictures," 217).

23. Bazin, *What Is Cinema?* 103.

24. Panofsky, "Style and Medium in the Motion Pictures," 218–19. O'Neill was troubled by the static quality of stage space and did try to "dynamize" it and to "spatialize" time. Disturbed by the dead time of changing sets in *Beyond the Horizon,* he prevailed on Robert Edmond Jones to design a new kind of fluid set for *Desire Under the Elms.* Still more interesting are his stage directions for *Strange Interlude* for which he insists that the arrangement of furniture in Nina's many residences remain the same through the years and up the economic ladder, thus indicating the permanence of her psychic wound and emphasizing the enclosure of her world and the entrapment of the men within that world, and it is the only world in the play. Darrell's journeys and Charlie's seem futile; their world is defined by Nina's. The film adapters seem not to have noticed O'Neill's intent.

25. Bazin, *What Is Cinema?* 102.

26. Leo Braudy, *The World in a Frame: What We See in Films* (Garden City, N.Y.: Doubleday and Co., Anchor Press, 1976), 35.

27. Bazin, *What Is Cinema?* 105, 107.

6

A Spokesman for America: O'Neill in Translation

Rita Terras

Eugene O'Neill's work has been staged more often and has had larger audiences in Europe than anywhere else in the world including the United States. Of a number of possible reasons for this phenomenon, two stand out immediately. First, there exist in European countries—such as France, Germany, Russia, and the Scandinavian countries—established legitimate repertory theaters that have a considerable following as well as assured financial support from their government, which enables them to experiment without the burdensome mandate of fiscal success; second, few foreign playwrights, and certainly no other American dramatist before O'Neill, offered European audiences the same mixture of familiar dramatic trends (Strindberg, Shaw, Georg Kaiser, and so on) *and* the exoticism of an as yet largely unknown American culture and subculture.

But a foreigner's understanding of an exotic America may be somewhat strange and produce unusual effects. O'Neill's friend Michael Gold reported about a 1923 *Anna Christie* production in Moscow that featured as an introduction various so-called Americans, dressed in Russian garb, prancing about the stage singing in English "Chinatown, my Chinatown" and then switching to "a queer version of 'Yankee Doodle Dandy' done gypsy style and accompanied by a guitar and concertina."[1] All this was obviously an attempt to transport the audience into an American atmosphere in the middle of Moscow. O'Neill's steady presence in European theaters during the past sixty years or so by no means guaranteed that all of the many productions of his plays achieved critical acclaim. They experienced their share of failures, sometimes disastrous failures, but they nevertheless seldom failed to lure audiences into the theater where they wished to learn, firsthand, what America is all about. O'Neill abroad, then, is more than a highly respected playwright. He is a spokesman for his country whose pronouncements are taken seriously and whose presentations shape opinions about and attitudes toward the United States. But outside the English-speaking world, O'Neill speaks to foreign audiences in translation, not in his original English. To study the influence of O'Neill abroad one must consider the means through which most of the world knows him: translations of his work. Therefore in the following article I propose to examine both the impact as a spokesman for America that O'Neill in translation has had upon Europe and the success or failure with which some translations of his plays transmitted the essence of the American dramatist to people abroad.

Much of what the world knows of America and its culture is dispensed through American literature, particularly those works of American literature that *in translation* become available to millions of people who are seriously seeking information about American history, about life in a capitalist society, about a civilization that appeals to almost everybody or, if not, arouses passionate antagonism. But the picture of America that translated American literature provides is selective. It is a well-known fact that writers and works accepted in other countries are not necessarily those most highly valued in their own country. Availability in translation has something to do with fame abroad, and translations are often done haphazardly, depending upon publishers' whims and the willingness of translators to work for very little money at a most demanding job.

When O'Neill first entered the literary scene, a number of his contemporaries were already well known on the European continent: Theodore Dreiser (1871–1945) with his novel *Sister Carrie* (1900), Upton Sinclair (1878–1968) with *The Jungle* (1906), and Sinclair Lewis (1885–1951) with *Babbitt* (1922). By then, the interest of European readers of American literature changed from nineteenth century curiosity about an exotic–romantic America with Indians, pioneers, and a gold rush to an acute interest in social issues around the time of World War I. The founding of socialist states, such as the Soviet Union, and strong socialist governments in the Weimar Republic in Germany, in France, and in Sweden ensured the success of those works in contemporary American literature that showed strong socialist tendencies indicting the meat-packing industry or the ruthless business practices of the middle class. Clearly, all of the authors I just mentioned were socialists or at least socialist sympathizers and presented the United States from a highly critical point of view. It is, therefore, no surprise that interest in O'Neill's early plays was shaped, to a large extent though not entirely, by an interest in the social issues presented in these plays—the plight of the lower classes, the racial question, the situation of women in bourgeois/capitalist society. Even the Soviet Russian encyclopedia of 1968 stresses O'Neill's place in the "radical, lower-bourgeois intelligentsia" of Greenwich Village and the beneficial influence of John Reed (who died in 1920 and was buried in the Kremlin wall) on O'Neill. Reed is credited with having acquainted the playwright with "socialist ideas in an anarchist version."[2] Actually, it is not at all clear that O'Neill was truly interested in Reed's socialism. He knew and liked him as one of the founding members of the Provincetown Players and the lover of Louise Bryant for whom O'Neill himself felt great affection at one time.[3]

In the same vein, the admittedly difficult-to-translate title *All God's Chillun Got Wings* is simply *Negr* in Russian, making clear where the main interest in the play should be from a socialist point of view. But O'Neill himself insisted that the specific social criticism discovered in his plays by foreign and—occasionally—even by domestic critics rests entirely on a misunderstanding of his intentions.[4] *The Hairy Ape* then was neither union propaganda nor O'Neill's attempt to imitate the German author Georg Kaiser in his plays *Gas* and *Die Koralle,* some of whose themes are unequivocally the confrontation of haves and have-nots or of man and machine.[5]

Continental Europe (as well as most of the rest of the world, with the exception of the English-speaking countries) does not know O'Neill in his own words. The fact is that more people know O'Neill in translation than in the original English. Public performances in a language other than the native language of the population of any given country are extremely rare and occur usually either in an academic setting or, in some instances, in opera houses. In general, one may say that if a translation is not available, a work of literature does not exist except for those people whose native language is that of the author. Bilingualism is relatively rare and has no real impact on this state of affairs. O'Neill's plays have been translated into at least thirty-two languages—most likely more. Among the known translations are renderings into five languages spoken in India (Tamil, Hindi, Marathi, Bengali, Telugu), into Arabic, Hebrew, Chinese, Japanese and Korean, Persian, Turkish, and many others. Missing from the list altogether are African languages. The editors of the only existing list of O'Neill translations, Horst Frenz and Susan Tuck, counted mainly, though not exclusively, translations that appeared in book form.[6] In addition, there are others, published in journals and sometimes existing in manuscript only. It is particularly difficult to obtain exact figures for the lesser known languages. To give an example: Frenz and Tuck's compilation lists only one translation into Estonian—*Pikk Päevatee Kaob Öösse,* meaning, in a literal translation back into English, *Long Day Trip Disappears into Night*[7]—whereas the *Estonian Encyclopedia* (1973) lists three additional plays as having been translated and performed in Tallinn, Estonia, during the country's independent existence from 1918 to 1944.[8] They are, with the dates of translation: *Desire Under the Elms* (1929), *The Moon of the Caribbees* (1938), and *Anna Christie* (1939). But even this is not a complete list. According to an oral report, *Ah, Wilderness!* enjoyed an unusually long run in a Tallinn repertory theater in the late 1930s. It is obvious that Frenz and Tuck received their information about Estonian translations from a source in the Soviet Union that did not bother to list anything done before Estonia became a Soviet Republic in 1944. Not mentioning *Ah, Wilderness!* in the *Estonian Encyclopedia* may simply be an oversight.

An analysis of Frenz and Tuck's list of translations yields the following information. Of all of O'Neill's plays, *Long Day's Journey into Night* (written in 1940) seems to have been translated into more languages (twenty according to Frenz and Tuck) than any other play. It is closely followed by *Mourning Becomes Electra,* translated into eighteen; *The Emperor Jones,* translated into seventeen; *Desire Under the Elms* and *Anna Christie,* both into sixteen; *Ah, Wilderness!* fifteen; *Strange Interlude,* fourteen; *Beyond the Horizon,* twelve; *A Moon for the Misbegotten* and *Ile,* eleven each; and *The Hairy Ape, The Moon of the Caribbees, The Great God Brown,* and *All God's Chillun Got Wings,* ten each. Translated into only one or two languages are *More Stately Mansions,* two; and *Thirst* and *Fog,* one each. Among other well-known and often performed plays of O'Neill, *The Iceman Cometh* and *A Touch of the Poet* were translated into nine and eight languages, respectively. Altogether, there seem to exist translations of at least thirty-seven plays. Thirty-five of them were translated into Spanish, which is the largest number of plays translated into any one language, followed by thirty-four plays into French, thirty into German, twenty into Japanese, fifteen into Russian as well as into Chinese, and eight into Swedish. Some translations were published under titles such as *The Sea-Plays* or *"Anna Christie" and other Plays* without listing exactly every play in the collection, which leads us to the safe assumption that several plays have been translated more often than the kind of listing now available will show.

If we look at the dates when they were written or published, it becomes obvious that the most frequently translated plays are not necessarily the latest ones nor the ones that received the greatest critical acclaim in this country. *Anna Christie* (translated into sixteen languages) and *Ile* (translated into eleven languages), for example, were always very popular abroad, but they are often dismissed as minor plays in this country. One might have expected that O'Neill's fame would have grown after he received the Nobel prize in 1936, particularly since the Nobel prize for literature has long been regarded as the highest distinction in the world that an author could possibly achieve, and O'Neill was only the second American author to be so honored (after Sinclair Lewis in 1930). Actually, of the later plays, only *Long Day's Journey into Night* and *A Moon for the Misbegotten,* O'Neill's last completed play (written 1941–43), were translated into more than ten languages; *A Touch of the Poet* (written between 1939 and 1942) was translated into only eight languages; *Hughie* (written in 1940) into only five; and *More Stately Mansions* into not more than two.

On the other hand, plays written and performed and published in the United States in the 1920s and early 1930s were very popular abroad, especially *Anna Christie* (1920) but also *The Emperor Jones* (1920), *The Hairy Ape* (1922), *All God's Chillun Got Wings* (1923–24), *Desire Under the Elms* (1924), *The Great God Brown* (1925), *Strange Interlude* (1927–28), *Mourning Becomes Electra* (1929–30), and *Ah, Wilderness!* (1932). Drawing conclusions from small sample statistics is risky, but it certainly seems that the Nobel prize did not enhance O'Neill's image in Europe except for Sweden. At the same time, there can be no doubt that some far-reaching changes in cultural policies affected O'Neill's reception in both Russia and Germany beginning around 1930 and continuing until after World War II in Germany and even longer in the Soviet Union.[9]

After the revolution of 1917, Russian art and literature, which had begun their avant-garde movement under Czar Nicholas II around 1910, continued to flourish in the new socialist society.[10] In the arts, movements such as suprematism (Kazimir Malevich), rayonnism (Natalya Goncharova and Mikhail Larionov), and constructivism (Sir Naum Gabo and Vladimir Tatlin) became well known not only in Moscow and Petersburg (Leningrad since Lenin's death in 1924) but also in Berlin, Paris, and Venice.[11] Russian futurism in art and literature turned out to be as exciting and imaginative as the futurisms of other European countries. The poets of the "Stray Dog Tavern" in Petersburg gathered once again after 1917, trying to adjust to or even to embrace the new social and political order of a Communist state. The chaos of revolution had brought with it—albeit for a brief period only—a complete freedom of creativity that, despite starvation and other hardships, energized and inspired the young generation of artists.[12] In this atmosphere of optimism and enthusiasm Alexander Tairov (1885–1950), one of Russia's most talented directors, founded in 1914 the Moscow Kamerny (Chamber) Theater, which was devoted to a cosmopolitan repertory, performed for the enjoyment and relaxation of its audiences.[13] Tairov was opposed to the Stanislavski method of meticulous realism. The Kamerny Theater was the first important stage to introduce O'Neill to a Russian–speaking audience. *Anna Christie* had been shown in 1923.[14] In 1926 Tairov produced *The Hairy Ape* (translated in 1925) and in 1927 *Desire Under the Elms* (translated in the same year), followed by *All God's Chillun Got Wings* in 1930 (production and translation).[15] All four plays were translated for the Kamerny by the translation team of N. M. Krymova and P. B. Zenkevich. P. B. Zenkevich is known as a member of the avant-garde acmeist group of poets, with Osip Mandelstam and Anna Akhmatova as its most prominent representatives.[16] Photographs of the productions of *The Hairy Ape* and *Desire Under the Elms* at the Kamerny Theater show a strong constructivist influence, a stage set consisting of a unistructure delineated by vertical and horizontal lines that are further emphasized through the use of light and shadow.[17] Also typical for this kind of set is the inclusion of the written word. To set the scene for an American play, the words *ENSOR I.T.E. LIMITED* appear not in Cyrillic but in Latin letters.

When in May 1930 Tairov toured Europe with his production of *Desire Under the Elms* and *All God's Chillun Got Wings,* O'Neill with his third wife, Carlotta, saw both plays in Paris and found the staging "damned interesting and imaginative," and, as Louis Sheaffer further reported, "in a backstage visit, felt an immediate rapport with Tairov and his actors."[18] What exactly "damned interesting and imaginative" meant, we do not know, for John Martin, the dance critic of the *New York Times,* who reviewed the two productions in Paris, gained a somewhat different impression. He reported on June 15 of the same year: "The scenery and costumes are shabby from much travel, and there is a general down-at-the-heel air about the whole business that would not be tolerated for an instant in New York and is not being received too cordially in Paris. . . . Certainly it is not the perfect 'theatrical' theater of one's dreams."[19] Most likely, O'Neill was, at the time, not aware of the shifts in cultural policies taking place in the Soviet Union around 1930. After Lenin's death in 1924, a struggle for leadership between Trotski and Stalin led to Stalin's victory and Trotski's dismissal from the party by 1927. Stalin almost immediately decreed an end to individual creativity and freedom in the arts. The newly developed doctrine of Socialist Realism demanded that art, literature, and the theater not only be realistic but also serve the cause of socialism and present an optimistic view of the future. Tairov survived the change in policy—many others did not. The Kamerny Theater changed from a cosmopolitan to a strictly Soviet Russian stage, and O'Neill, though at the time a proper champion of proletarian causes, apparently lacked the required enthusiasm for the future building of a classless society and therefore disappeared as a translatable author until Khrushchev came to power, denounced Stalin's policies, and prepared the way for, among other things, a number of new O'Neill translations into Russian. From 1961 to 1975 at least seven plays were translated.[20]

The German story is somewhat similar. The name O'Neill was first heard by Hugo von Hofmannsthal (1874–1929), himself a well-known Austrian playwright and the librettist for most of Richard Strauss's operas. He heard the name at the 1921 Salzburg Festival, which he had cofounded with Max Reinhardt the year before. As he told us in his 1922 essay "Dramaturgical Reflections," "A few Americans in our audience . . . aroused my curiosity . . . by relating the plots of *The Emperor Jones* and *The Hairy Ape.*" Hofmannsthal reported that he proceeded to read several O'Neill plays (he read English very well) and found them "throughout . . . essentially of the theatre."[21] The essay was published in Berlin, where O'Neill's plays were soon to make frequent appearances on various stages, with varying success. (They were also performed in other German cities, such as Cologne and Essen). Also, in 1923 Alfred Kerr, the famous drama critic for the established *Berliner Tageblatt,* together with a friend, Gustav Kauder, returned to Berlin from a trip to New York, where the two men had seen several O'Neill plays. They, too, generated considerable enthusiasm for the foremost American playwright. Gustav Kauder immediately proceeded to translate into German *The Emperor Jones* (1923) and *The Moon of the Caribbees* (translated in 1924). Between 1923 and 1932 nine plays were translated by several different translators and also performed: *The Emperor Jones* and *Anna Christie,* translated in 1923 and performed in Berlin in 1923; *The Moon of the Caribbees,* translated and performed in

1924 (directed by Erwin Piscator); *The Hairy Ape*, 1924); *Desire Under the Elms* and *All God's Chillun*, 1925; *The Great God Brown*, 1926, performed in 1928 in Cologne; *Strange Interlude*, 1929; and *Before Breakfast*, 1932.[22]

The first production to reach any Berlin stage was a sentimental version of *Anna Christie* in which Anna ended up shooting herself. It was done in a botched German translation by—strange as this may sound—a Hungarian (Melchior Lengyel), whose talents as a translator were evaluated at the time of performance by the German journalist Rudolf Kommer as follows: "Apart from his admiration of the play" the translator's "qualifications as a literary go-between were limited to a Berlitz acquaintance with English and German. What he may have guessed in English, he was utterly unable to express in German."[23] *Anna Christie* closed after three performances. The Berlin production of *The Emperor Jones* in Kauder's excellent translation also failed because Berlin directors did not hesitate to experiment freely with newly developed expressionist concepts, but audiences were not always willing or able to accept strange interpretations of a play and radical innovations on the set. Rudolf Kommer this time commented that the producers apparently "thought they could only cope with the primeval forest by entrusting its execution to a neo-expressionist of the most radical brand. The result was so perplexing that even an Elizabethan signboard, if added to the scenery, could not have convinced the audience that it was sitting in front of a forest. . . . Strange are the ways of producers."[24] Horst Frenz quoted another German critic as having said that the so-called jungle (actually a kind of dome, as O'Neill had described it) had had "the effect of an (apartment) courtyard hung with dirty laundry."[25] Apart from the ineffective set, the play had other faults that led to misinterpretations culminating in the idea—as one critic in the conservative newspaper *Deutsche Zeitung* put it—that the play was an attempt to ridicule the monarchy (still close to the heart of many Germans in 1924) with the help of cheap sensationalism and outrageous sets.[26]

The last of the major German productions of O'Neill's early plays was *Strange Interlude* in 1929 with Elisabeth Bergner, a famous actress, as Nina. It, too, caused a sensation. Bergner was a success, but the German critics "yowled and hooted." They actually found *Strange Interlude* too literary—which it is with its whispered asides—because, having become accustomed to expressionistic productions, they now preferred the "*primitive*" O'Neill.[27] By 1929 the dramatist's reputation as an expressionist playwright had been firmly established in Germany, and as such, he became persona non grata on the German stage as soon as Hitler came to power and denounced all expressionist art as degenerate art.[28] Ironically, *Strange Interlude*, which displeased critics so much in 1929, should have been, and *could* have been—exactly the kind of play Nazi Germany after 1933 might have appreciated. *Strange Interlude* shows some similarity of attitude and ambience to some short stories by Rudolf Binding (1867–

1938), a much revered German author of the 1920s, 1930s, and 1940s. The Nazi mentality ought to have found appealing a play featuring the ghost of a war hero hovering in the background and the story of a woman consciously breeding a healthy offspring with her lover after aborting the possibly mentally deficient fetus fathered by her husband.

Having been banned from the German stage for twelve years, O'Neill was resurrected after World War II by the theater department of the American High Commission, the military government in charge of administering the American Zone of Germany from 1945 to 1949, when the Federal Republic and the German Democratic Republic came into being. Together with several O'Neill translations, the commission sponsored translations of Faulkner's recently revised *The Sound and the Fury* and a number of Hemingway novels. The latter were very successful in the American Zone and in the Federal Republic, whereas the forced O'Neill revival did not "take" in the late 1940s. *Anna Christie* was a total disaster in 1945, and the German reaction to *Ah, Wilderness!* in 1947 was an incredulous "what could this lame discussion possibly mean to us, here in Germany" sitting on mounds of rubble with no future and nothing to eat.[29] *Mourning Becomes Electra* earned some critical acclaim the same year but wasn't successful otherwise. O'Neill did not become popular again until the late 1950s and early 1960s, when the economic miracle had occurred and postwar German literature had its own beginnings with Günter Grass, Heinrich Böll, and playwrights such as Heinar Kipphardt, Peter Weiss, Rolf Hochhuth, and the two Swiss dramatists Max Frisch and Friedrich Dürrenmatt. Two 1957 and 1958 productions of *Long Day's Journey into Night* (in a new translation) experienced the first complete success of any O'Neill play in Germany. Since 1958, the publication and production of new and revised translations of O'Neill abound in the Federal Republic, and even the German Democratic Republic published a first volume of translations with at least seven plays in 1972.[30]

O'Neill's disappearance from the German and Russian stages happens to coincide with a twelve-year span during which he did not release a single new play—the so-called silent years from the critically unsuccessful production of *Days Without End* in 1934 to the premier of *The Iceman Cometh* in 1946. There exists, however, no relationship between the politically motivated events in the Soviet Union and in Germany and O'Neill's personal choice of silence in the 1930s and early 1940s. During this time, O'Neill was constantly visible on the American stage with productions of earlier plays, while he was totally invisible in Germany and Russia. Moreover, a comparison of translations into German and Russian with translations into Spanish, the language that can boast of more O'Neill translations than any other, shows that the Spanish translations—uninhibited by political events—appeared in a normal manner all through the 1930s, 1940s, 1950s, and 1960s. Most of them were published in Argentina.[31]

So far, we have seen that O'Neill has been as successful an author in translation as he has been in the original. His appeal to non English-speaking audiences began early on in his career as America's foremost dramatist and, with some interruptions, continues into the present. The success or failure of his plays abroad were often influenced by political events beyond the control of both the author and the translator. But in addition to their dependence on sociopolitical circumstances, translations owe much of their acceptance or rejection to the ability of the translator to convey correctly what the author intended to say. It is therefore worthwhile to take a closer look at the art of translating O'Neill in the second part of this chapter.

Translation has become a serious, sometimes even profitable, business in recent times. Giving in to the demands of mass consumption with its need for instant gratification, translations have received considerable attention. It is not enough for the serious translator of important literary works to have a firm grasp of two languages. The translator must also have an intimate knowledge of the form as well as the content of the work to be translated. His integrity with regard to the author's text must be beyond reproach. Finally, beyond all that *can* be acquired, the translator of poetry—in the widest sense—must be somewhat of a poet himself, an insight first voiced by the German Romantics around 1800. In 1928 Carlotta Monterey—after it was arranged for a Monsieur Calmy to adapt *Strange Interlude* into French—expressed succinctly what is most important for a good translator: "The man," she wrote, "who does [translate] *Lazarus*," a play she particularly liked, "must not only know (in the *finer sense*) French & English—but he must be in his bones a poet! A real poet!"[32] O'Neill himself distrusted translators, perhaps not without good reason. On the occasion of the French production of *The Hairy Ape,* in October 1929, he maintained that the play "can't ever really be translated. It is bound to lose in translation just the quality . . . that is most worthwhile—its rhythm of colorful dialogue, its dynamic drive of language. And its emotional significance and meaning is nothing the French rational mind could ever get in a million years."[33] What O'Neill says here is also true for his other plays and for translations into languages other than French. Linguistic features are tremendously difficult to capture and to reproduce in another language, but cultural differences, such as those existing between the rational French and the irrational Irish/American approach to human existence, pose an even greater problem for the translator—as well as for a director and all others involved in a foreign production.

This brings us to the important question of translation, transmission, transformation, or adaptation: What is it that the good translator does? The translator will try to be as faithful to the text as possible without sacrificing the spirit of the whole work. An adaptation, that is, a negation of values in the original in order to accommodate values existing in another culture, is not the translator's task. Whether it is the task of a producer or director is another question that will have to be decided on the basis of a particular situation. Transformation of linguistic features, rather than literal translation, is often necessary to retain the spirit of the work. A model may demonstrate what a translation cannot do, can do, and must not do.

If we think of a work of literature as a sphere that permits a critic to interpret the many aspects of the work by selecting several tangents reflected off that sphere, the translation of the work in question would constitute a second sphere formed at the intersection of a limited number of tangents from the original sphere. The critic working with the original will find that all tangents of interpretation are at his disposal and that many of them will intersect (a Freudian approach will be overlapping with the strictly textual, the feminist with the sociological, and so on). The work in translation, however, is not more than an approximation to the original and has fewer tangents open to interpretation. A strictly textual approach to criticism, for instance, is impossible because the actual words of the author are no longer present. At the same time, the transposition of the work from one language to the other causes a reflection of tangents from the new sphere that have nothing to do with the original but are part of the cultural background of the second language. The good translator will try to emphasize as many aspects of the original as possible and avoid the intrusion of interpretative tangents from the other culture.

To illustrate the above, consider the following as an example of what a translator must not do: In *Long Day's Journey into Night* O'Neill gives stage directions mentioning living room, dining room, kitchen, porch, and so on. "To live" in English can mean either to live one's life or to live at a certain place. In German, the first is *leben* and the second *wohnen*. "Living room" is usually called *Wohnzimmer* or *Wohnraum*. One interpreter of O'Neill argued that "living room" in this particular play means not simply *Wohnzimmer* but also *Lebensraum*, that O'Neill meant more than just living space (*Wohnzimmer*), that he also wanted to point out that in the living room of the Tyrone family all of life happens.[34] If the translator were to accept the latter idea of *Lebensraum* for "living room" and subsequently to translate "living room" with the word *Lebensraum*, this would bring with it insurmountable complications in the form of the intrusion of tangents into the sphere of the translated work that are totally unrelated to O'Neill's original. Namely, the word *Lebensraum* in modern usage has connotations that O'Neill surely never intended to introduce into a play about a family or—in fact—his own family. *Lebensraum* became a slogan in Nazi Germany for German imperialism in World War II. *Lebensraum* designated the attempt by the Nazis to win new living space for coming generations of Germans in Eastern Europe and particularly in the Ukraine. Clearly, a translation of living room with *Lebensraum* is impossible because it totally confuses the issue. The common and infinitely more sensible *Wohnzimmer* or *Wohnraum* must be retained. Otherwise, it would violate the spirit of the play.

Among the important aspects of a work that the translator can preserve are—contrary to O'Neill's opinion—"its rhythms of colorful dialogue, . . . its dynamic drive of language." In *The Hairy Ape* and in other plays, O'Neill reproduces, whenever appropriate, the spoken rather than the written idiom in a variety of dialects. He often contrasts them with the more formal spoken language of a semi-educated or fully educated person. The difference between the written language and the vernacular arises out of nonstandard grammatical arrangements, out of the inclusion of a large number of idioms, as well as from the unusual pronunciation of certain words. In scene seven of *The Hairy Ape*, Yank, the protagonist—he is a stoker—speaks to the secretary of Local 57 of the Industrial Workers of the World union. His manner of speech depends heavily on the pronunciation of "d" for "th" and "t" for "th," as in "*d*at" for "*th*at," "wi*t*'" for "wi*th*," "*d*en" for "*th*en," and "*t*ings" for "*th*ings." He also says "oi" instead of "er" in "n*oi*ve" instead of "n*er*ve," and he likes to use "you*se*" instead of "you." Finally, he is in the habit of combining words that are normally separated, such as "want*er*" for "want to" or "off*en*" for "off of." Unlike the apparently inadequate French translation of this particular play, the German translation of 1924, by Frank Washburn and Else von Hollander (obviously the combined effort of a native speaker of English and a native speaker of German), takes all of these linguistic quirks into consideration and manages, in most cases, either to reproduce a vernacular similar to the original one or to substitute words and phrases of equal value and quality. For instance, for "*d*at/*th*at" they use not simply the German word "das," but "da*t*" or "e*t*," a dialect version of "es." This means that they substitute "t" for "s" whereas in English a substitution of "d" for "th" occurred. They also include pronunciations such as "se" for "Sie," and they reproduce the feature of combined words such as "want*er*" meaning "want to" by using the German "wollt'*r*" for "wollt ihr." They often leave out the final "t" in the German words "ist" and "nicht," as is common in the vernacular. In addition, the translators correctly inserted a grammatical "error"—as an uneducated German would do—into the sentence "Blow it offer the oith," saying "Runter von *die* Erde muss da*t*." The correct form would be the dative "von der Erde." For the idiomatic phrase "Yuh call me," in the sense of "if you need to know," the translators use a literal translation of "if you need to know," but they soften it by the careless pronunciation of "*se*," "*et*" and "woll*n*." This example is from *The Hairy Ape* or *Der haarige Affe,* scene 7:

YANK. *D*en yuh sure got your n*oi*ve wit you*se*.
   Donnerwetter, Mensch, feige seid ihr *nich!*

SECRETARY. Just what was it made you want to join us? Come out with that straight.

Welchen Grund haben Sie, bei uns Mitglied zu werden? Rücken Sie mal raus mit der Sprache!

YANK. *Yuh call me?* Well, I got n*oi*ve, too! Here's my hand. Yuh want*er* blow *t*ings up, don't y*ur*? Well, *d*at's me! I belong!
    Wenn *se et* unbedingt wissen woll*n*. Feige bin ich auch *nich!* Hier *is* meine Hand! Alles in die Luft sprengen, dat woll*t'r* doch, *nich?* Schön, da*t is* genau mein Fall! Dazu taug ich.

SECRETARY. You mean change the unequal conditions of society by legitimate direct action—or with dynamite?
    Woll'*n* Sie die Ungerechtigkeiten der Gesellschaft auf gesetzlichem Wege abschaffen—oder durch Dynamit?

YANK. Dynamite! Blow it off*en* d*e oith*—steel—all *de* cages—all *de* factories, steamers, buildings, jails—*de* Steel Trust and all *d*at makes it go.
    Dynamit! Runter von *die* Erde muß da*t*—Stahl—all Käfige—all die Fabriken, Dampfer, Häuser, Gefängnisse—der Stahltrust und all da*t* andere, wa*t* damit zusammenhängt.[35]

O'Neill's flair for highly poetic, evocative titles is evident throughout his work. His attention to the names of his plays is no accident. In the words of one critic, titles are like "a lighthouse, signaling the way to port through the fog and darkness which surround so many works of contemporary art."[36] The titles often correspond to the text of the play itself, where they are spoken at a significant moment. The titles' poetic value rests on a variety of poetic features. Obvious is the alliteration in *A Moon for the Misbegotten, More Stately Mansions, Marco Millions, The Great God Brown.* Many titles show visual imagery as in *The Iceman Cometh, Desire Under the Elms, A Touch of the Poet,* or *Long Day's Journey into Night,* with the latter being particularly effective through the creation of the strong contrast between day and night. A slightly dated grammatical construction such as the genitive (possessive) case in *Long Day's Journey* or *All God's Chillun* or the use of an archaic form such as "cometh" gives a sentence importance. Grammatical features in a text in one language can usually be reproduced fairly easily in a related language, and most European languages—including English but excluding the Finno-Ugrian group— are related. It is true that the attempt to reproduce grammatical features of O'Neill's work in the language into which it is being translated is not always made. For instance, the French rendering of *Long Day's Journey into Night* as *Long voyage vers la nuit* lacks not only the significant genitive but, in consequence, also the contrast between day and night, that is, the full effect of the visual image. The Finno-Ugrian languages produce—at least to ears unfamiliar with their sound system— surprising effects. In Finnish, one of the least contrived of O'Neill's titles, *In the Zone,* translates into the infinitely more poetic *Vaaravyöhykkeessä.*
    Alliteration is often more of a problem, but not totally impossible to reproduce, since there are many cognates of English words in related languages, for instance, in German, which permits alliteratively faithful

translations such as *Der grosse Gott Braun* and *Marcos Millionen*. Surprisingly, O'Neill's intention to give the title *Mourning Becomes Electra* the dual meaning of "it befits—it becomes Electra to mourn" and, second, in an ironic sense, "mourning (black) is becoming to her"—is entirely expressible in German also, where "Trauer" has all the connotations of "mourning" and where the latest translation sounds as poetic as the original English. Nevertheless, the first translator of this play did not recognize O'Neill's sophisticated intention and conveyed only the second sarcastic and less important meaning in *Trauer steht Elektra gut* (1931). Not until years later did a second translator come up with the wonderfully poetic and expressive title *Trauer muss Elektra tragen* (1947).[37] *A Touch of the Poet* is an idiomatic phrase and idioms almost never translate literally into another language. The title has been translated into German in two ways, neither of them fully satisfying (*Ein Hauch von Poesie, Fast ein Poet*). The Russian translation, on the other hand, is effective though further removed from the original than the German. It preserves the poetic spirit of *A Touch of the Poet*. Translated back into English, it reads: "The Soul of a Poet." One may wonder if the unfortunate translation of the title *Desire Under the Elms*—in which the word *desire* (*Begehren* in German) is given as *Gier*, the equivalent of "lust" or "craving," frequently applied to animal behavior—may not be the reason for a German critic's 1929 one sentence dismissal of this particular play. He simply described it as follows: "[*Gier unter Ulmen*] with its zoo full of country people, fanatics of the soil, of power, of sex."[38] Of all of O'Neill's titles, *A Moon for the Misbegotten* proved to be more troublesome to translators than any other one. It translates fairly well into some languages closely related to English such as Danish, *Maane for de mislykkede* ("Unlucky Ones"), or Dutch, *Een maan voor de misdeelten* ("Those with a Raw Deal"). Both have the alliteration. The Swedish and German versions lose some poetic value but at least preserve the significance of the word *Misbegotten* in *olycksfödda* ("Those without Luck") and *Beladenen* ("The Burdened"). The Spanish translator simply decided to call the play *Una luna para el bastardo*, even though O'Neill certainly refrained from using the inappropriate word *bastard*.[39]

Finally, I would like to address briefly the question of the alternatives of a diachronic or a synchronic approach to translation, which for O'Neill's work didn't matter until recently, when his early plays began—linguistically speaking—to age; now even his late plays show some signs—again linguistically speaking—of being out of step with contemporary usage. The great number of recent Bible translations attests to the fact that a synchronic approach in translating historic texts is fashionable because one assumes that a layperson's comprehension of a biblical text is impossible unless it can be read in his own contemporary idiom. Others will disagree, pointing out that the revelatory nature of the Bible requires linguistic distancing to aid an intuitive, perhaps poetic, understanding of the text. In other words, the latter group insists on the diachronic approach with some kind of recognition of the fact that—linguistically speaking—the Bible is a historic and not a contemporary document. Such linguistic recognition does not have to be historically accurate; it must simply show that some kind of historicity exists. The diachronic approach, then, seems to come closer to what I propose as a good translator's goal: to try to be as faithful as possible to the text without sacrificing the spirit of the whole work. But can it always be done? Does the translator of today possess the linguistic tools to reproduce the vernacular common to the 1920s? He must, if he wants to satisfy the playwright, Eugene O'Neill.

NOTES

1. Louis Sheaffer, *O'Neill: Son and Artist* (Boston: Little, Brown and Co., 1973), 109.

2. See under "Eugene O'Neill" in *Kratkaya Literaturnaya Entsiklopediya*, ed. A. A. Surkov, vol. 5 (Moscow: Izdatel 'stvo "Sovetskaya Entsiklopediya," 1968), 439–41.

3. See Louis Sheaffer, *O'Neill: Son and Playwright* (Boston: Little, Brown and Company, 1968), 345–59, 363–65.

4. See Eugene O'Neill, "What the Theatre Means to Me," in *O'Neill and His Plays: Four Decades of Criticism,* ed. Oscar Cargill, N. Bryllion Fagin, and William J. Fisher (New York: New York University Press, 1961), 107.

5. Horst Frenz, *Eugene O'Neill* (Berlin: Colloquium Verlag, 1965), remarked (38) that Tairov in interpreting *All God's Chillun* was poetically as well as politically motivated. He added a number of songs and a scene concerned with class struggle and the oppression of blacks. See also 34–36.

6. Horst Frenz and Susan Tuck, eds., *Eugene O'Neill's Critics: Voices from Abroad* (Carbondale: Southern Illinois University Press, 1984), 200–218. This list is the source for much of the documentation in this chapter, particularly the foreign titles of translations of O'Neill.

7. Ibid., 217.

8. See under "Eugene O'Neill" in *Eesti Nõukogude Entsüklopeedia,* vol. 5 (Tallinn: Valgus, 1973), 505.

9. Ideology kept O'Neill out of China during the Cultural Revolution, when virtually all foreign literature was banned.

10. On the Russian avant-garde, see John Milner, *Vladimir Tatlin and the Russian Avant-Garde* (New Haven: Yale University Press, 1983).

11. See ibid. for Malevich and suprematism (esp. 104–7); Goncharova, Larionov and rayonnism (esp. 51); and Gabo, Tatlin and constructivism (esp. 181–216, 225).

12. For this brief period of creative freedom after the revolution, see Nikolai Gorchakov, *The Theater in Soviet Russia,* trans. Edgar Lehrman (New York: Columbia University Press, 1957), 100ff.; and Marc Slonim, *The Russian Theater from the Empire to the Soviets* (Cleveland: World Publishing Co., 1961), 228–56.

13. For Tairov and the Kamerny, see Sheaffer, *O'Neill: Son and Artist,* 357–58; and Nikolai Gorchakov, *The Theater in Soviet Russia,* 88–93.

14. Sheaffer, *O'Neill: Son and Artist,* 109–10.

15. Gorchakov, *The Theater in Soviet Russia,* 231–32.

16. For acmeism, see *Handbook of Russian Literature,* ed. Victor Terras (New Haven: Yale University Press, 1985), 3–8; for Mandelstam, see ibid., 271–73; for Akhmatova, see ibid., 14–16.

17. Frenz and Tuck, *Eugene O'Neill's Critics,* photographs on 42 and 72.

18. Sheaffer, *O'Neill: Son and Artist*, 357.

19. Ibid., 358.

20. Frenz and Tuck, *Eugene O'Neill's Critics*, 217–18.

21. Hugo von Hofmannsthal, "Dramaturgical Reflections" (1922), in Frenz and Tuck, *Eugene O'Neill's Critics*, 4 (see n. 6). According to Hoffmannsthal, he heard about *The Hairy Ape* in the summer of 1921, yet the play was not written until December 1921 (Sheaffer, *O'Neill: Son and Artist*, 72). It is true, however, that O'Neill had written earlier a short story about his stoker friend Driscoll that bore the same title (Sheaffer, *O'Neill: Son and Artist*, 69). The visitors to the Salzburg Festival may have discussed this story.

22. Frenz and Tuck, *Eugene O'Neill's Critics*, xiv and 206; Rudolf Kommer, "Eugene O'Neill in Europe," in *Eugene O'Neill and His Plays*, 266–68 (see n. 4).

23. Frenz and Tuck, *Voices From Abroad*, 205; Kommer, "Eugene O'Neill in Europe," 266–67.

24. Kommer, "Eugene O'Neill in Europe," 267–68.

25. Frenz, *Eugene O'Neill*, 29: "die 'Wirkung eines mit schmutziger Wäsche verhangenen Hinterhofes.'"

26. Ibid., 88–89: "Das Stück sei ein Versuch, mit Hilfe von Sensationen und wilden Bühneneffekten das Kaisertum lächerlich zu machen," wrote the *Deutsche Zeitung*.

27. Sheaffer, *O'Neill: Son and Artist*, 351.

28. Although no O'Neill plays were staged in Germany, literary critics continued to be interested in O'Neill throughout the 1930s. See Frenz, *Eugene O'Neill*, 89.

29. Ibid., 90: "Was sollen wir Deutschen mit dieser lauen Diskussion anfangen?"

30. Frenz and Tuck, *Eugene O'Neill's Critics*, 205.

31. Ibid., 200–201, 214–15.

32. Sheaffer, *O'Neill: Son and Artist*, 304–5.

33. Ibid., 350.

34. Ulrich Halfmann, *Unreal Realism: O'Neills dramatisches Werk im Spiegel seiner szenischen Kunst* (Francke Verlag: Bern, 1969), 59.

35. English: Eugene O'Neill, *The Hairy Ape*, in *The Plays of Eugene O'Neill*, vol. 1 (New York: Random House, Inc., Modern Library, 1982), 248; German: "Der haarige Affe" in *Eugene O'Neill: Meisterdramen* (Frankfurt: S. Fischer Verlag, 1963), 94.

36. Wojciech Natanson, "O'Neill's Comeback," in Frenz and Tuck, *Eugene O'Neill's Critics*, 121 (see n. 6).

37. Sheaffer, *O'Neill: Son and Artist*, 338. See also Eugene O'Neill, *Seltsames Zwischenspiel*, Marianne Wentzel, trans., Hellmut Schlien, ed. (Emsdetten: Verlag Lechte, 1957), 8.

38. Erik Reger, "The Georg Kaiser of America," in Frenz and Tuck, *Eugene O'Neill's Critics*, 32 (see n. 6). The play was translated and staged in Berlin in 1925.

39. The translation of this particular title into Polish seems to have had a strong influence on the evaluation of various Polish productions of *A Moon for the Misbegotten*. See Natanson, "O'Neill's Comeback," 120–21.

Part Two

Art and Life —
The Wellsprings of Genius

7

Eugene O'Neill's
American *Eumenides*

Richard F. Moorton, Jr.

There is general agreement among scholars that the first two plays of
O'Neill's *Mourning Becomes Electra* follow the *Agamemnon* and *Libation
Bearers* of the *Oresteia* with reasonable fidelity. In Aeschylus's
Agamemnon, the king returns from the war only to be murdered by
Clytemnestra in collusion with Aegisthus. Just so, in O'Neill's
Homecoming, on his return from the Civil War, General Ezra Mannon is
murdered by his wife, Christine, with a poison she got from Adam Brant.
Likewise, as Orestes with the support of Electra kills Aegisthus and
Clytemnestra in *The Libation Bearers*, so Orin is incited by Lavinia to
shoot Adam Brant in *The Hunted*, in grief for which Christine commits
suicide. But in *The Haunted*, O'Neill ends his trilogy with Orin's suicide
and Lavinia's virtual self-incarceration, rather than the public acquittal of
his protagonist in a trial by jury through which Aeschylus exonerates
Orestes in *The Eumenides*. This difference has naturally led critics like
Barrett Clark, Father Joseph P. O'Neill, and Virginia Floyd to conclude
that in the third play of his adaptation of the *Oresteia* O'Neill has abandoned Aeschylus altogether.[1] These scholars would seem to find support in
O'Neill's own words on the subject. In a letter to George Jean Nathan
written during the composition of the trilogy O'Neill explained that if the
secret that the work was modeled on Aeschylus were to leak out it would
be "injurious" and "misleading," since "beyond the general plot outline of
the first two plays there is nothing of the Greek notion about it now. I have
simplified it until all its Greek similarities are out—almost."[2] But this
statement looks suspiciously like others in which (presumably with the
intent of protecting his reputation for originality) O'Neill sought to mini-
mize his artistic dependence on authors like Freud and Georg Kaiser whom
scholars rightly see as influences on his work.[3] In a virtual about-face, in
his very next letter to Nathan, O'Neill stresses that he has been struggling
not to purge his work of its parallels with Aeschylus but to assimilate the
Greek spirit to his American trilogy, "to get enough of Clytemnestra into
Christine, of Electra in Lavinia, of Orestes in Orin, etc. and yet keep them

American primarily; to conjure a Greek fate out of the Mannons themselves."[4] He was steeped in the details of the *Oresteia* and intent upon creating an American correlative to the destiny of the house of Atreus. My thesis is that in spite of his statement to the contrary O'Neill consciously or unconsciously followed Aeschylus to the end by patterning the third play of his American trilogy on the third play of the Greek trilogy that he had made his model. It is true that O'Neill did not intend, like Aeschylus, to save his young avengers from their Furies, but like *The Eumenides* O'Neill's *Haunted* is a play of judgment, in this case a private judgment whose stages of development are remarkably parallel in structure to the development of the public judgment of Orestes in Aeschylus's *Eumenides*.

At the beginning of *The Eumenides,* the priestess of Apollo at Delphi, after a brief prologue, enters his temple. She soon comes out, aghast at what she has seen inside, the bloodstained Orestes surrounded by the troupe of Furies, dressed in black and oozing rheum. Distraught by this defilement of the holy of holies, she exits. I believe that O'Neill has modeled the initial episode of *The Haunted* upon this scene. The play opens before the Mannon mansion, whose Greek revival facade by design imitates a temple front. Before the house Seth Beckwith and four townsmen are getting drunk, a possible parody of the prophetic ecstasy in which the Pythia of Apollo prophesies. On a bet, Abner Small goes into the house to brave the ghosts of the Mannons, and like the Pythia he soon emerges from the temple facade full of horror. He has had a similar encounter with the ghosts of the Mannons, which, like the Furies, hound the guilty, as Lavinia asserts in her climactic speech at the end of the play.[5] Small's vision of Ezra Mannon is dressed, like the Furies, in black, or, as Small puts it, "like a judge" (134), a foreshadowing of the fact that *The Haunted* no less than *The Eumenides* will be a play of judgment.

After the Pythia exits, the doors of the temple open to reveal the spectacle within. In parallel fashion, as Small exits the sealed mansion, Peter and Hazel Niles arrive to open up the house for Lavinia and Orin, returning from the South Seas. Both openings are revelations of the defilement of purity behind sacred exteriors.

As the temple opens, we see Apollo, who directed Orestes to kill Clytemnestra and Aegisthus and has purified him of the pollution, now protecting Orestes from the Furies, whom he has cast into a deep sleep. Similarly in O'Neill, the house in which the Mannon ghosts lurk is now approached by Lavinia, who prompted Orin's murder of Adam Brant, and Orin, whom she urges to confront the now powerless ghosts with equanimity. Their trip to the idyllic South Sea Isles was intended to purify them, as Orestes' trip to Delphi purified him of the physical pollution of murder. But unlike Apollo, who sends Orestes to Athens for judgment, Lavinia erroneously supposes that this purification has released them from their Furies, as we learn when she exclaims "The dead have forgotten us! We've forgotten them!" at the end of Act one, scene one (138).

But Orin has not forgotten the absent Christine, from whom he craves forgiveness, as he says before and after Lavinia's exclamation. His mother's painful absence amounts to a kind of presence. Orin's guilt over Christine is stirring up his conscience, that is, the Mannon Furies. So next in *The Eumenides* the ghost of Clytemnestra enters to arouse the Furies to avenge her against Orestes. Therefore Apollo must return to defend the man he incited to murder from the Furies. O'Neill follows Aeschylus as Lavinia defends Orin from the reawakening demands of his conscience in Act one, scene two of *The Haunted*. In each scene, the advocates of the murdered fathers, Apollo and Lavinia, engage in a terse debate with the apologists of the dead mothers, the Furies and a guilt-wracked Orin. In this scene of *The Haunted*, Orin begins to show again the "morbid spells" of guilt and brain fever he had begun to overcome, O'Neill's analogue to the madness the Furies send upon Orestes at the end of *The Libation Bearers* after he has killed his mother.

In the next scene in *The Eumenides,* Orestes appears in Athens before the statue of Athena to seek judgment. He calls upon Athena, who will be his judge, to set him free. Athena, the goddess of the polis and therefore the symbol of both cosmic and civic justice, arrives to solicit statements from both the accusers, the Furies, and the accused, Orestes. Orestes responds to Athena's exhortation with a concise but comprehensive statement of the facts of the case and calls upon her to judge whether he did right or wrong. Athena then convenes an Athenian court, the prototype of the Council of the Areopagus, to hold a trial.

Act two of *The Haunted* shows important parallels to this scene. Orin sits in the study below the portrait of his father dressed as a judge. He addresses the dead patriarch of the Mannon family as "Your Honor" (149), as Orestes had called upon Athena, the goddess of city justice. Orin asks if the old judge really wants to know "the truth, the whole truth and nothing but the truth" (149), an allusion to the pretrial testimony that Athena asked from *both* sides, so that the whole truth might be known. Like Orestes, Orin is minded to seek judgment. When Lavinia enters, he tells her that he is taking up the study of law like his father, particularly the law of crime and punishment. But unlike Orestes, Orin has admitted his guilt and joined forces with his ghostly Furies. He urges Lavinia to "confess and atone to the full extent of the law," since "that's the only way to wash the guilt of our mother's blood from our souls" (152), an allusion to the Greek rites of purification in *The Eumenides*. All this he enjoins in the name of "our father, the Judge" (152), the Mannons' family version of Athena. As Athena exacted a statement of the tribulations of his house from Orestes, so Orin confides that at the "earnest solicitation" of Ezra the Judge, he has written a history of the family in his capacity as the last male Mannon, just as Orestes is the last male of his father's house. Now the spokesman for the dead patriarch, Orin cross-examines Lavinia about her guilty actions in a way similar to Athena's cross-examination of the witnesses in *The*

Eumenides. He is intent on justice for them both: He continues his incriminating confession to ensure that Lavinia will pay for her acts either through public justice or self-punishment, and he offers, without immediate success, to help her plot his death.

In the subsequent trial scene of *The Eumenides,* the jury, that is, the Council of the Areopagus, assembles with Athena presiding to hear Orestes' trial. Correspondingly, O'Neill's description of the Mannon study for Act three this time mentions not only the portrait of Ezra, the judge, but the pictures of all the Mannons, who form both a chorus of Furies and a jury of conscience (157). To drive the point home, O'Neill has Seth tell Lavinia at the beginning of the act that Hannah the maid senses the presence of ghosts. We know that the court of conscience has assembled.

The trial will be held in the courtroom of the soul, not the city, as in Aeschylus. O'Neill subtly reminds us that he has chosen a venue distinct from if parallel in function to that of Aeschylus when he makes Peter remark early in this act that he must attend a council meeting. He has been summoned to *The Haunted*'s civic counterpart of the Aeschylean public sector, the Council of the Areopagus. O'Neill's case, however, will be decided not in the arena of public justice but in the parallel though separate sphere of private justice. To achieve this, Orin must threaten to publicize the crimes of the house. When Lavinia learns that Orin has given a copy of his devastating family history in a sealed envelope to Hazel, who is to open it if he should die or Lavinia should marry Peter, Lavinia capitulates to get it back. Orin tries first to forever join Lavinia to him with an unbreakable bond of guilt through incest, from which Lavinia recoils. Then he proposes that they find peace together through a public confession, but she still will not accept her guilt. Next Lavinia, now the very image of her mother and full of hatred for Orin, wishes he were dead. In this Orin sees a judgment on his head. The moment is precisely parallel to that when the jury in *The Eumenides* is polling to reach the verdict that Orestes and the Furies await:

> ORESTES. This is the end for me. The noose or else the light.
> FURIES.   Here is our destruction, or our high duties confirmed. (746–47)[6]

In Aeschylus, Orestes is acquitted and the Furies are deprived of vengeance. In O'Neill, a self-condemned Orin commits suicide with a pistol as his mother had, and the grim offices of the Mannon ghosts are thereby confirmed.

In the concluding portion of *The Eumenides,* Athena and the Furies debate over whether the Furies will soften their anger and be converted to a life force fructifying society, as Athena wishes, or turn their blighting anger against the city because it has acquitted the matricide. In the end the Furies are persuaded to be transformed, to exchange their black clothing for garments of reddish-purple, a life color, the color of blood and of the grape,[7] and to accept a place of worship near the temple of Erechtheus, an early patriarch king of Athens.

The concluding act of *The Hunted* contains a parallel conflict, though with different consequences. Lavinia is determined to repudiate the Mannon ghosts and the mansion, in her words "a temple of Hate and Death" (171), by marrying Peter Niles. Like Athena, she argues for the triumph of life over death and vindictiveness. The title of the trilogy tells us that she will fail. In Orin's suicide the victory of the Mannon ghosts is evident, and Lavinia's fight against them must ultimately prove futile. They are, after all, within her.

A sign of their victory is already apparent, for Lavinia has exchanged her green dress for black, in observance of Orin's death. The symbolism of this color exchange is the reverse of that of the Furies in *The Eumenides*. The Furies begin intent on retributive justice and wear black as a sign of their grim resolve. But their would-be victim escapes, and they allow themselves to be converted to guarantors of life, a change symbolized by their assuming red garments. Contrariwise, Lavinia begins *The Haunted* with the intention of escaping the Mannon Furies through the affirmation of life, to signify which she is dressed in a life color, green. But when she impels Orin to commit suicide, Lavinia enacts the aboriginal role of the Furies and thereby confirms the futility of her flight from the Mannon past. The black she then dons foreshadows the fact that she will invert the Furies' movement from death to life, symbolized in their assumption of red raiment, by moving from the affirmation of life to the surrender to death as she has turned from the wearing of green to the wearing of black.

The debate between Athena and the Furies is coordinate with the argument between Lavinia and Hazel Niles in Act four. In this exchange Hazel speaks for the Mannon ghosts, Lavinia against them. Hazel urges Lavinia not to marry Peter because she will ruin his life—that is, by denying that Lavinia can escape her past Hazel asserts the power of the Mannon ghosts. Lavinia threatens to shoot Hazel for urging her to consult her conscience—and we must remember that Athena, Lavinia's counterpart in debate, threatens the Furies with her father's thunderbolts to persuade them to relent. Hazel responds that as a Mannon Lavinia can't be dead to honor and justice and reveals that she has told Peter about Orin's fateful envelope. As Lavinia gradually realizes that her ghosts cannot be laid to rest—and we must remember that Aeschylus's Furies (who, like Lavinia, are persuaded against their inclination) also only gradually give in—she sends Peter away and vows to spend the rest of her life in the sunless Mannon mansion: "I'll have the shutters nailed closed so no sunlight can ever get in. I'll live alone with the dead, and keep their secrets, and let them hound me, until the curse is paid out and the last Mannon is let die" (178). Lavinia's affirmation of death and darkness in the house of Mannon at the end of the play is in striking contrast to the prayer of the converted Furies at the end of the *Oresteia* as they accept the hospitality of Athens and call for sunshine and happiness to fill the land of Attica (916–27). At the last the Furies are enshrined near the Athenian temple of Erechtheus, in residence as benign guardians beneath the ground of Athens, whereas Lavinia is entombed in the false temple of the Mannon mansion. Yet even in this divergence there is a patent symmetry.

The overall parallelism between the two plays can be conveniently represented in a comparative chart.

A TABULAR COMPARISON

	The Haunted	*The Eumenides*
Act 1,		
Scene 1:	Small meets ghosts in mock temple, exits	The Pythia meets Furies in temple, exits (1–63)
	Peter & Hazel open mansion	The temple doors open
	(Trip to Islands = purification = Trip to Delphi)	
	Lavinia & Orin confront ghosts	Apollo & Orestes confront Furies (64–93)
	Orin's guilty conscience	Clytemnestra rouses Furies (94–177)
Act 1,		
Scene 2:	Lavinia & Orin debate	Apollo & Furies debate (178–234)
Act 2:	Orin before Ezra's portrait	Orestes before Athena's statue (235–396)
	Orin & Lavinia before Ezra:	Orestes & Furies before Athena:
	Orin's confessional manuscript	Orestes' confessional statement (397–565)
Act 3:	Public justice avoided:	Public justice undergone:
	Trial by conscience (the gathered ghosts):	Trial by jury (the Council of the Areopagus):
	Orin self-condemned	Orestes acquitted (566–777)
Act 4:	(Lavinia doffs green, dons black)	
	Hazel debates with Lavinia	Furies debate with Athena,
	Lavinia's threat	Athena's threat (778–891)
	The ghosts are unconverted	The Furies are converted (892–995)
	Lavinia confined	The Furies ensconced (996–1047)
		(The Furies don red)

It is apparent from this diagram that there is a close correspondence not only between the sequences of incidents in the two plays but also between their sequences of structural units. Albin Lesky has pointed out that "the *Eumenides* shows a structure of four approximately equal blocks, the first two of which depict the outbreak of the conflict occasioned by Orestes' deed, while the final two contain the solution of this conflict for men and gods."[8] These four blocks correspond precisely to the four acts of *The Haunted*, the first two of which depict the outbreak of the conflict occasioned by the acts of violence in *The Hunted*, while the second two depict the resolution of this conflict. In dramatic function, Act one of *The Haunted* parallels Orestes at Delphi, Act two matches Orestes at Athens, Act three is coordinate with Orestes' trial, and Act four corresponds to the final settlement with the Furies. This correspondence between the latter thirds of trilogies, one of which was manifestly and professedly modeled on the other, is certainly not accidental. But to point out this correspondence is not to explain why O'Neill patterned *The Haunted* on *The Eumenides* at the same time so closely and yet in so transformed a fashion that the fact has gone undetected for more than half a century. To answer this question we must ascertain in a way hitherto unattempted the nature of the task O'Neill faced in transplanting the *Oresteia* to American soil.

One vital fact to the inquiry was noticed by a critic who, like others, drastically underestimated the kinship between *The Eumenides* and *The Haunted*, Walter Prichard Eaton: "Certainly O'Neill could not find any externalized modern counterpart of the Furies. There was nothing for him to do but to make the tragedy of Orestes the tragedy of conscience and a broken mind and that of Electra the terrible realization that in wreaking her vengeance she had not, after all, escaped the house of Mannon but had immured herself forever within its walls as in a living tomb."[9] Eaton here made the important observation that in *The Haunted* O'Neill has internalized in the psyches of his protagonists the punitive forces that in Aeschylus were dramatized as the Furies, external goddesses of retribution. But Eaton's remark gives the impression that O'Neill made this change simply because the modern world has rejected the naive polytheism of the Greeks. A more powerful analysis of the relationship between *The Eumenides* and *The Haunted* can be achieved in the light of an important fact not utilized by previous critics: The task of adapting Aeschylus's trilogy to the modern world required O'Neill to transfer a plot conceived in the shame culture of Greek antiquity to the fundamentally distinct guilt culture of Puritan New England, a task whose exigencies O'Neill's adaptation shows he understood, at least on an intuitive level, extremely well.

The anthropological terms *shame culture* and *guilt culture* were first popularized by Ruth Benedict in *The Chrysanthemum and the Sword*, a book written after World War II to explain the "inscrutable" Japanese to their American conquerors.[10] She undertook the same task that the American interpreter of Aeschylus must assume, making a shame culture intelligible from the alien perspective of a guilt culture. Benedict characterized the difference between the cultural types this way:

A society that inculcates absolute standards of morality and relies on men's developing a conscience is a guilt culture by definition. . . .

True shame cultures rely on external sanctions for good behavior, not, as true guilt cultures do, on an internalized conviction of sin. Shame is a reaction to other people's criticism. A man is shamed either by being openly ridiculed and rejected or by fantasying to himself that he has been made ridiculous. In either case it is a potent sanction. But it requires an audience or at least a man's fantasy of an audience. Guilt does not. In a nation where honor means living up to one's own picture of oneself, a man may suffer from guilt though no man knows of his misdeed and a man's feeling of guilt may actually be relieved by confessing his sin.[11]

Classical scholars have understood since E. R. Dodd's study *The Greeks and the Irrational* that the ancient Greeks were, like the modern Japanese, a shame culture.[12] In the shame culture of the Greeks the good man, or *agathos,* is he who possesses honorable status, or *timê,* the product of the communal recognition of his *aretê,* roughly translatable as "physical and mental prowess" (not "virtue," at least not in the popular value system). The *agathos* who cannot successfully resist challenges to his *timê* suffers a diminishment of status and therefore, as the Greeks saw it, of his worth as a human being.

When Clytemnestra kills Agamemnon in the first play of the *Oresteia,* she deprives him not only of his life but of that which gave it value, his honor.[13] When *The Libation Bearers* opens, Agamemnon's fellow victims in this shame are his loyal son Orestes, an exile without his patrimony and thus a man without the *timê* that otherwise would be his due, and his loving daughter Electra, maltreated by her mother and deprived of a noblewoman's due, a fruitful marriage to an *agathos.* Thus in *The Libation Bearers* Orestes says that the fate that Electra describes was inflicted on Agamemnon "unworthily," *atimôs* (434), and asks rhetorically if Clytemnestra will not pay for inflicting this "dishonor" on Agamemnon, *patros d' atimôsin* (435).[14] The chorus then tells Orestes of the mutilation of his father's corpse, which they call his father's shameful anguish, *patrôious duas atimous* (443).[15] When Electra describes her own shameful treatment, she says, "Meanwhile I / Stood apart, dishonored," *egô d' apestatoun / atimos* (445–46). The only way that the dishonor of Agamemnon and his children can be redressed is through vengeance against those who caused it, Clytemnestra and Aegisthus. But to avenge his family's honor and assume his place at the head of his family and community, Orestes must kill his mother, which the Greek reverence for blood ties forbade. Tellingly, the crowning horror with which Apollo has threatened Orestes to get him to kill his mother and redeem the *timê* due to Agamemnon and his heirs is that if Orestes does not obey, he will, after being afflicted with a horrible disease, die "dishonored and unloved by all," *pantôn d' atimon kaphilon* (295). When Orestes kills Clytemnestra, his mother's dying curse sends the Furies against him at the end of *The Libation Bearers.*

The Furies are not projections of Orestes' guilt over killing his mother. They are dread goddesses charged with exacting retribution for the shedding of kindred blood. Their status or *timê* in the cosmic order depends upon their successful execution of their task, the restoration through vengeance of the honor of those killed by kin. Thus when the ghost of Clytemnestra stirs up the Furies against Orestes in *The Eumenides,* she explains her urgency by declaring that because of their negligence she is dishonored among the other dead: *egô d' huph' humôn hôd' apêtimasmenê / alloisin en nekroisin* (95–96). Because the verdict goes against them, the Furies lose face and accordingly complain not about the wrong done to Clytemnestra but about the dishonor they each have suffered (*egô d' atimos:* 780, 810).[16] Athena attempts to forestall their shame in terms appropriate to a shame culture. She points out that the Furies were not defeated, since the votes were equal, and that this involved no dishonor, *atimia,* to the dread goddesses (794–96). She also offers them a new domain in Attica to confirm their *timê.*[17] When the goddesses begin to be persuaded, they ask explicitly what *timê* will be theirs if they accept (894),[18] and when they have accepted, the chorus of Athenian women assembled to escort them to their new abode hail them honorifically as lovers of *timê* (*philotimoi:* 1033).[19] So throughout the shame-culture trilogy, the *Oresteia,* humans and gods alike are motivated by the primary impulses of Greek culture, the desire for honor and the abhorrence of shame.

Scholars debate to what extent the values of the *Oresteia* are part of a moral order resting on disinterested principles of right and wrong rather than prudent self-interest.[20] Zeus punishes human *hubris,* arrogant transgression of the human and cosmic order, but as the ruler of the cosmos he can be argued to have a personal interest in keeping his house in order, so to speak. In any case, whether or not the code of human behavior in the *Oresteia* is a moral code, it is maintained through the external sanction of divine enforcement and human enforcement (whether through vendetta or tribunal) rather than the internal sanctions of conscience punishing transgressors with guilt. Agamemnon feels anxiety at the thought of treading on the purple cloth Clytemnestra spreads before him not because of pangs of conscience but because he fears divine retribution for his arrogance. Neither Clytemnestra nor Orestes ever shows a trace of guilt for having murdered those close to them.[21] Offenders against the communal code in the *Oresteia* face retribution not from their consciences but from others (both human and divine) with a vested interest in enforcing that code. The *Oresteia* treats the problem of human responsibility quite appropriately in terms natural to a shame culture.

When O'Neill set out to adapt Aeschylus's *Oresteia* in an American trilogy set in Puritan New England, he was faced with the problem of reenacting the Greek plot in a culture that was not merely more legally developed than that which Aeschylus had depicted but different in kind. Ruth Benedict singled out American Puritanism as a consummate example of a guilt culture in which the behavior in individuals is regulated by norms internalized in the form of the individual conscience.[22] Abram Kardiner pointed out that the impetus to this particular internalization of norms came from the Protestant Reformation:

As far as impulse control was concerned, the Reformation made the psychological task more difficult. Man had to become his own judge, for with the break with the church went the opportunity to keep the conscience externalized. The internalization of conscience had an equivocal effect on social stability, because it did not operate on those hidden forms of aggression concealed in commercial practice. It could only operate on those impulses which fell under disciplinary ban in childhood—chiefly the pleasure drives. Calvin, more than Luther, became the mouthpiece for the claims of the rising bourgeois class.[23]

Calvin became the prophet of the Puritan bourgeoisie, libidinally repressive but commercially aggressive, which O'Neill depicts in the Mannon family of his American *Oresteia* with more sociological and psychological acumen than critics generally recognize. The Mannons stifle their erotic drives but ruthlessly exercise their impulses to acquisition and power. Their most persistent arbiter of behavior is not social institutions or community opinion but individual conscience.

Thus each Mannon is motivated by guilt rather than shame even, in a fine irony, when attempting to break free of the guilt-ridden Puritan ethic.[24] Ezra Mannon feels guilty about his honoring death over life, Christine Mannon feels guilty about murdering a repentant man and about what collaboration in the murder does to her lover ("Adam! You make me feel so guilty!" [*The Hunted*, 110]), Adam Brant feels guilt for helping Christine kill Ezra with poison, a coward's weapon ("It serves me right, what has happened and is to happen! It wasn't that kind of revenge I had sworn on my mother's body!" [*The Hunted*, 110]), and Orin feels guilty about killing Brant and precipitating his mother's suicide and realizes that Lavinia's claim to have a clear conscience is hollow: "I hate the daylight. It's like an accusing eye! No, we've renounced the day, in which normal people live—or rather it has renounced us. Perpetual night—darkness of death in life—that's the fitting habitat for guilt! You believe you can escape that, but I'm not so foolish!" (*The Haunted*, 150)

Eventually, Orin awakens Lavinia's latent guilt, as she complains: "You're becoming my guilty conscience too!" (152) Even after Orin's suicide Lavinia cannot escape her conscience. Her lifeless manner at the beginning of Act four reveals that she feels guilty over Orin's death, and to this is soon added her guilt for what she is doing to Peter and her realization that her love for Peter is a surrogate for her love of Adam Brant, the relative whom she helped to murder.

Precisely because all of the Mannons are motivated by conscience more than honor, they look ultimately to self, not society, for judgment. This is the reason that O'Neill, with unerring instinct, declined to conclude his trilogy with a play of public judgment, as Aeschylus had. In a shame culture the propriety or impropriety of a normatively problematic act must ultimately be decided by persons other than the doer, if it has come to light, and it does not constitute a normative problem for the doer if others do not learn of it. Thus Orestes' public trial is a natural forum for ascertaining the correctness or incorrectness of his actions in the context of Greek norms. In a guilt culture the primary responsibility for the moral judgment of acts lies with the conscience of the individual who contemplates them. If individual acts transgress laws designed to codify the interests of the community, public judgment may ensue, but the conscience of individuals is still the arbiter of morality though not legality—hence our saying "You can't legislate morality." *Mourning Becomes Electra* is a tragedy of conscience, specifically the pathological conscience of the Puritan ethic, which O'Neill portrayed as a perversion of the libido substituting power for love as the supreme human value. As a tragedy of conscience it is a private tragedy, symbolized by the masklike visages of the Mannons, separating the family members from one another and the whole family from the rest of humanity. O'Neill would have had nothing to gain and everything to lose by ending such a guilt-culture tragedy in a courtroom, a public legal arena ill suited to resolve private moral dilemmas.

A tragedy of conscience like *Mourning Becomes Electra,* however, has at least as fundamental a stake in judgment as a tragedy of honor like the *Oresteia.* Thus O'Neill was moved to end his American *Oresteia* with *The Haunted,* a guilt-culture play that internalizes the public judgment of *The Eumenides* with the private decisions of conscience by which Orin and Lavinia seal their fates. Since *The Haunted* is functionally analogous to *The Eumenides,* O'Neill was able to parallel his great original with remarkable if scarcely blatant fidelity.

As a result of their implications in their mothers' deaths, both Orestes and the children of Ezra Mannon are pursued by avenging entities, Orestes by the Furies and Lavinia and Orin by the Mannon ghosts, that is, their own vividly imagined superegos. Both the Greek hero and his American counterparts seek a preliminary purification, Orestes at the Delphic shrine of Apollo, the god of purity, and Lavinia and Orin in the South Sea Islands, the symbol of the innocence of childhood and the natural man. Purification is in both cases inadequate by itself to free the fugitives from the negative consequences of their actions. Therefore both the Greek and American protagonists must submit their cases to judgment. Orestes is acquitted by a public tribunal, the instrument of communal justice appropriate to a shame culture. But Lavinia and Orin are found guilty by their own intransigent consciences. A weary Orin submits with relief, but Lavinia struggles to escape. When Orin implores her to join him in confession and atonement (which, as Benedict observes, can bring relief to the guilt of a guilt-culture man), Lavinia is tempted (as a shame-culture woman would not be), but she declines. In defiant words that mark her as the guilt-culture woman she is, Lavinia cries to Hazel: "I'm not asking God or anybody for forgiveness. I forgive myself!" (174). But the internalized Furies of guilt that are her ghosts are too strong, and in the end Lavinia condemns herself to lifelong solitary confinement in the prison of her own guilty conscience, a guilt culture's version of a living hell.

In Lavinia's world there is no Apollo to take responsibility for the murderous imperative that led to the deaths of Adam and Christine and no

Athena nor civil jury capable of removing from her psyche the burden of judgment. She lives in a culture in which the decisive judgment of souls comes from within, not without. But the judgment that she and Orin face is no less inevitable than that which Orestes undergoes, and therefore O'Neill was able to craft in *The Haunted* a play faithful both to its great model, the third drama of Aeschylus's trilogy, and the American moral landscape to which he transplanted its plot. It is appropriate to conclude that the third play of Eugene O'Neill's *Mourning Becomes Electra* is the American playwright's American *Eumenides*.

NOTES

This essay was first published in *Classical and Modern Literature* 10, no. 4 (Summer 1990): 359–72. It is reprinted here with the permission of the editors. Minor changes of style and documentation have been made to enable the reprinted text to conform in format with the rest of the volume. Note 21 is new.

1. Barrett H. Clark, "Aeschylus and O'Neill," *English Journal* 21, no. 9 (November 1932): 706–7; Joseph P. O'Neill, "The Tragic Theory of Eugene O'Neill," *Texas Studies in Literature and Language* 4, no. 4 (Winter 1963): 486–87; and Virginia Floyd, *The Plays of Eugene O'Neill: A New Assessment* (New York: Frederick Ungar Publishing Co., 1987), 397.

2. Eugene O'Neill, letter to George Jean Nathan, 21 February 1931, in *"As Ever, Gene": The Letters of Eugene O'Neill to George Jean Nathan,* ed. Nancy L. Roberts and Arthur W. Roberts (Rutherford, N.J.: Fairleigh Dickinson University Press, 1987), 118, 120.

3. For O'Neill and Freud, see chapter 4, "Masking Becomes Electra: O'Neill, Freud, and the Feminine," and chapter 11, "The Author as Oedipus in *Mourning Becomes Electra* and *Long Day's Journey into Night* " (in this volume). For O'Neill and Georg Kaiser, see Mardi Valgemae, *Accelerated Grimace: Expressionism in the American Drama of the 1920s* (Carbondale: Southern Illinois University Press, 1972), 27–40; and Horst Frenz, "O'Neill and Georg Kaiser," in *Eugene O'Neill: A World View,* ed. Virginia Floyd (New York: Frederick Ungar Publishing Co., 1979), 172–85.

4. O'Neill to Nathan, 7 April 1931, in *"As Ever, Gene,"* 121 (see n. 2).

5. Eugene O'Neill, *Mourning Becomes Electra* in *The Plays of Eugene O'Neill,* vol. 2 (New York: Random House, Inc., Modern Library, 1982), 178.

6. Unless otherwise noted, all line references to and quotations from the *Oresteia* are taken from Richmond Lattimore's translation in David Grene and Richmond Lattimore, eds., *The Complete Greek Tragedies,* vol. 1, *Aeschylus* (Chicago: University of Chicago Press, 1959), 35–171.

7. The validity of this interpretation depends upon which translation of *The Eumenides* O'Neill used in his reading for *Mourning Becomes Electra*. The Greek text at this point is problematic, and depending upon the interpretation, the reddish cloaks are put on either the Furies or the Athenian women escorting them. Pre-1932 English translations of *The Eumenides* are about equally divided in making either the Furies or the mortal women don the robes. For a good explanation of the textual difficulty see Oliver Taplin, *The Stagecraft of Aeschylus: The Dramatic Use of Exits and Entrances in Greek Tragedy* (Oxford: Clarendon Press, 1977), 412–13.

8. Albin Lesky, *Greek Tragic Poetry,* trans. Matthew Dillon (New Haven: Yale University Press, 1983), 89.

9. Walter Prichard Eaton, "O'Neill—'New Risen Attic Stream'?" *American Scholar* 6, no. 3 (Summer 1937): 311. On 310, Eaton wrote of O'Neill's "final almost complete discarding of the third play in Aeschylus' trilogy as a model."

10. Ruth Benedict, *The Chrysanthemum and the Sword: Patterns of Japanese Culture* (Cambridge, Mass.: Riverside Press for Houghton Mifflin, 1946).

11. Ibid., 222–23.

12. E. R. Dodds, *The Greeks and the Irrational,* Sather Classical Lectures, vol. 25 (Berkeley: University of California Press, 1951). As stated in his second chapter, "From Shame-Culture to Guilt-Culture" (28–63), Dodds believed that though Homeric society was a shame culture, by the fifth century Greece was evolving into a guilt culture. However, subsequent scholars have maintained, correctly in my view, that classical Greece remained predominantly a shame culture throughout the fifth century: See, for example, Arthur W. H. Adkins, *Merit and Responsibility: A Study in Greek Values* (Oxford: Clarendon Press, 1960), 153–71; Hugh Lloyd-Jones, *The Justice of Zeus,* Sather Classical Lectures, vol. 41 (Berkeley: University of California Press, 1971), 24–27; Michael Gagarin, *Aeschylean Drama* (Berkeley: University of California Press, 1976), 24–26. For the persistence of shame-culture values in the modern Mediterranean region, see J. G. Peristiany, ed., *Honour and Shame: The Values of Mediterranean Society* (London: Weidenfeld and Nicolson, for the University of Chicago Press, 1966).

13. For the presence of shame-culture values in Aeschylus, see Gagarin, *Aeschylean Drama,* 24; Adkins, *Merit and Responsibility,* 162–63, 169 n. 5; and R. P. Winnington-Ingram, *Studies in Aeschylus* (Oxford: Alden Press for Cambridge University Press, 1983), 97–98.

14. The transliterated Greek is relevant because it documents the presence of a derivative of *timê, atimosin,* and hence the concept of honor, in the original text, a fact that should have been reflected in whatever translation O'Neill used. A likely candidate is Herbert Weir Smyth's translation of the *Oresteia* in *Aeschylus,* vol. 2, Loeb Classical Library (New York: G. P. Putnam's Sons, 1926) 6–371. This edition includes the Greek and the English translation on facing pages. It is interesting to note that O'Neill first decided to write an Electra play in 1926, a year in which he spent time in New York, where Smyth's edition had been published and where it must have been readily available in the book stores (Virginia Floyd, *Eugene O'Neill at Work: Newly Released Ideas for Plays* [New York: Frederick Ungar Publishing Co., 1981], 185; Louis Sheaffer, *O'Neill: Son and Artist* [Boston: Little, Brown and Co., 1973], 187ff., 232ff.). What would have made Smyth's edition particularly attractive to O'Neill is the fact that it was a scholarly work that included the Greek text. In *O'Neill: Son and Artist* (197), Sheaffer said that in 1926 O'Neill began the study of Greek with the intention of reading Greek tragedy, and he needed no more than a knowledge of the alphabet and a Greek-English dictionary to investigate key value terms in the Greek text.

15. Lattimore translated *patôious duas atimous* inadequately as "the mutilation of your father." Smyth, more satisfactorily, rendered the Greek as "the ignominious outrage done to thy father."

16. In both cases Lattimore translated *"egô d' atimos "* as "I, disinherited." Smyth was again closer to the shame-culture connotation of the original in his translation, "I, bereft of honour."

17. In "Aeschylus and O'Neill" (707), Clark wrote of Aeschylus's "avenging Furies, placated by a mere bribe (this at least is a modern touch)." This flippant appraisal is an illustration of the serious misreadings into which a critic can fall when interpreting a play whose cultural dynamics he does not understand. In the Greek shame culture, the impeccable generosity and tact of Athena's offer both accord to the Furies the respect that is their due and enrich her own polis of Athens with the patronage of the Furies' formidable powers.

18. Lattimore translated *timê* as "definite powers." Smyth again was more reliably literal: *timê* = "honour."

19. Lattimore translated *philotimoi* as "aspiring." Again Smyth was preferable: *philotimoi* = "lovers of honour."

20. Those who see Aeschylus's tragic theater as fundamentally lacking a structure of moral judgment in the sense specified in the text include Adkins, *Merit and Responsibility*, 155, 162, 169 n. 5; Gagarin, *Aeschylean Drama*, 24; and Eric A. Havelock, *"DIKAIOSUNE:* An Essay in Greek Intellectual History," *Phoenix* 23, no. 1 (Spring 1969): 49–70, esp. 68–69 (however, Gagarin may have implicitly modified his position in an article that argues for a kind of morality in Homer, "Morality in Homer," *Classical Philology* 82, no. 4 [October 1987]: 285–306). Those who believe that there is a well-established concept of justice, and thus morality, in Aeschylus include Lloyd-Jones, *The Justice of Zeus*, 84–103; Winnington-Ingram, *Studies in Aeschylus*, esp. 73–77; Philip Vellacott, "Has Good Prevailed? A Further Study of the *Oresteia*," *Harvard Studies in Classical Philology* 81 (1977): 113–22; and John J. Peradotto, "The Omen of the Eagles and the *ETHOS* of Agamemnon," *Phoenix* 23, no. 3 (Autumn 1969): 237–63.

21. This needs some qualification. Orestes' emotional distress after killing his mother in *The Libation Bearers* can be interpreted as a reaction of guilt. But such an interpretation would not compromise my thesis. Lloyd-Jones (*The Justice of Zeus*, 25–26) points out that all cultures contain elements of both guilt and shame and that a culture is designated a guilt or a shame culture according to whether guilt or shame is the dominant cultural sanction of behavior. Orestes' scruples over killing his mother do not survive in *The Eumenides*, where he shows utterly no remorse over her death.

22. Benedict, *The Chrysanthemum and the Sword*, 223–24.

23. Abram Kardiner with the collaboration of Ralph Linton, Cora Du Bois, and James West [pseud.], *The Psychological Frontiers of Society* (New York: Columbia University Press, 1945), 439.

24. *Mourning Becomes Electra* is permeated with the language of guilt. In *An O'Neill Concordance*, vol. 2 (Detroit: Gale Research Co., 1969), 713–15, J. Russell Reaver documents thirty-nine appearances of "guilt" and its derivatives "guiltily," "guiltiness," and "guilty" in the text and stage directions of *Mourning Becomes Electra*.

8

Searching for Home
in O'Neill's America

Kristin Pfefferkorn

In *Long Day's Journey into Night* the four Tyrones reside in a summer cottage that is not their permanent home. As an actor's family they spend most of the year on tour living in hotels. Yet Mary Tyrone's desire for a better, more permanent home plays so dominant a role in their incessant quarrels and self-recriminations that the play cannot be fully understood without grasping what "home" means for Mary, for O'Neill, and for American society in general. In this chapter, therefore, I mean to trace a number of the crucial meanings of *home* and to read *Long Day's Journey* as a text in which the interplay of various senses of home is a cardinal issue.

Despite the fact that even popular wisdom knows that "a house is not a home," there usually can be no home without a house, and for Mary Tyrone the two are nearly interchangeable. As a result, the distinction between these two concepts will often appear blurred, and my discussion will proceed without the crisp separation that under other circumstances might be desirable. In addition, although we tend to assume that the idea of home has roughly the same meaning the world over, there are, in fact, national and regional differences. What most obviously sets the United States apart in this respect are the actual circumstances associated with the idea of home and, therefore, of the meaning that idea has for Americans. Comparing what we Americans take for granted about the notion of "home" with what Europeans take it to mean may serve us as a first approach to the subject.

In the Bavarian countryside where I grew up, for instance, the mountains are dotted with farmhouses built five, six, or seven hundred years ago. Today's farmers can look back on some twenty or so generations of forebears who were all born and who all died under the same roof and were buried in the same nearby ground. *Home* under these conditions means a particular place one's family has owned for centuries, and *being at home* means being rooted in the very earth of that place. One's belonging to that earth is so ancient that no memory of any other place one might have called "home" survives. In such a world the bond between the land and the people living on it is so profound that it is common to call people by the name of their land rather than by their given names.

In contrast, people in the United States live with a split consciousness of belonging. We are all Americans, but some of us are Italian–Americans and others are Chinese–, Polish–, or German–Americans. All of us, with the exception of the Native American Indians, live with a more or less clear awareness of that other place that we or our forefathers left in order to try our luck in the new world—a world more to our own taste, more of our own making. Most of us here willingly exchanged our ancient rooted-ness for a new freedom of choice, a freedom of movement. Even those whose ancestors did not elect to come here but who were forced from their homes or stolen from their villages and brought here against their will now live with the conscious awareness of having roots also somewhere else than in the place where they were born and grew up. Whether we are Irish–, Asian– or Afro–Americans, the very hyphen in our designation bears witness to our multiple heritage, to our doubled sense of belonging. But whether we chose this separation from our roots or whether we did not, we all came to prize our freedom vastly more than any sense of belonging. The young colony, set in a sparsely populated continent, invited us to strike out farther and farther. Moving on held out the promise of a better future to recent arrivals and earlier settlers alike: There would be no telling how far we could go or how well we might fare if only we would pick ourselves up again and, again, leave our past behind and move on, move west, unafraid of the new and strange world we might find. One aspect, then, of what it means to be at home in America is to feel our sense of belonging afflicted by an inner tension between our past history and our hopes for the future. Not that in other places people are entirely free of that tension. Here, however, it is an essential part of what shapes our character.[1]

Progress—the idea of moving on—is an idea we are committed to as Americans. Yet we are also trying ever again to hold on, to sink roots, to build homes. We attempt to resolve the contradiction by acting like a nomadic people; we buy and live in mobile homes and own Silver Bullets, vans, campers, and VW buses in which to travel across this land. But unlike a nomadic people, we do not travel in a communal group and so do not carry our cultural traditions and roots with us. Rather, we travel as individuals or, at best, in small family units. Even when we buy a home for ourselves and our nuclear family, we most frequently buy it merely as a "starter home," which we intend to sell as soon as we can turn a profit with which to buy another, better and bigger home, until we outgrow that, too, and seek an even larger, more stately residence, and so on and on.

In other words, we Americans are paradoxical creatures who desire progress and change and forever want to be on the move in the deeply held conviction that standing still is a falling back or a loss of our place in the climb up the hierarchy of success, but we also desire to hold on to a sense of belonging, to a feeling of being at home, of having deeply sunk roots. To manage somehow to have both, we attempt to grow ever new roots, to settle again and again not just into new houses but, indeed, into new homes, to become at home over and over again in the new places we have moved to. The very idea of home thus changed. Having been originally the name for the one—and only—place on earth that could claim us and have a hold on us, it now has become a mere buzzword that recalls to us only our nostalgic wish to feel at home but no actual place that *is* our home. In fact, we now harbor the paradoxical belief that we can be at home anywhere and everywhere that we find it useful or desirable to go.

Since moving on to new places is thought to be an expression of freedom, the ability to leave is taken to signify that we are free. Because homes tie us to specific places, they are often experienced ambivalently, particularly by American men who tend to think of the home as both a reassuring shelter and a millstone around their necks or a prison of sorts that limits their free choices and curtails their freedom of movement. As that all-American boy Huck Finn had already observed while traveling down the Mississippi with Jim: "We said there warn't no home like a raft, after all. Other places do seem so cramped up and smothery, but a raft don't. You feel mighty free and easy and comfortable on a raft."[2] But not being able always to escape life by sailing on a raft and yet desiring—even if just for a short while—to forget the responsibility and lack of freedom a home entails, American men often withdraw to all-male clubs and barrooms which offer a respite from home and home life. Conversely, hotels serve the traveling salesman, businessman, or actor by providing him with a "home away from home" without, however, settling any of the obligations of real home life on him—as G. B. Shaw had one of his characters quip: "The great advantage of a hotel is that it's a refuge from home life."[3]

But if we are actually and psychologically on the move and make no particular place our home, we tend to shift the ties that bind and anchor us away from the places we happen to inhabit to the people with whom we inhabit them. The security that individuals in more traditional and stable societies derive from having and knowing "their place"—both actually and socially—we tend to demand from those with whom we share our journey. As Tennessee Williams has Hannah Jelkes observe in *The Night of The Iguana:*

We make a home for each other, my grandfather and I. Do you know what I mean by a home? I don't mean a regular home. I mean I don't mean what other people mean when they speak of a home, because I don't regard a home as a . . . well, as a place, a building . . . a house . . . of wood, bricks, stone. I think of a home as being a thing that two people have between them in which each can . . . well, nest–rest–live in, emotionally speaking.[4]

But all too often this demand becomes unreasonable, and the very security we seek is lost. Overburdened by being asked to supply not only the sense of connectedness we feel in close relationships but also the sense of belonging that usually is provided by being at home in a place, we turn away from each other. We move away either literally or psychologically and distance ourselves, thus paradoxically leaving and losing not only the places that have some claim on us but also the relationships that bind us closely to one another.

If to have many homes, and none, is a mark of the American soul, then Eugene O'Neill, in this respect, was a typical American: Born in a hotel room in New York in 1888, he died in a hotel room in Boston in 1953. He found this fact so ironic that his last words before losing consciousness were "I knew it, I knew it! Born in a goddamn hotel room and dying in a hotel room!"[5] In fact, much of O'Neill's life was spent in hotels, particularly during his early childhood when he was traveling with his parents while his father was on tour. Later he divided his life between being away at a series of schools for nine months of the year and spending his summers with his family at the Monte Cristo Cottage in New London. The rest of his life was no more stable. In 1909 he matriculated at Princeton and soon flunked out. Not being able to find the sort of inner settledness that often is the result of an unambivalent religious faith (he renounced his Catholicism as a boy), Eugene O'Neill lived several years on the run from himself and his life. Nor did his marriage in 1909 to Kathleen Jenkins, who was expecting his child, change O'Neill or settle him down. He left that very year on a gold-prospecting expedition to Honduras. The next year he shipped on a Norwegian barque as a seaman to Buenos Aires and worked at odd jobs in the Argentine, little more than "a bum on the docks," as he said. In 1911 he took care of mules on a cattle steamer to South Africa and returned to New York penniless, taking up lodgings at Jimmy the Priest's flophouse. He shipped out again, this time to England. When he returned to the United States he got so drunk at a party that to his own surprise he found himself waking up in New Orleans, where his father's company was performing at the time. Asking his father for money, he was offered a job as a bit player instead, and at the end of the season both returned home to the family's cottage in New London, where O'Neill took a job as a reporter with the New London *Telegraph*.

Only when a bout with tuberculosis in 1912 necessitated a stay in a sanatorium did his desire to regain his health lead O'Neill to impose a strict discipline of hard work and exercise on himself, which from then on determined his life and gave it a semblance of structure and stability. He now read and wrote prodigiously, and in Provincetown in 1916 his play *Bound East for Cardiff* was the first of his works to be produced on the stage. Having divorced Kathleen Jenkins in 1912, O'Neill married Agnes Boulton in 1918 and moved to Cape Cod to work more intimately with the Provincetown Players. O'Neill now divided his time between New York and the Cape. By 1922 he was making $850 a week in royalties, and in the attempt to settle down and live in the style his mother desired, yet never quite managed to persuade her husband to adopt, O'Neill bought a farm in

Ridgefield, Connecticut. But already in 1924 the O'Neills had moved on again and were living in Bermuda.

The restlessness marking O'Neill's life was no mere surface characteristic. It pervaded his life in all of its aspects. In 1927 his marriage to Agnes Boulton came to an end. He left her and their two children, Shane and Oona, to court Carlotta Monterey. Carlotta's account of the beginning of this courtship suggests that in seeking her out O'Neill was looking for a way of settling down, of finally coming home. "He never said to me, 'I love you. I think you are wonderful.' He kept saying, 'I need you. I need you. I need you.' And he did need me, I discovered. He was never in good health. He talked about his early life—that he had had no real home, no mother in the real sense, or father, no one to treat him as a child should be treated—and his face became sadder and sadder."[6]

In 1928 Agnes Boulton sought a divorce from O'Neill. To escape the publicity and scandal that ensued and surrounded his affair with Carlotta, O'Neill left for a whirlwind tour around the world. In 1929 he settled in Le Plessis, France, and married Carlotta. But by 1932 the O'Neills had returned to the United States and built a house, Casa Genotta on Sea Island off the coast of Georgia. Only four years later the O'Neills were traveling again. In 1936 O'Neill received the Nobel prize, and he and Carlotta moved to Oregon. But already in the next year they left for California where they began to build Tao House. Since Taoism is a philosophy that stresses the illusory nature of permanence and the reality of change, the house is aptly named to reflect O'Neill's underlying restiveness. But there is something odd—and perhaps intentionally ironic—in O'Neill's giving his house a name that fundamentally denies the possibility of permanence and, therefore, of the possibility of settling down. It is not surprising, then, that O'Neill did not spend the rest of his days at Tao House. He and Carlotta sold the house in 1944 and moved first to San Francisco, then to New York, and finally to a shorefront cottage in Massachusetts. During these years O'Neill's relationship with Carlotta was similarly volatile: It shifted continually from alienation to reconciliation and back again. Still, she was with him when he died of pneumonia in that hotel room in Boston.

Like so many Americans O'Neill was driven throughout his life by the paradoxical desires of simultaneously moving on and settling down. Yet in contrast with most Americans, for O'Neill traveling seems to have been merely an outward manifestation of an inner nervousness that was part of his true journey: his travels into the soul. O'Neill's voyage was inward; his goals were not geographic but artistic. Being on the move and traveling had for O'Neill none of the abandon or spirit of adventure and curiosity with which most of the members of his generation, who sought to distract themselves by traveling, went abroad. Having tried to escape himself as a young man, O'Neill later in life did not make the mistake that St. Augustine criticized when he said that "men go abroad to wonder at the heights of mountains, the huge surges of the sea, at the broad gliding rivers, at the expanse of the ocean, at the cyclic courses of the stars, and yet they pass by themselves without wondering" about the nature of the self and its relationship to the world.[7]

O'Neill did not go abroad to wonder at the world. There was nothing about him that was of the tourist, or of the reporter braving the Civil War, or of any of the other masks that the members of the lost generation wore as expatriate Americans in Europe. O'Neill went to Europe in much the same spirit in which he traveled or moved from town to town and state to state in America. He did not pass by himself without wondering. In his most important plays his journey inward extends beyond himself to his entire family. For despite—or rather because of—his restless life O'Neill knew that no amount of traveling allows us ever wholly to leave ourselves and our past behind—try as we might.

As Americans we, or our forbears, came here carrying with us not only the cultural heritage of the places we left but also whatever private burdens prompted us to leave the lands of our births. It is a weight that is not easily borne, nor is it easily thrown off. The promise held out to the newcomer and to the citizen alike is the possibility of a new start. We literally can go West to a never-before-seen land, or we can journey to new places in the spirit, to new places in our conscience. If we have sinned or been sinned against, we trust that we can start anew. Thus James O'Neill, Sr., who was an Irish immigrant, and his wife, Mary Ella Quinlan O'Neill, who was the daughter of Irish immigrants, believed in the American dream, in the possibility of ever new beginnings. They expected spiritually, intellectually, and psychologically to be able to start anew—even while paradoxically also feeling the weight of the past burden the present. Especially Ella O'Neill was painfully aware of that burden. Yet she continued to hold on to the hope of a new start—or a return to her innocence—and so suffered from, in addition to her many other afflictions, the disjointedness of her beliefs in this respect. The degree to which we can turn away from the past and its hold on us differs not only from individual to individual but also according to the cultural heritage to which we belong. Whereas Northern Europeans seem to have assimilated American ways easily, other groups have held on more tenaciously to the views, moods, and traditions they brought with them. It would appear that immigrants took on the ways of their new places, of their new hometowns with relative ease, if their original cultural heritage had a value structure that focused on the community rather than on the family. Scandinavians, for instance, and Northern Europeans in general tended to become assimilated within a generation or two. But the more family oriented the original culture was, the greater the tendency to perpetuate and hold on to the old ways. Southern European immigrants and the Irish, all of whom have strong commitments to the family and relatively little sense of the larger community, tended to maintain their cultural traditions even in the new world. The Irish especially seem to have held on to the ways of the "Old Country," possibly because they, more than any other Europeans, were family oriented.

In the first place there were no clans in ancient Ireland, with the family being the basic unit although the family was not a one generation affair. According to Sean O'Faolain in his *The Irish—A Character Study,* the basic family unit was symbolized by the hand. "The limits of the sacred nexus were symbolized by the hand. The palm was the common ancestor; the joints of the finger were his descendents into his grand-children; the finger-nails were his great grand-children." These families, moreover, were not inclined toward communal enterprises, such as the founding of cities, and it was the Normans, Danes, and Tudors who first constructed every Irish town of any consequence that exists.[8]

The Irish O'Neills share this family-oriented outlook; they, too, were conscious of being Irish first and American second and thus felt the power their Irish past had over the present. In *Long Day's Journey into Night,* when Tyrone entreats Mary for God's sake to forget the past, O'Neill has her reply, "Why? How can I? The past is the present, isn't it? It's the future, too. We all try to lie out of that but life won't let us."[9] Although Mary's answer is not meant primarily to recall their immigrant heritage, it will turn out—as we shall see—to be that heritage that, at least in part, bedevils them all, Tyrones and O'Neills alike.[10]

For Ella Quinlan O'Neill, her Irish–Catholic cultural heritage meant the well-being of her family within the context of a well-settled Catholic home. Yet James O'Neill's acting profession meant that the family always had to be on the road. The resulting unsettledness strained family relationships often to the point of breaking. Having to live life on the move from engagement to engagement, from town to town and hotel to hotel, the O'Neills/Tyrones turned, or tried to turn, both toward one another and away from each other. In *Long Day's Journey into Night,* the stage representation of the O'Neills' family life, the lack of a settled home and life on the road are the focal point of Mary's troubled discontent. Although hotel living was part of the problem, it also had its attractions. The O'Neills/Tyrones split their responses to hotel life evenly between them. It suited the father (or so the mother claimed) and was dreaded by the mother who blamed her own and her family's problems on it: "He [Tyrone] thinks money spent on a home is money wasted. He's lived too much in hotels. Never the best hotels, of course. Second-rate hotels. He doesn't understand a home. He doesn't feel at home in it. And yet, he wants a home. He's even proud of having this shabby place. He loves it here" (*Long Day's Journey,* 61).

Thus whereas for an Irish–American family, with its family-oriented value structure, hotel life as such is in itself deplorable because, even at its best, it cannot offer a real foundation for family living, a second-rate hotel is an out and out insult to the idea of family, since all that is implied by it— lack or loss of home, drunken bouts in its bar, debauchery, and so on—are in direct opposition to the hegemony of the family. In accusing Tyrone not only of the misguided idea that money spent on a home is wasted money but of then not even knowing or caring to stay at the best hotels, Mary is accusing him of doing very real harm to his family. Speaking directly to her husband she attempts to explain how troubled she is about not having a proper or real home, at having to live in hotels:

Oh, I'm so sick and tired of pretending this is a home! You won't help me! You won't put yourself out the least bit! You don't know how to act in a home! You don't really want one! You never wanted one—never since the day we were married! You should have remained a bachelor and lived in second-rate hotels and entertained your friends in barrooms! (*She adds strangely, as if she were now talking aloud to herself rather than to Tyrone*) Then nothing would ever have happened. (67)

The "nothing" Mary refers to is her own marriage and the consequent troubles that beset her and her family's life—most of all the drug addiction that was caused by a cheap *hotel* doctor who, taking the easy way out, prescribed morphine to soothe her pain. For Mary the lack of a home is thus, on the one hand, a symbol for all the ills that beset her family and, on the other hand, the cause and foundation of those ills. Her own drug addiction, her infant son Eugene's death, and the dissolute life of her two grown sons—all somehow could have been avoided if only Tyrone's acting career and temperament had not demanded a life on the road. Even the more conciliatory tone she eventually attempts is bitter and ultimately even more accusatory than her direct attacks:

Never mind. The summer will soon be over, thank goodness. Your season will open again and we can go back to second-rate hotels and trains. I hate them, too, but at least I don't expect them to be like a home, and there's no housekeeping to worry about. It's unreasonable to expect Bridget or Cathleen to act as if this was a home. They know it isn't as well as we know it. It never has been and never will be.
TYRONE. (*bitterly, without turning around*) No, it never can be now. But it was once, before you— (72)

Tyrone does not understand, or does not want to understand, Mary's complaint. Each blames the other for not providing the home both claim they want and miss. But the truth of their situation lies deeper and is carefully veiled by either and hidden in its full power from both. Thus ostensibly due to the father's acting profession, hotel life offers them an emblem of their life and relation to one another, although it certainly does not provide them with anything like a refuge from home life.

But the real problem with the O'Neills/Tyrones' life is that, although it does not allow them to escape from one another, it does facilitate their escaping from themselves and hiding from what troubles them most deeply. In an essay in the *New York Tribune* on the subject of his own darkly hopeful view of life, Eugene O'Neill speaks harshly about the need to be unrelenting in the pursuit of one's self-possession. In criticizing the "spiritual middle classers," who prove their "compromising insignificance" by pursuing "pretty" dreams and "mere attainable" goals, O'Neill wishes upon them the success they seek as a punishment for their small aspirations.

Settling for success to O'Neill is true failure because "stopping at success" rather than pushing on to a "greater failure" spells the arrival at a dead end where no further growth can occur. Only in the quest for the unattainable can human beings realize "a hope worth living and dying for" and so attain themselves. For only in such a quest can human beings find "the spiritual guerdon of a hope in hopelessness" that lifts them beyond themselves and thus offers them a perspective from which to find themselves.[11]

Here, in a wholly American tradition, striking out and moving on is discussed in terms of success. O'Neill stresses the need to risk even beyond success, since to settle merely for success is actually failure. Real success, thus, lies in overcoming the need for success. This is an American voice believing in the American myth that there is nothing that in principle is unattainable. We therefore must dare to risk ourselves and attempt to attain what appears unattainable, for then even failure becomes success.[12] By implication, though, the piece also serves the son to judge and criticize his father for dreaming too small, too safely. Yet James O'Neill, Sr., the Irish immigrant, had reasons for "stopping at success," as Eugene O'Neill himself acknowledges in *Long Day's Journey into Night* when he has Tyrone say to Edmund:

My mother was left a stranger in a strange land with four small children. . . . There was no damned romance in our poverty. Twice we were evicted from the miserable hovel we called home, with my mother's few sticks of furniture thrown out in the street, and my mother and sisters crying. I cried, too, though I tried hard not to, because I was the man of the family. At ten years old! . . . [My mother's] one fear was she'd get old and sick and have to die in the poorhouse. (147–48)

Because of this early experience with being homeless in most of the senses that we can have lost our home—being fatherless, being an immigrant in a strange land, and literally being without a roof over his head—the elder O'Neill makes exactly the sort of mistake that according to *Long Day's Journey* he later came to regret. He dreamed too small and greedily when he bought the rights to the *Monte Cristo* play and built his career and success on that role.

That God-damned play I bought for a song and made such a great success in—a great money success—it ruined me with its promise of an easy fortune. . . . I'd lost the great talent I once had through years of easy repetition. . . . Yet before I bought the damned thing . . . I studied Shakespeare as you'd study the Bible. . . . I loved Shakespeare. I would have acted in any of his plays for nothing, for the joy of being alive in his great poetry. And I acted well in him. I felt inspired by him. . . . What the hell was it I wanted to buy, I wonder, that was worth— (149–50)

James O'Neill/Tyrone thus lost what ultimately would have been of greatest value for his life: his talent. And so he also lost himself, and in some sense, that means the only home none of us can afford to lose.

O'Neill apparently felt so deeply about this issue that he planned to structure the entire set of *Cycle* plays around it. In a public interview he said that he was

going on the theory that the United States, instead of being the most successful country in the world, is the greatest failure. It's the greatest failure because it was given everything, more than any other country. . . . Its main idea is that everlasting game of trying to possess your own soul by the possession of something outside of it. . . . This was really said in the Bible much better. We are the clearest example of "For what shall it profit a man if he gain the whole world and lose his own soul?"[13]

Obviously, O'Neill's claim here is not political. As O'Neill matured he had given   up any sustained interest in social and political issues because, as he said, "most of us have something within us that prevents us from accomplishing what we dream and desire. . . . I suppose that is one reason why I have come to feel so indifferent toward political and social movements of all kinds."[14]

In addition, as both *Long Day's Journey* and the essay in the *New York Tribune* make clear, the question had deep personal significance for him and constituted a groping toward and coming to terms with, on the one hand, his own family and family history, and, on the other hand, the "force behind," that is, with fate or providence, whether these be understood in terms of a personal god or our biological inheritance. In a letter to Arthur Hobson Quinn, O'Neill speaks not only of being very much aware of this "Mystery" at the foundation of all life but also of the "eternal tragedy of man in his glorious, self-destructive struggle to make the force express him" so that man would not appear to himself to be, like an animal, an "infinitesimal incident in its expression." It is O'Neill's "profound conviction" that no other subject is "worth writing about."[15]

Thus O'Neill was not interested in "the relation between man and man" but only "in the relation between man and God."[16] In the character of Mary Tyrone, the two themes of home and of man's relationship to a greater power come together. Through her life and through her voice O'Neill shows us that these are such interconnected issues that neither can be grasped fully without also exploring the other. In Mary Tyrone's character O'Neill gives us his most sustained treatment of the depth of meaning the question of home has and how it throws into relief the question of the fatedness of human life.[17]

For Mary, then, the idea is linked and intertwined with several other issues that beset her life. Her desire for a "real home" is reflected in her obsessive litany about the insufficiency of the summer cottage Tyrone built for them: "I've never felt it was my home. It was wrong from the start. Everything was done in the cheapest way. Your father would never spend the money to make it right" (44). Mary's passion for a home must be considered in the context of her attempt at defining and understanding herself. At a time when American men sought to constitute themselves according to an Emersonian notion of self-reliance,[18] American women understood themselves in terms of their interrelatedness with others— mostly their own families but also the larger community. Nor did they take this different approach only because they were taught the female Victorian virtue of dependency. Indeed, the only arena in which a woman could and did exercise (an often pitifully limited) independence was in the running of "her" home. To the degree that a woman succeeded in making a good home for her family, she was a good woman; to the degree that she failed to do so, she failed herself as well as those that depended on her and so became responsible for all the ills that could befall them. In 1869 Frances Power Cobbe defined the relationship a woman, according to a widely held and popular belief, should have to her home: "The more womanly a woman is, the more she is sure to throw her personality over the home, and transform it, from a mere eating and sleeping place, or an upholsterer's showroom, into a sort of outermost garment of her soul, harmonized with all her nature as her robe and the flower in her hair are harmonized with her bodily beauty."[19]

This is a view of the home that makes of it a sign or symbol of a woman's character and nature. Popular wisdom here closely resembles what Renaissance physicians called the doctrine of signatures. It asserts a more than merely accidental likeness between a sign and what it signifies. Taking an object's outer appearance to be a sign for its inner nature and claiming that inner and outer reality stand in a harmonious relation to each other, the proponents of this doctrine thought the outer, phenomenal appearance of an entity expressed its inner force, power, and essential character.[20]

Being denied the opportunity to make a "real home" for her family by both her husband's professional need to be "on the road" and by his miserly temperament, Mary Tyrone feels she is cheated of her prerogative to make of her house a sign or symbol of herself. Such a representation of the self is felt—by whatever turns and twists of the psyche and its atavistic tendencies to believe in magic—to be no mere image of the self but to possess an active force of its own with which it affects, in turn, that of which it is the sign. Tyrone's failure to provide Mary with a house that is a proper expression of herself is in this view tantamount to denying her the means for her cure.

Not surprisingly, then, Mary is involved in struggling with what "home" under these conditions can possibly mean to her. Mourning the lack of a "real home," that is, of a home that properly reflects her, she is so ambiguous in her expressions that we are left uncertain whether it is a physical, solidly built, and socially acceptable house she desires or a home in the spiritual realm—or both. Associating everything that troubles her (from bad servants to the loss of her soul) with the lack of a real home, she vacillates between two positions: On the one hand she blames Tyrone for this lack, and on the other hand she is not certain to what degree she also may have abdicated her responsibility as homemaker and so have no one to blame but herself. As a result, the exchanges on who is to blame for what in *Long Day's Journey into Night* are wrenching. Sooner or later all four members of the Tyrone family blame another member for something they can neither forget nor entirely forgive. But they also tend to shift blame abruptly—and often back to themselves. Yet it is not at all clear whether anyone can be justly blamed and held responsible or whether all their troubles are of no one's making but simply a matter of fate. In the person of Mary this question finds its most excruciating expression as she continually interweaves it with her desire for and lack of a proper home.

Starting out by blaming herself for falling in love with Tyrone in the first place, for the death of her son Eugene because she left him with her parents—a home she on other occasions idealizes and considers a safe haven—and for her own drug addiction, Mary soon moves on to denying all responsibility and blaming her husband. She blames him for not giving her the house she desires and thus laying the foundation for all the evils that befalls them; for getting drunk too much, for being jealous of his own children, and for trying to separate her from them—thus undermining the family even more; for starting his sons on the road to drunkenness; for not caring about his family as much as his shady deals in real estate; for liking hotel living; and for being miserly and thus getting the cheap hotel doctor who prescribed morphine and started her addiction. But in the end all this amounts to one and the same complaint: that Tyrone does not understand the importance of having a real home and thus ultimately does not understand her.

In a rare outburst of recrimination at someone other than a family member Mary then turns her frustrated anger against the family doctor.

I know all about Doctor Hardy. Heaven knows I ought to after all these years. He's an ignorant fool! There should be a law to keep men like him from practicing. He hasn't the slightest idea— When you're in agony and half insane, he sits and holds your hand and delivers sermons on will power! . . . He deliberately humiliates you! He makes you beg and plead! He treats you like a criminal! He understands nothing! And yet it was exactly the same type of cheap quack who first gave you the medicine—and you never knew what it was until too late! . . . I hate doctors! They'll do anything—anything to keep you coming to them. They'll sell their souls! What's worse, they'll sell yours, and you never know it till one day you find yourself in hell! (74)

In blaming her loss and state of alienated and disenfranchised selfhood on "the doctors," Mary can be said to ascribe to them a role akin to the devil's. For like him the doctors both entice the soul to sin and administer punishment: They taunt her with her affliction and give her the drug that keeps her addicted, thus better to punish her. Yet if Mary's addiction is the form of her punishment, as she in one sequence of exchanges suggests, then it is also the means by which she is ever again made aware of her fallen state. With fine irony the terror of Mary's life thus reflects her sin. For the issue of her addiction is crucial to Mary's dilemma as a frustrated homemaker. Since a true home is a projection of a good woman's soul, Mary's inability to have a home must be due to her losing herself in her addiction and its morphine-induced haze—a state facilitated by her doctors.

But as a smuggler's double-bottomed suitcase hides what he is really transporting, so this scene's meaning is double layered and hides under its direct assault another accusation. It becomes plain before the tirade is over that it is Tyrone, after all, at whom the blame is really directed. Not only is he obviously responsible for hiring the original "cheap quack" of a hotel doctor who started Mary on her road to ruin, but he, too, delivers sermons on willpower and humiliates her—as when he shamelessly does a handyman's work in his oldest suit where all the neighbors can watch him—and worse, he too makes her beg and plead for her cure—her home, which she clearly views as essential to her very worth as a human being—but nonetheless keeps it from her because of his miserly love for money, which causes him to sell his soul (as he does when he buys the *Monte Cristo* play) and to sell hers, too, by settling for less than good treatment until it is too late and she is lost.

Dimly aware of the real target of her accusations and therefore overcome by guilty confusion, Mary stammers, "Forgive me, dear" (75). But she resumes affixing blame a few moments later, this time turning on her son Jamie for deliberately infecting the infant Eugene and killing him: "I've always believed Jamie did it on purpose. . . . I know Jamie was only seven, but he was never stupid. He'd been warned it might kill the baby. . . . I've never been able to forgive him for that" (87). Yet no sooner has she voiced this terrible suspicion than Mary turns the tables again and once more lays claim to being the only one at fault, simultaneously excusing and blaming herself:

It was my fault. I should have insisted on staying with Eugene and not have let you persuade me to join you, just because I loved you. Above all, I shouldn't have let you insist I have another baby to take Eugene's place, because you thought that would make me forget his death. I knew from experience by then that children should have homes to be born in, if they are to be good children, and women need homes, if they are to be good mothers. I was afraid all the time I carried Edmund. I knew something terrible would happen. I knew I'd proved by the way I'd left Eugene that I wasn't worthy to have another baby, and that God would punish me if I did. I never should have borne Edmund. . . . I've been so frightened and guilty— (88)

Once again Mary returns compulsively to the theme of home, without which there can be neither good children nor good mothers. Once again concealed in her self-blame there is a blaming of James for luring her to him on tour and thus causing her to abandon Eugene to his death; for imposing another child on her, which resulted in her drug addiction; and for denying her the home in which she could find fulfillment.

Her consciousness of her own guilt in her afflictions does not stop her from blaming others, even for things they cannot control. All along Edmund has been made to feel responsible for her addiction just by being born, and now she implies that it is her worrying about his illness that has once more caused her to succumb to the destructive forgetfulness of morphine. Checking herself, she pleads that she is not using Edmund as an excuse for her own weakness: "Promise me, dear, you won't believe I made you an excuse." To this Edmund, as unforgiving as Mary herself, replies bitterly: "What else can I believe?" (93)

The ascription of guilt and innocence jumps back and forth. Even for a mere onlooker it is dizzying; what it might feel like to be involved in this dance of accusation of errors, faults, and transgressions is all but unimaginable. Eventually, everyone has blamed everyone else; and everyone has been blamed and excused, shackled and driven away, by the guilt and innocence alternately proclaimed. Yet this maze of recriminations and bitter unforgiving is ultimately due to Mary's inability to decide whether we are responsible for our acts at all. Although sometimes she uses guilt manipulatively, mostly she doubts that we are free to choose what we do and wonders whether, on the contrary, we are bound by situations, by conditions, by social and psychological realities that are not of our own making and over which we have no control: "But I suppose life has made him [Jamie] like that, and he can't help it. None of us can help the things life has done to us. They're done before you realize it, and once they're done they make you do other things until at last everything comes between you and what you'd like to be, and you've lost your true self forever" (61). Because she is a woman and a drug addict, Mary, more than any other member of the Tyrone household, is aware of the limits set to our free will, to our freedom of choice, and to our actions. As a consequence she vacillates between accusing and excusing, between affixing blame elsewhere and feeling guilty. But whether she blames the calamity of her self-alienation on herself, others, or fate, the conviction that she has perhaps irretrievably lost her true self, her soul, haunts her life.

The problem, as Mary sees it, is that as long as we remain alienated from ourselves we cannot be at home anywhere and, conversely, that we cannot truly integrate ourselves as long as we are not at home somewhere. For her, the self is not fashioned in near holy self-reliance but only in the interaction with other selves. Human nature has a social dimension. Even in our inmost character we are, according to Mary, inseparable from the community to which we belong. As a result, the sort of home that is an image and reflection of our nature mediates our position in the community and so becomes an aspect of what shapes and forms us. The standing the Tyrones have in the community is expressed by the fact that the house they live in is not a real home but merely a summer cottage. Nor is lacking a proper home, for Mary, merely lacking a symbol of belonging. Rather, the symbol *is* how we belong, and so she can think and say that if only they had a true home, none of the ills and wrongs in their lives would have befallen them. Not only would the circumstance of the Tyrones' lives then have been changed, but the Tyrones themselves would have been different in their individual natures, characters, and characteristics. Eugene would not have died, she would not have fallen victim to morphine, Tyrone would not drink too much and be a social boor, and the boys would have better prospects for marriage than those with which their footloose and uprooted upbringing has provided them, and finally, even Edmund would not have contracted tuberculosis—somehow it, too, could have been avoided.

Mary's view on the importance, value, and meaning of the role the individual plays in society begins to emerge in an exchange with Edmund. As she looks out the window and observes her son Jamie wince with shame at having to do yard work out front, where all can see, in the company of a father dressed in the oldest suit he owns, she is in agreement with Jamie that Tyrone's behavior is undignified and below their station:

They've started clipping the hedge. Poor Jamie! How he hates working in front where everyone passing can see him. There go the Chatfields in their new Mercedes. It's a beautiful car, isn't it? Not like our secondhand Packard. Poor Jamie! He bent almost under the hedge so they wouldn't notice him. They bowed to your father and he bowed back as if he were taking a curtain call. In that filthy old suit I've tried to make him throw away. (*Her voice has grown bitter*) Really, he ought to have more pride than to make such of show of himself. (43)

O'Neill gives to Mary the voice of Greek tragedy, in which the ethical role of the community is given its due. For Mary is aware of the ethical significance of their social standing. Indeed, the precarious tension between self and society in the American attitude toward ethics is presented by O'Neill in Mary's contradictory beliefs that, on the one hand, the independent individual conscience is the proper arbiter of conduct and, on the other hand, ethics is a matter of community standards. But it is this latter, pre-Christian voice heard in Greek drama that is peculiarly Mary's own. As a woman she sees even the self in terms of community-centered values; as a drug addict, she is painfully aware of the superficiality of all exaggerated claims of self-reliance. In her moral self-understanding, therefore, Mary vacillates between a socially defined sense of shame and a personal and inwardly experienced feeling of guilt. For Mary, what the neighbors say is as serious a moral index as the voice of conscience.[21]

Because Edmund does not grasp the complexity of Mary's ethical position, he responds inadequately when he defends his father by suggesting that the Chatfields are of no account since outside of this "hick burg" no one has heard of them. For Mary, it does not matter whether they are important in the world at large. Here, they are members of the community, and in terms of the community it does not matter whether it is its most important or least significant member who is passing by. Pride in oneself and one's family can be taken only if everyone behaves as custom, tradition, and public opinion require. Not behaving according to these community standards establishes the Tyrones as outsiders who do not belong. Tyrone's shabby suit worn out front and his doing work below his standing by clipping his own hedge mark him and his family as different no less than his theatrical profession and his stinginess in caring for his own. Even Edmund's response to Mary's complaint is the response of an outsider who feels disconnected from the community he lives in and therefore, in part, finds it wanting.

Mary, who desperately longs to belong somewhere and thus to be at home someplace, agrees only in passing with Edmund that the Chatfields are big frogs in a small pond. Almost immediately she returns to her insight that people like the Chatfields stand for something after all: They have presentable and representative homes of which they need not be ashamed! They, in fact, not only have homes but they belong.

Still, the Chatfields and people like them stand for something. I mean they have decent, presentable homes they don't have to be ashamed of. They have friends who entertain them and whom they entertain. They're not cut off from everyone. . . . But [Tyrone] never wanted family friends. He hates calling on people, or receiving them. All he likes is to hobnob with men at the Club or in a barroom. Jamie and you are the same way, but you're not to blame. You've never had a chance to meet decent people here. I know you both would have been so different if you'd been able to associate with nice girls instead of— You'd never have disgraced yourselves as you have, so that now no respectable parents will let their daughters be seen with you. (43–44)

Turning back from the window, Mary now also turns from her position of wanting to be a fully accepted member of this town. In the never straightforward manner in which the Tyrones interact and trace out intricate patterns of involvement, mother and son next trade places in their views. Avowing that she always hated this town and never wanted to come here in the first place, Mary now blames Tyrone for liking it here and building this most inadequate and inappropriate home, whereas Edmund defends the town, saying that he prefers to spend his summers here rather than in a New York hotel because this is the only home he has ever known.[22]

By focusing on her own loneliness and on her own understanding of what the social dimension of their life should be, Mary avoids noticing clearly that not all the members of the Tyrone household are as cut off from other people as she herself is. Tyrone and his sons have their various barroom drinking buddies. Whatever Mary may think of them and whether or not she approves of them, these chums do provide company to her men. To the degree that Mary is aware of this, she finds it appalling. To her way of thinking the social standing of these drinking companions and "ladies" is a threat to the social well-being of the family and therefore also to the psychological and spiritual health of her family and herself. To her husband and sons, on the other hand, drinking with just these sorts of companions provides the respite from home life she herself finds in the haze of morphine. Being the only one who is entirely isolated from people outside the family and who is utterly alone and without anyone to talk to, Mary responds by isolating herself even more: She withdraws into the fog of her addiction. Being the kind of man who is willing to settle for what O'Neill called "mere success," Tyrone is also willing—and able—to settle for the lesser ways of being at home. His career as the Count of Monte Cristo and his drinking buddies offer him all the sense of belonging he needs. Feeling at home on the stage and in barrooms, he is incapable of understanding the deeper, more complex, and more subtle sense in which Mary needs to be at home and to belong. Therefore, neither can he imagine what it would take to achieve it, nor does he experience the impoverished social atmosphere they live in as a burden.

Mary, on the contrary, does. Because of *his* lack, she is doomed to be homeless and friendless and to have no one with whom to share even the unimportant gossip of the day, much less something so important as her pain at Edmund's illness: "If there was only . . . some woman friend I could talk to—not about anything serious, simply laugh and gossip and forget for a while— " (46). But except for her occasional visits to the doctor, she has no one to talk to but the maids, who even as maids are not very good and are merely inadequate help. But at least they offer some outside contact and allow some issues to be brought up that otherwise would remain unexpressed and only vaguely thought.

CATHLEEN. Speaking of acting, Ma'am, how is it you never went on the stage?
MARY. (*resentfully*) I? What put that absurd notion in your head? I was brought up in a respectable home and educated in the best convent in the Middle West. Before I met Mr. Tyrone I hardly knew there was such a thing as a theater. I was a very pious girl. I even dreamed of becoming a nun. I've never had the slightest desire to be an actress. . . . I've never felt at home in the theater. Even though Mr. Tyrone has made me go with him on all his tours, I've had little to do with the people in his company, or with anyone on the stage. Not that I have anything against them. They have always been kind to me, and I to them. But I've never felt at home with them. Their life is not my life. It has always stood between me and— (101–2)

Although Mary's loneliness is in part due to the unsettledness her husband's acting career entails, it now turns out also to result from her not belonging to and not feeling at home in the world of the theater. It is a community that even after all these years is alien to her. That seems due to the fact that their social standing is in Mary's eyes inferior to her own. Thus having married Tyrone not only doomed Mary to live in hotels but also brought her such a diminished standing in the community that she remained friendless, as she painfully reminds Tyrone:

At the Convent I had many friends. Girls whose families lived in lovely homes. I used to visit them and they'd visit me in my father's home. But, naturally, after I married an actor—you know how actors were considered in those days—a lot of them gave me the cold shoulder. And then, right after we were married, there was the scandal of that woman who had been your mistress, suing you. From then on all my old friends either pitied me or cut me dead. (86)

But the depth of Mary's loneliness runs deeper than having neither an appropriately appointed home nor friends to receive in it. To make up for her loss of home and friends Mary idealizes the past and fantasizes about her childhood home, her father's house. It now appears to her to have been perfect. In that "real" home she had been sheltered from the harshness of life: Surrounded by a caring family and friends and thus well tied into the interrelatedness of all the members of the community, Mary had felt safe and protected. Although it cannot be doubted that this is just how Mary remembers her father's love and the home he made for his family, she also uses this memory against Tyrone and the life he offers her. "In a real home," she tells him, "one is never lonely. You forget I know from experience what a home is like. I gave up one to marry you—my father's home" (72). But Tyrone realizes that her memory here is taken up as a weapon against him and so he defends himself by showing it up for the idealization it is. As he remarks to Edmund: "You'd think the only happy days she's ever known were in her father's home, or at the Convent, praying and playing the piano. (*Jealous resentment in his bitterness*) As I've told you before, you must take her memories with a grain of salt. Her wonderful home was ordinary enough. Her father wasn't the great, generous, noble Irish gentleman she makes out" (137).

Although having ideals is necessary to keep before us a model after which, at least, to try to fashion the circumstances of our lives, giving up on these actual circumstances, withdrawing from them entirely, and substituting for them a nostalgically enhanced ideal is to pervert the role and practical function ideals have. By withdrawing within her morphine fog to distance herself from her family, Mary Tyrone uses her nostalgic and idealized memory of being at home in her father's house to avoid facing the real world and making a home, however imperfect, here and now. Mary's attachment to the childhood home she has lost parallels in some respects the structure Kierkegaard laid out for an ideal love.23 When a "young swain," having fallen in love with a princess, discovers that their union is impossible, he resigns himself to giving her up. By a movement of idealization he exchanges his temporal love for an eternal one, thus keeping his love unassailed by the changes and ruinations of reality. Like so many of us, Mary Tyrone, too, longs for what could be and for what once was— or was sufficiently so to allow her the idealized memory she now nurtures of the home in which she grew up. Being an ideal, the perfect home Mary inhabits in her imagination is one that no one should be able to take from her; it should be more securely hers than anything she actually lives with and possesses. Then, how did it happen that she lost it? Unable or unwilling to resign herself—as Kierkegaard's young swain resigned himself—Mary never voluntarily gives up hoping for a proper home in the real world. In contrast to the "Knight of Resignation," Mary tenaciously insists on holding on to what circumstances will not allow her to have and thus not only fails to gain what she most desires, a real home, but in her lament also loses herself.

Even when Mary conflates the loss of social standing with her marriage to Tyrone and with the lack of a real home and associates both with
his acting career and their life in the theater (that is, with the need of
having to make *her* life on the road and in cheap hotels), she only touches
on the surface of her troubles. What acting and the theater meant to a
young woman with pious leanings who was brought up in a convent during
the midnineteenth century is stated in the preface of the Ursuline manual
for the education of young ladies used in convents such as that which as
Ella Quinlan/Mary Tyrone attended. It warns young ladies about the perils
of sin and about the necessity to avoid not only sinning but the occasion for
sin. Whereas there are many such occasions, none is either more tempting
or beset by more dire consequences of evil than the theater.

> Plays and theatrical amusements may be counted among the most dangerous oc-
> casions of sin which young persons have to avoid in the world. . . . By St. Augustine they
> are styled "the pest of souls, the ruin of virtue and decorum," and St. Chrysostom
> denominates them "the fuel of the passions and the pomps of Satan, which Christians
> solemnly renounce." Notwithstanding this, it is a melancholy truth, that there are persons
> now found, who are so insensible to the real interests of their daughters, sisters, and other
> female friends, as to authorize, and even procure their presence at such diversions. An
> eminent prelate of the present day . . . expresses just astonishment at the inconsistency of
> those parents, who first, by a Christian education, provide their children with the means of
> saving their souls, and afterwards expose them to the evident risk of being eternally lost,
> by permitting them to frequent stage representations. "Those parents," continues he,
> "deserve no pity, if their children ultimately disappoint their hopes; because they have to
> reproach themselves with . . . implanting those [lessons] of the world, the flesh, and the
> devil, by conducting them to the head school, where these lessons are taught, viz. the play-
> house.". . . A steady determination never to assist at theatrical amusements, should be one
> of their [the young persons'] most particular resolutions on entering the world. They are
> not ignorant of the various and solid reasons which exist for making and keeping such a
> resolution. Among those the two following should be particularly impressed on their
> minds:
>   First, the risk they run, by frequenting the theatre, of losing what should be dearer to
> them than life itself, the grace of God, and the love of virtue; because, as St. Augustine
> observes, "it is at the theatre that the flesh and the devil assault the minds and the hearts of
> young people, by every means calculated to instil the poison of vice, to enervate the soul,
> and flatter the passions, by a general and simultaneous movement of all the allurements and
> charms of the senses."
>   Secondly, the bad example which the appearance of a well-instructed Catholic would
> give in a play-house, as likewise the scandal which it may occasion, by leading others to
> indulge without scruple in amusements, of which they before hesitated to participate.[24]

What impressionable, docile young girl brought up on such teaching
could marry an actor and not feel devastating guilt? Since Mary was such a
young girl, she is even in middle age still struggling with the consequences
of her youthful disregard of the teachings of the church. The many
transgressions she blames herself for—not being a good mother and
homemaker, joining her husband on tour and so allowing her infant son to
die, her drug addiction and the lying it taught her—can therefore all be
viewed as the consequences of her original disobedience. In marrying an
actor Mary freely chose to make the occasion for sin a permanent condition

of her life.[25] Falling in love with Tyrone, then, is not the wonderful, romantic event she likes to imagine it was, as she says: "(*Bitterly* [to herself]) You're a sentimental fool. What is so wonderful about that first meeting between a silly romantic schoolgirl and a matinee idol? You were much happier before you knew he existed, in the Convent when you used to pray to the Blessed Virgin. (*Longingly*) If only I could find the faith I lost, so I could pray again!" (107).

The happiness that was Mary's before she met Tyrone, then, was not merely due to the idealized shelter her earthly father's house provided nor to the friends she received in that home but to the home she had in her heavenly father's house and to the community of the faithful to which she then still belonged. After marrying Tyrone, Mary gave up her churchgoing, as Cathleen the maid tells her: "Sure, you never darken the door of a church, God forgive you" (102). But having lost the church is still not Mary's greatest loss. Rather, Mary's ultimate and most tragic homelessness is due to her losing her faith and, thus, her soul and losing it so thoroughly that she cannot even remember what it is she has lost. For what homelessness could be worse than not being able to remember that what was lost, and is now being searched for, is being at home in one's own soul? Not knowing this *is* the very loss of home Mary mourns.

MARY. [to Edmund] I've never understood anything about it, except that one day long ago I found I could no longer call my soul my own. (*She pauses—then lowering her voice to a strange tone of whispered confidence*) But some day, dear, I will find it again—some day when you're all well, and I can see you healthy and happy and successful, and I don't have to feel guilty any more—some day when the Blessed Virgin Mary forgives me and gives me back the faith in Her love and pity I used to have in my convent days, and I can pray to Her again—when She sees no one in the world can believe in me even for a moment any more, then She will believe in me, and with Her help it will be so easy. I will hear myself scream with agony, and at the same time I will laugh because I will be so sure of myself. (93–94)

But this still relatively hopeful lament soon gives way to a more urgent despair as Mary more powerfully feels the loss of her faith. "If only I could find the faith I lost, so I could pray again!" (107). By the time the play winds down to its conclusion, though, Mary is so despondent that she has thoroughly withdrawn into the past and no longer recognizes Tyrone. Believing herself to be back at the convent, she looks at her hands and seeing that they are too stiff and too swollen to play the piano, she plans to seek help from Sister Martha. But there is meaning in her madness, for in contrast to the doctors who have sold her soul and keep her in bondage to her affliction, Sister Martha, who is "old and a little cranky," has "things in *her* medicine chest that'll cure *anything*" [emphasis mine]. Sister Martha not only dispenses medicines but also exhorts her patients "to pray to the Blessed Virgin," which speeds the cure and will make ostensibly Mary's hands, but on a deeper level her whole self, "well again in no time" (171).

Yet Mary cannot return to the past wholly until she has undone the event that set all her and her family's suffering into motion. Earlier in the play she merely mused that if Tyrone had only stayed a bachelor "then nothing would ever have happened" (67), but now she ritually acts out the undoing of her past. Like a sleepwalker who moves not knowing fully the why or wherefore of her actions, she carries her wedding gown down from the attic and lets Tyrone persuade her to surrender it to him, thus unconsciously enacting a symbolic rite of "unwedding" Tyrone by returning to him the white gown that announced to the world her innocence—an innocence that was destroyed by her marriage to him. In returning this emblem of her marriage to him, Mary symbolically returns to the time before she met Tyrone. In the darkly yet urgently felt need to effect a different outcome for her life, she treats the famous actor with just the sort of "*shy politeness of a well-bred young girl toward an elderly gentleman*" that she then would have exhibited as she now allows Tyrone to rid her of her "*bundle*" (a word whose mundane, unromantic connotations are no accident).[26] Regarding the wedding gown with puzzled interest she says: "It's a wedding gown. . . . I remember now. I found it in the attic hidden in a trunk. But I don't know what I wanted it for. I'm going to be a nun—that is, if I can only find—" (172).

Suspended in a time consciousness that is neither wholly of the past nor wholly of the present but somehow contains both at once—as Mary had already recognized earlier when she claimed that the past is the present—she does not know what she wants with a wedding gown because it is not marriage she wants any more than a divorce. What she does want is what none of us can really have; a second chance, a truly new beginning by making what has happened undone. Mary seeks to regain the self she was before she lost her innocence, before she married Tyrone and set into motion the events that followed her marriage as inexorably as fate or providence would have it. But although Mary can still symbolically act out her deepest desire, she is beyond being able to state it, beyond being able to name her loss: "What is it I'm looking for? I know it's something I lost. . . . (*Looking around her*) Something I miss terribly. It can't be altogether lost. . . . (*Looking around her*) Something I need terribly. I remember when I had it I was never lonely nor afraid. I can't have lost it forever. I would die if I thought that. Because then there would be no hope" (172–73).

So Mary is homeless in every conceivable sense. Most directly and simply she lacks the kind of house that can be a proper home. But she is also homeless because there is no community to which she belongs. Neither with her husband's theatrical troupers nor with the good burghers of New London does she feel at home. Even within her own family Mary is isolated and alone and not at home. Not only is she a woman in a family circle of men and thus lacking female companionship, but whereas her husband and sons can indulge their alcohol addiction by keeping each other company when getting "stewed," Mary must slink off and hide herself when she is giving in to her own need for morphine. In addition, she then has to lie to herself and to others about it. Society somehow tolerates and even approves of men giving in to drink together; it provides bars—places where one can communally lose oneself. But drug addiction makes of a woman a "fiend" who must indulge alone. Since a priest would understand her no better than her doctor or her menfolk do, Mary has also lost being at home in the church. Finally, Mary is homeless because she has lost herself, her faith, and so also her soul.

O'Neill shared in almost all of these senses of homeless. He, too, had no house of his own—the houses he did own, and splendidly appointed ones some of them were, belonged to his second and third wives more than to him. Carlotta in particular planned, built or renovated, and furnished a number of homes for O'Neill.[27] Although, like his father, O'Neill did belong to the theater community and had friends among them (no matter how loosely or lightly most of these relationships were tied), and although, also like his father he had drinking buddies, neither seems to have offered him the sort of deep friendship or sense of home that people can give to one another. Only in his marriage to Carlotta does O'Neill appear to have found a measure of belonging such as Hannah Jelkes shares with her grandfather. Like his mother, O'Neill lost both the church and his faith, but unlike her he did not entirely lose himself. This, no doubt, was due to his art. In his work O'Neill risked himself again and again beyond success and tried to reach beyond the limits of social, commercial, and even artistic acceptance. As a result it cannot be said of him—as he said of his father— that he gained the world and lost his own soul. Indeed, insofar as all poetry and all art are a means of paying respect and doing homage, they are a form of secular prayer. Since in his dramas O'Neill was not interested in the relation "man has to man" but only in the relation man has to "the Force behind," it can be said that whereas O'Neill may have lost the Catholic faith, he never lost his faith or the ability to write his "prayers."[28] So the home Mary Tyrone unsuccessfully looked for, and Ella Quinlan O'Neill regained in rekindled faith after overcoming her addiction in a convent, Eugene O'Neill found in his work.

NOTES

1. Whereas the Russians love their *mother* Russia and the Germans their *father*land, we have chosen, because of our doubled consciousness of belonging, to think of our home country as our *Uncle* Sam—a kinship more removed in emotional ties, commitment, and direct connection than the parental one.

2. Mark Twain, *The Adventures of Huckleberry Finn* (New York: Harper and Row, 1951), 126 (ch. 18).

3. George Bernard Shaw, *You Never Can Tell*, act 2, in *Bernard Shaw: Collected Plays with Their Prefaces*, vol. 1 (New York: Dodd, Mead and Company, 1975), 729.

4. Tennessee Williams, *The Night of the Iguana*, in *The Theatre of Tennessee Williams*, vol. 4 (New York: New Directions, 1972), 356–57.

5. Louis Sheaffer, *O'Neill, Son and Artist* (Boston: Little, Brown and Co., 1973), 670. I owe this quotation and many other good suggestions to the most helpful assistance of the editor.

6. Seymour Peck, "A Talk with Mrs. O'Neill," reprinted from the *New York Times*, 4 November 1956, in *O'Neill and His Plays: Four Decades of Criticism*, ed. Oscar Cargill, N. Bryllion Fagin, and William J. Fisher (New York: New York University Press, 1961), 93.

7. St. Augustine, *The Confessions*, book 10, chapter 8.

8. John Henry Raleigh, "O'Neill's *Long Day's Journey into Night* and New England Irish-Catholicism," in *Partisan Review* 26, no. 4 (Fall 1959): 576. In his article Raleigh went so far as to claim that *Long Day's Journey into Night* is as much a cultural document of Irish Catholicism as a family history (574).

9. Eugene O'Neill, *Long Day's Journey into Night* (New Haven: Yale University Press, 1955), 87.

10. As O'Neill himself once put it, "One thing that explains more than anything about me is the fact that I'm Irish." (Louis Sheaffer, *O'Neill: Son and Playwright* [Boston: Little, Brown and Co., 1968], 10).

11. Eugene O'Neill, "Damn the Optimists," in *O'Neill and His Plays*, 104 (see n. 6); this article is reprinted from the *New York Tribune*, 13 February 1921.

12. On another occasion, O'Neill had this to say about success in failure (Sheaffer, *O'Neill: Son and Artist*, 182):

The tragedy of life is what makes it worthwhile. I think that any life which merits living lies in the effort to realize some dream, and the higher that dream is, the harder it is to realize. Most decidedly we must all have our dreams. If one hasn't them, one might as well be dead—one is dead. The only success is in failure. Any man who has a big enough dream must be a failure and must accept that as one of the conditions of being alive. If he ever thinks for a moment that he is a success, then he is finished. He stops.

13. Ibid., 442.

14. From an interview with Oliver M. Sayler published in *Century Magazine*, January 1922; quoted in *O'Neill and His Plays*, 107 (see n. 6).

15. See the letter to Arthur Hobson Quinn, 3 April 1925, published in Quinn's *A History of the American Drama from the Civil War to the Present Day*, vol. 2, rev. ed. (New York: F. S. Crofts and Co., 1936), 199, and quoted in *Selected Letters of Eugene O'Neill*, ed. Travis Bogard and Jackson R. Bryer (New Haven: Yale University Press, 1988), 195.

16. From conversational remarks quoted by Joseph Wood Krutch in the introduction to *Nine Plays by Eugene O'Neill* (New York: Random House, Inc., Modern Library, 1932) and reprinted in "On Man and God," in *O'Neill and His Plays*, 115 (see n. 6). This interest in the relationship between man and God seems to accord ill with Carlotta's remark that O'Neill was not at all a religious man and never thought of going back to religion (see Peck, "A Talk with Mrs. O'Neill," 95). According to Carlotta, however, O'Neill believed in the possibility of the existence of a personal God until the very end: see Sheaffer, *O'Neill: Son and Artist*, 668.

17. The theme of home and fate play prominent and complex roles in plays such as *Ile, Beyond the Horizon, Desire under the Elms, Mourning Becomes Electra, A Touch of the Poet, More Stately Mansions*, and *A Moon for the Misbegotten*.

18. The generation of O'Neill's father is the generation that formulated and shaped the ideas with which O'Neill grew up. Most Americans then still lived a rural life and believed in the superiority and inviolateness of the individual and thought freedom to be an American's birthright. In agreement with this conviction they believed the individual had

the right as well as the responsibility to constitute himself more or less out of his own resources—not only was this thought possible, but it was a worthy and honorable thing to do. Any less, any sign of dependency, would have been suspect as an indication of a lack of freedom and a challenge to the very foundation of the ideals of this nation.

American writers of this day dealt more or less exclusively with the question of the individual. A thinker like Emerson wrote an essay entitled "Self-Reliance," and William James pondered the power of a single individual over the whole community in "The Importance of Individuals." Novelists as well were preoccupied with the quest of the lone individual. For example, Melville chronicled the struggles of Captain Ahab with the forces of nature and evil in the white whale in *Moby Dick,* and Hawthorne traced the confrontation of individual and community in *The Scarlet Letter* much as O'Neill himself does in *Desire Under the Elms.*

19. Frances Power Cobbe, "The Final Cause of Women," in *Woman's Work and Woman's Culture,* ed. Josephine Butler (London: Macmillan, 1869), 10–11; quoted by Elizabeth Wilson, *Adorned in Dreams: Fashion and Modernity* (Berkeley: University of California Press, 1987), 123.

20. The doctrine of signatures was used by Renaissance physicians and alchemists to describe a state in which outer physical characteristics accurately reveal an inner, nonphysical, and ideal reality or force. The shape of an herb or fruit thus can be an indication of its healing power. Accordingly, walnuts, for instance, are good "brain food" because the peeled kernel resembles the human brain. Much folk wisdom tends to operate on the basis of this intuition that the phenomenal reality of the world, the figure or shape of a given thing, truly expresses its inner essence or nature.

21. I agree with the view that Richard F. Moorton, Jr., has expressed in chapter 7, "Eugene O'Neill's American *Eumenides*" (in this volume), that in *Mourning Becomes Electra* O'Neill is interested in exploring the difference between the Greek notion of an ethic of shame and the Judeo-Christian idea of an ethic of guilt. O'Neill continues this exploration in *Long Day's Journey into Night.* The frankly autobiographical drama offers O'Neill the opportunity to work through the implications of Greek tragedy—with its emphasis on fate and its concern for the relation that holds between the individual and the community—for an Irish–American family.

22. Later in the play Edmund seems to appropriate his mother's sense of the ethical importance of the opinion of others when he berates his father in terms of communal values for his stinginess in selecting a state home for Edmund's cure: "But to think when it's a question of your son having consumption, you can show yourself up before the whole town as such a stinking old tightwad! Don't you know Hardy will talk and the whole damned town will know! Jesus, Papa, haven't you any pride or shame?" (145).

23. Søren Kierkegaard, *Fear and Trembling,* 52–54 in *"Fear and Trembling" and "The Sickness unto Death,"* trans. and ed. Walter Lowrie (Garden City, N.Y.: Doubleday and Co., Anchor Press, 1954).

24. *The Ursuline Manual, or a Collection of Prayers, Spiritual Exercises, etc., Interspersed with the Various Instructions Necessary for Forming Youth to the Practice of Solid Piety; Originally Arranged for the Young Ladies Educated at the Ursuline Convent, Cork. Revised by the Very Rev. John Power, D.D., and Approved by the Most Rev. John Hughes, D.D., Archbishop of New York* (New York: Edward Dunigan and Brother, (James B. Kirker), No. 371 Broadway, 1859), 20–22 (for the sake of clarity, minor changes in punctuation have been made in this quotation). I owe a debt of gratitude to Camille Hanlon of Connecticut College for bringing the existence of this manual to my attention and then providing me with her family's copy. It is interesting to note that an Ursuline convent was also Eugene O'Neill's first school (see Croswell Bowen, "The Black Irishman," in *O'Neill and His Plays,* 66 [see n. 6]).

25. We should remember that Ella O'Neill was finally able to overcome her drug addiction and recover her health by temporarily leaving her family and entering a convent, in spite of the objections of her husband, who had been discouraged by the failure of earlier attempts at cures in sanatoria. After her cure in the convent, Ella attended church regularly. So in the end she saved her soul and recovered her home in the church by going back to the

spiritual life from which she had been led by her marriage to the actor James O'Neill (Sheaffer, *O'Neill: Son and Playwright,* 280–81).

26. I know of a case of an ex-nun hospitalized for mental illness who spent her days kneeling before a toilet removing imaginary hosts one by one from her mouth and flushing them down. When she had removed the last one, thus completing the symbolic annihilation of her "marriage to Christ," she was cured. She and Mary Tyrone perform the same kind of ritual action renouncing vows in a quest for spiritual health but in opposite directions: the ex-nun moves from the sacred to the secular world, whereas Mary seeks her well-being by symbolically returning from her secular marriage to her girlhood in the church.

27. Weirdly echoing Mary in *Long Day's Journey,* Carlotta's remarks to José Quintero on the subject of home in his book *If You Don't Dance They Beat You* (Boston: Little, Brown and Co., 1979) provide striking support for my thesis in this chapter:

Do you know how many homes I made for O'Neill? Oh, they were such beautiful homes. I selected everything myself, to the last piece of furniture. He didn't help me, wouldn't put himself out the least bit. *He didn't know how to act in a home* [Quintero's italics]. *He never really wanted one . . . never, since the day we were married.* (236)

See also the conclusion of chapter 3, "Causality in O'Neill's Late Masterpieces," in this volume.

28. As Sheaffer put it in *O'Neill: Son and Artist,* "Basically, this Catholic apostate used the drama as a confessional; his chief objective was certainly not popular success, not even critical acclaim or literary immortality, but his own salvation" (47).

9

"Get My Goat": O'Neill's Attitude toward Children and Adolescents in His Life and Art

Lowell Swortzell

O'NEILL'S CHILDHOOD

O'Neill's own childhood surely would not have prepared him for a comprehensive knowledge of children, their emotional values, and their psychological needs. "The truth is," he once said looking back at his own experience, "that I had no youth."[1] His was a childhood totally overshadowed by the demands of his father's theatrical career. Although the boy himself did not appear on stage with James O'Neill during his annual tours of *The Count of Monte Cristo* until he was twenty-four years old, his life from the beginning was regulated by the same seasonal engagements, rehearsal periods, and touring schedules. In addition, the little free time that the matinee idol had to spend with his sons often was not pleasant: "God deliver me," he once exclaimed nonplussed, "from my children!"[2] For the first seven years of his life, O'Neill was left in the care of a nurse who became a surrogate mother far more influential than the absent Ella O'Neill. Sarah Sandy's love of melodramatic fiction, particularly that of Dickens and Poe, helped formulate Gene's early taste in literature, and her love of Gothic horror also conditioned his sense of the dramatic. In later life he recalled that she told him stories drawn from current murders as well as fanciful tales of terror of her own creation, which were often truly frightening.[3] Even so, she was also a source of comfort and affection, perhaps the only such source at this age, as he acknowledged in adulthood in a chart diagramming his youth and adolescence. Apparently drawn when he underwent psychoanalysis in the 1920s, the diagram may be found as an appendix in Louis Sheaffer's *O'Neill: Son and Playwright*.[4] The line that runs from birth to age seven is labeled "Mother love," with a note reading, "meaning Nurse love." His mother spent so much time on tour with her husband that the boy scarcely saw her from September through May.

He cut the line at seven years old with the note "complete break—school." Two days after turning seven he arrived at a boarding school, now without either mother or nurse to comfort him. At the Academy of Mount St. Vincent in Riverdale, New York, he experienced "outbursts of hysterical loneliness," which recurred upon his return each fall for the five years he remained there.[5] With a total of only sixty boys, the school's classes were small, but since he had never spent time with other children, he did not make friends easily. Instead of playing, he chose to read and dream of a friend who accompanied him: "There was me and one other in this dream . . . and during the day sometimes this other seemed to be with me and then I was a happy little boy," he remembered years later.[6] Subconsciously, he had created the friend he needed but did not know how to find. He was no more socially adept as a teenager; he once invited a classmate to accompany him to Monte Cristo cottage for Easter vacation only to leave his houseguest to his own resources while he spent the entire week reading by himself. He simply did not realize that he was expected to entertain a friend.[7]

His best friend, as we might infer from *Long Day's Journey into Night,* was his brother Jamie, ten years his senior and also often away at school except for the summer holidays.[8] When Gene was at Riverdale, however, the brothers were only an hour apart and could see each other for frequent visits. So began the close relationship that eventually led the younger brother to be introduced to nights of riotous drinking, to prostitutes, and to the general hellraising of his highly accomplished mentor. In *Long Day's Journey,* Jamie's love-hate relationship with his brother constitutes one of the great paradoxical dilemmas of the play. Jamie recognizes that his brother is his only hope of accomplishing something of which he can be proud and which might give his life meaning. At the same time, he cannot forgive him for being the cause of their mother's drug addiction. In real life, Eugene must have realized this dichotomy even at an early age and, drawn as he was to his brother's worldly and often amusing cynicism, still recognized the possibility of becoming a victim of his self-hate and destruction.

The facts of O'Neill's childhood are clear enough: a saga of loneliness, isolation, the unfulfilled desire to belong, the passion for reading, the love of swimming and the sea, and the prolonged absences of his parents. However true this may be, Louis Sheaffer, one of O'Neill's biographers, insisted that even with a penurious father, a drug-addicted mother, and a wastrel brother, there still had to be times of joy and laughter.[9] The Gelbs, O'Neill's other major biographers, reported that James could be a generous and even indulgent father.[10] They cited a toy railroad "which ran on a track surrounding his house. It was not a miniature electric train, but a coal burning model in which he could sit and ride around his yard." They said the young O'Neill "delighted" in this gift even though he had to stoke the engine and carry the fuel himself. Sheaffer, however, denied the boy this fun when he reported the train was a hoax, a bit of human interest invented by James's press agent, a man named appropriately enough for a press agent, A. Toxen Worm: "The railroad originated, and remained, in Mr. Worm's mind."[11] Sheaffer added that Eugene must have found the story "an interesting piece of fiction." "Interesting," indeed, for once more he found himself the victim of his father's theatrical career, again manipulated and on this occasion even exploited by the demands of fostering the star's image before his public. If the twelve-year-old boy read the story, the irony of its fabrication would be less interesting than heartbreaking as he thought what might have been his childhood pleasures and realized the extent to which they had been missed. The story makes us question if any of James's gifts were real and to what extent the joy and laughter might also have been inventions of Worm's mind.

In the diagram of his childhood and adolescence, O'Neill labels the role his father played before the age of seven as "indefinite hero" and indicates that from early childhood his father would provide him whiskey and water to soothe the nightmares caused by his terror of the dark. He writes on the diagram: "This whiskey is connected with protection of Mother—Drink of Hero Father." No doubt the adult O'Neill was digging at the roots of his advanced alcoholism by attributing it to his father's notion of comfort. He further notes that during this period before seven "the world of reality" was "practically unrealized" except for the terror of it, emphasized by the murder stories told by the nurse and by his own traumatic fear of being alone in the dark. He adds that these nightmares also brought the delight that came from feeling the "protecting influence" of his mother, nurse and the nuns, which, except for the nuns, largely ended at the age of seven. At Christmastime with his parents on the road, he frequently spent the holidays with his former nurse so that her influence continued sporadically for the next portion of his life.

In the chart his father progresses from an "indefinite hero" to a "fantasy hero," the illusion having ended with the belief that his father was the real cause of his being shipped off to school. This notion results in "resentment and hatred" of James O'Neill during the period between seven and adolescence. In the teenage part of the chart, a new phrase accompanies the word *hatred:* "Defiance of Father." At this point, O'Neill became a rebellious teenager, contesting almost every value of what to the public must have appeared a sheltered and privileged life: an English governess, expensive schools (his father did not stint on education), a summer home in fashionable New London, splendid clothes, and every book a voracious reader could desire. Indeed, these elements under normal circumstances should have resulted in a happy youth if it were not for the more damaging facts that made them seem unimportant.

A parallel line in the diagram cuts across the vertical line representing adolescence, abruptly ending it with a description reading "Discovery of Mother's inadequacy." In the summer of 1903, when O'Neill was fifteen, and after a period of particularly heavy rain and fog that had virtually paralyzed New London and had resulted in relentless ominous warnings from the local lighthouse, Ella O'Neill, having consumed her current drug supply and because of the weather unable to obtain more, ran from the cottage to the river determined to drown herself. Rushing after her, father and sons subdued her struggle and slowly helped her back to the drab house she hated because its simplicity so greatly humiliated her.[12] On that unforgettable night (brilliantly recalled in *Long Day's Journey*), Eugene learned for the first time the secret his family had successfully withheld from him: His mother was a drug addict. The disclosure resulted in a loss of faith not only in his parents but also in his God, the God of the Catholic church he had been reared to revere both at home (his parents were ardent worshippers) and in school by the nuns who had controlled his life.

His faith had begun to falter well before this eventful evening, for he had long witnessed his mother's strange and erratic behavior. As he had watched her suffer throughout the years, he had begun to question how a woman of such strong belief who constantly prayed for deliverance from her pain could be overlooked so completely by her God. What was the point of continuing his own prayers for his mother when they too went unanswered? He had had enough of Catholicism at home and in church and refused to return to De La Salle School, insisting he would attend instead a nonsectarian boarding school. He had not divulged his true feelings to his family and throughout the summer had accompanied them to Mass, giving lip service each Sunday. But now he considered this a hollow, deceptive gesture that he could not reenact and so refused henceforth to worship again, in defiance of a God in whose existence he no longer believed.[13]

From this point on the teenager was more desolate in his loneliness than ever before. Already hating his father, he now viewed his mother's "Inadequacy," as he termed it on the chart, as a cause for another "break." He indicates that at this point he also broke away from the Nurse as a Mother value, leaving only Jamie, hardly a reliable counselor on any subject except debauchery, as an ally. Jamie, moreover, was never available on a regular basis.

The longest line of the diagram deals with reality and is perhaps the most significant self-diagnosis O'Neill makes about his childhood and adolescence. His youthful nightmares induced by fear of the dark and the Nurse's stories merge, as he matures, into a fear of reality itself. The earlier fears had been modified by the "protecting influence" of mother, nurse, and nuns, all three sources of comfort removed from fifteen years onward. The final notation reads, "Reality found and fled from in fear— Life of fantasy and religion in school—Inability to belong to reality." It is this same inability that plagues Brutus Jones, Yank in The *Hairy Ape*, Robert Mayo in *Beyond the Horizon*, and a series of characters running all the way through to the denizens inhabiting Harry Hope's back barroom, to Erie Smith, the loner of *Hughie*, and, of course, to the four haunted Tyrones of *Long Day's Journey*.

The realization that he did not belong and the recognition of the need to find a place of comfort and security took him first to the writing of poetry and short stories and then to plays. Eventually, the theater and his determination to become a serious artist in it replaced his allegiance to both family and church and became his temple of worship and source of redemption.

O'NEILL'S CHILDREN

For a man who experienced the worst traumas of childhood arising from a sense of rejection, loneliness, and a fear of the dark and who periodically awoke from nightmares so terrifying that their impression remained with him as an adult, O'Neill made little attempt to provide his own children with the protection, comfort, or understanding he had missed. Just as he seemed unaware of how to entertain a houseguest, he appeared equally unsuited to play the role of father, to know what was expected of him, or even what to say. He admitted that he didn't know how to talk to children.[14] A teenage friend of Eugene O'Neill, Jr., remarked that what he liked most about the playwright was that he spoke to him as an equal, "none of that talking down because you were a kid."[15] But he was ill at ease with youngsters and became quickly annoyed by their noise, energy, and constant demands for attention. To work, O'Neill required absolute silence from early morning until early afternoon when he appeared for a swim or for lunch. With children anywhere in the house absolute silence was impossible, as he discovered in the summer of 1926 at Loon Lodge in Maine, where it was necessary to build a one-room studio, actually a shack it seems, at a safe and silent distance from the menage of children who plagued him.[16]

His first child could not have been a problem since he didn't see the boy until he was twelve years old. Born in 1910, Eugene, Jr., was the offspring of O'Neill's first, brief marriage to Kathleen Jenkins, which took place in 1909, well after the baby had been conceived.[17] Outraged by what he considered to be the work of a gold digger, James O'Neill arranged for Gene to leave for a mining expedition in Honduras almost immediately after his marriage. Divorce proceedings, which gave Kathleen full custody of the child, followed in 1912; she did not seek alimony or child support. Not until ten years later when O'Neill's success was well known did she request assistance and then only for the boy's education. Kathleen had remarried in 1915, to an office clerk who also had a son just slightly younger than her own. Taking his stepfather's last name, her son was known as Richard Pitt-Smith and was not told the true identity of his natural father. Although the boy seems to have been fond of his stepfather and at first was happy enough at home where he was spoiled by a doting grandmother, he became increasingly rebellious and like his father before him was sent to a private military school—with much the same results. He ran away several times, pleading with his mother to allow him to remain at home. Each time that she sent him back his sense of rejection increased.

At the time O'Neill agreed to finance the boy's education, a meeting was arranged between father and son. The grandmother who had brought Richard from Long Island waited downstairs in the lobby of the O'Neill's apartment house while the boy, who had just learned the nature of his visit, went upstairs. O'Neill, afraid conversation might be difficult, had asked Kenneth Macgowan to be present to help him if he faltered. However nervous both father and son must have been, the conversation progressed comfortably through a discussion of baseball and a comparison of their school experiences. O'Neill seemed to like the boy, no doubt impressed by his good looks and intelligence, and invited him to spend part of his holidays with him the following summer. So warmly had the friendship developed that soon thereafter the boy wished to be known by his real name, Eugene Gladstone O'Neill, Jr.

This happy beginning continued when the son transferred from the military academy to a preparatory school and distinguished himself academically, as later he would at Yale where he became a promising classicist. Although drawn to his father, he never grew close to his half brother and sister, both considerably younger than he, whom he got to know during summer visits in Provincetown, Maine, and Bermuda. A united family became less likely when O'Neill separated from his second wife and later married Carlotta Monterey, who shortly thereafter made her lifework the protection and seclusion of O'Neill so that he could write in the silence and serenity that had eluded him during the last years of his marriage to Agnes.

O'Neill continued to see his son occasionally; when he was traveling in Europe in 1929, the young man came to the chateau the O'Neills had rented near Tours. O'Neill gave him Peaked Hill Bars, his beloved home near Provincetown, which had been a present from his father. But from the time that Eugene, Jr., received his doctorate in classics from Yale in 1936, both his career and his relationship with his father deteriorated. Three unsuccessful marriages and an ever-increasing drinking problem kept him in constant financial difficulty. His brilliant reputation as a classicist dimmed into part-time teaching, and a sudden interest in a career in radio also soon faltered. Carlotta made it increasingly difficult for Eugene to ask for money or to communicate at all with his father, and it is likely that O'Neill did not know the extent of the torments that surrounded his son. It is just as likely that had he known, he would not have made any effort, other perhaps than financial, to save him. His eldest son committed suicide at the age of forty in a classic Roman ritual in his bathtub, but, apparently changing his mind, attempted to drag himself to the telephone to call for help. The telephone had been disconnected for failure to pay the bills. He left a note beside an empty quart of bourbon that read, "Never let it be said of O'Neill that he failed to finish a bottle. Ave atque vale."[18]

Perhaps because he lived eighteen years longer, the decline and fall of O'Neill's second son, Shane Rudraighe (1919–77), is even a sadder study in self-destruction.[19] Agnes Boulton, O'Neill's second wife, describes in her account of the early years of their marriage the happiness and sense of fulfillment O'Neill seemed to feel during the summer of her pregnancy. At first, he insisted the doctor had made a mistake, but as the time for her delivery came closer, he accepted the reality that the two joyous lovers would be three in the autumn. When Shane was born, he said, "It'll be *us* still, from now on, Us—alone—but the three of us . . . —a sort of Holy Trinity, eh, Shane?" The last line of the book captures this moment: "And when he bent over to kiss me good night he kissed the little black head too, and I saw a real tenderness in his eyes."

But before uttering his affection, O'Neill already had christened his son not Shane the Proud, the name he must have had in mind when he drew it from his own ancient Irish ancestry, but Shane the Loud, the name he exclaimed as the baby cried his first screams. Holding the newborn infant, he asked, "Where do I put him, Doc? He's kicking me!"[20] Then he remembered that he had forgotten to buy a crib. Shane was to become louder and to continue to kick at life throughout his infancy and childhood, as he began to undergo much the same pattern of behavior as his father and older brother.

Early on, a visitor remarked that she felt sorry for Shane,

a touching child, wandering around at the edge of the sea when children should be taken in by their parents. I remember one afternoon when I found him sitting listlessly on the dock. He was so delighted when I asked if he'd like to come inside and have me read to him. Neither Gene nor Agnes, as far as I could see, paid much attention to him. Gene once told me he didn't know how to talk to children and felt he couldn't have any connections with him until he grew up.[21]

The factor of loneliness was already established for this exceptionally beautiful golden-haired, sensitive child.

Another striking parallel followed in the person of Shane's nurse, a Mrs. Clark he affectionately called "Gaga," who became his beloved surrogate mother until Agnes felt their bond had become too close. She endeavored to weaken it, however, without strengthening her own. When O'Neill left Agnes in 1927, Shane suffered the double emotional shock of losing a father he adored in spite of his aloofness and also the separation from Mrs. Clark, who became ill and returned to her home. Shane was shipped off to boarding school and, not surprising in this family chronicle, was soon pleading to come home. O'Neill had every opportunity to spot the child's dilemma, for although about to leave the country with Carlotta on an extended tour of the East, he regularly corresponded with both Shane and Oona, his second child with Agnes. One of the boy's letters described a happy day he had had with "Gaga" who took him to the zoo, aquarium, and the Museum of Natural History. O'Neill replied warmly that he, too, had had a nurse who took him to these exact same places. His identification with his son must have been complete at that moment, along with the remembrance of the loss of his nurse and the acute pain that resulted. Shane would endure the same misery, for soon "Gaga" was dead, and his father's letters stopped coming.

Shane's academic record at Lawrenceville School, which he entered at the age of twelve, reflected his instability. As before, Carlotta became a wall between son and father, determining what letters O'Neill would see and sometimes replying in his place, freely sending advice to unsympathetic eyes. Shane believed his stepmother intercepted the congratulatory message he sent when O'Neill won the Nobel prize in 1936, for the playwright never received it.[22] After leaving Lawrenceville for another school in Colorado where he did no better, Shane became interested in a career as a writer but received no encouragement from his father. He returned to Lawrenceville only to drop out again with poor grades.

His adult life reflected this same cycle of rambling failure and disillusionment, heightened by alcohol and drugs, several suicide attempts, three marriages, the death of his first child due to conditions the police described as "neglect," increasing arrests as a disorderly person, more suicide attempts, and, in his last years, an oblivion into which he dropped from public view only to be reported dead six months after he had jumped from an apartment building while having an argument.[23]

O'Neill's third child was born in Bermuda, the daughter of Agnes whose name when translated into Irish became Oona.[24] An exceptionally beautiful baby, she impressed her father who cabled Macgowan that he predicted a great future for her in grand opera, a reference to Oona's ability to scream and cry.[25] When at the age of four her parents separated, she, like Shane, underwent a long period of stress, which drew her closer to her mother throughout her childhood. O'Neill wrote to her sporadically, but visits could be as much as eight years apart. Both Carlotta and Gene were favorably impressed when, at the age of fourteen, she arrived at Tao House for a short visit: They found her well mannered, sensitive, and intelligent. They enjoyed the shy, attractive young lady precisely because they could treat her like an adult, which was a new and curious experience for Oona and very much to her liking.

Educated largely at the Brearley School in New York City, she was accepted at Vassar College but never attended, choosing instead to pursue a career in the theatre. This eventually took her to Hollywood and her meeting with Charles Chaplin, then in the midst of a sensational paternity suit. The O'Neills had not been pleased with the publicity her theatrical career had garnered, believing that she was exploiting her father's name. And when at the age of eighteen she married the fifty-four-year-old Chaplin, O'Neill was furious and never spoke to her again, later excising her from his will. Except in her early childhood, she had had little direct association with her father save through letters and several infrequent, if pleasant, visits. By marrying a man her father's exact age and moving to Switzerland where she became the mother of eight children, she had escaped the curse of the lonely, fear-ridden, self-destructive O'Neill men. Unlike them, she had found someone she deeply loved and the comfort of knowing she belonged.

He "has always been honest, amusing and charming. As well as grateful for our care and affection. Our other children have never given us that much!" "He's the only one of our children who never disappointed us."[26] So claimed Carlotta, obviously not referring to Gene's three children or to her own daughter by her previous marriage about whom she displayed little interest. She once proclaimed in her usual grandiloquent manner that she "loathed" children.[27] The so-called child to whom both O'Neills were emotionally devoted for twelve years was their beloved Dalmatian, named Silverdene Emblem but affectionately known as "Blemie." Handsome, intelligent and loyal, the dog joined them while they lived at Le Plessis, the chateau in which they settled at the time of their marriage in 1929.

Although Carlotta would not allow the servants to wear shoes because the noise might disturb the playwright at work, Blemie had the run of the house and of their lives. From Hermes in Paris they ordered a collar, leash, overcoat, and raincoat tailored to Blemie's measurements. In addition, they bought him a four-poster bed with handmade sheets and a special bathtub for his exclusive use.[28] Devoted to both master and mistress, Blemie was also attentive to guests and became the official host, looking after everyone with genuine interest. Rewarded for his care, according to the gardener at Tao House, "The dog had steak every day of the year."[29] Periods of Blemie's sickness are noted in the O'Neill correspondence. In old age, when his senses became impaired and he was lamed by a fall, they carried him about. They also spoiled him more than ever, with Carlotta still insisting, "He is the only one of our children who has not disillusioned us— and always seemed conscious (and grateful) of our efforts to do all we could for his welfare and happiness!"[30]

After they buried Blemie in a special grave at Tao House, Gene wrote "The Last Will and Testament of Silverdene Emblem O'Neill," in which the dog consoles his master and mistress: "It is time I said goodbye, before I become too sick a burden on myself and on those who love me. It will be a sorrow to leave them, but not a sorrow to die. Dogs do not fear death as men do. We accept it as part of life, not as something alien and terrible which destroys life."[31] When Eugene O'Neill, Jr., died, neither Gene nor Carlotta attended his funeral, although they sent flowers. The loss, however, prompted no such statement or evidence of grief as this for Blemie.

Perhaps out of embarrassment or even shame, O'Neill sometimes insisted that he was a good father. When writing Agnes in Bermuda while he was in New York with Carlotta, he would plead his love for the children, saying he missed Shane and Oona "like hell at times! Don't sneer. I love them as much as you do—perhaps more—in my oblique, inexpressive fashion."[32] He predicted that when older, they would find out that he had been a good father, "when they really come to know me and about me." O'Neill claiming to be a good father is perhaps as ironic as Elia Kazan's claim that he was faithful to his first wife except in the physical sense.[33] O'Neill was a good father except in the paternal sense. In his guilt-ridden conscience, he knew how lousy he was and said as much to Macgowan: "I was never cut out, seemingly, for a pater familias and children in squads, even when indubitably my own, tend to 'get my goat.' "[34]

O'Neill's "oblique, inexpressive fashion," it should be noted, was not limited to children, for as Carlotta revealed, O'Neill rarely said he loved her. In fact, he seemed to avoid the word in direct address, yet left impassioned love letters filled with testimonies of his deep and abiding affection about the house for her to find.[35] Love, for O'Neill, was something unspoken, an emotion that he could express best in his writing, which, as we now know, was the only place he fully lived.

Then, we must ask, to what extent did he overcome his guilt and become a responsible parent in his plays? Were the children he created the same noisy specimens that got his goat in real life, or were they the children he insisted he loved? As a writer, was he better equipped to meet his obligations as a father?

CHILDREN AND ADOLESCENTS IN O'NEILL'S PLAYS

Although no attempt is made to be complete in the following survey of O'Neill's dramatic progeny, we will examine the major and a few minor figures. The earliest group appears in a 1913 one-act play, the unproduced *Warnings,* part of a collection entitled *Ten "Lost" Plays of Eugene O'Neill* (1964).[36] The Knapps live in the Bronx with their five children, a singularly depressing lot: Charles, fifteen; Dolly, fourteen; Lizzie, eleven; Sue, eight; and a one-year-old crying baby. Their poverty results in constant squabbling and selfish behavior, which makes them truly hateful.

On the other hand, Davie, aged nine, and Ruth, aged seven, who appear the next year in the full-length work *Servitude* (1914), are allegedly *"healthy, noisy, delightful children,"*[37] although the reader may not find them so in the following exchange with their mother:

RUTH. I'm goin' to play I'm the Princess . . .
MRS. ROYLSTON. And are you going to be the Prince, Davie?
DAVIE. Nope; I'm goin' to be the dragon.
MRS. ROYLSTON. But the dragon was very, very wicked.
DAVIE. Tha's why I wanta be him. (102)

Fortunately, at this point they are whisked off to play in the sandpile before they can be any more delightful and are never seen again.

In the early one-act plays, Mary in *The Rope* (1918) is the only child worth noting, and she is largely a plot device by which the much sought-after gold can be ironically thrown into the ocean at the end. O'Neill clearly does not like her: "*She is a skinny, overgrown girl of ten, with thin, carroty hair worn in a pigtail. She wears a shabby gingham dress. Her face is stupidly expressionless. Her hands flutter about aimlessly in relaxed, flabby gestures.*"[38] He sees to it quickly enough that the reader does not take kindly to her either as she plays with her doll and proves to be meddlesome. The first line of the play says it all, as her grandfather shakes his cane after her, shouting, "Out o' my sight, you Papist brat!" (578).

Of the four Carmody children in *The Straw* (1918–19), Mary, aged eight, is the most developed and important to the play; the others, ranging in age from ten and eleven to fourteen, are largely present for family atmosphere. A "*delicate, dark-haired, blue-eyed, quiet little girl,*" [39] Mary likes to read while the others are filled with high spirits like their father. When their elder sister, Eileen, at the age of eighteen, leaves for the Hill Farm Sanatorium for Tuberculosis, she expresses regret that she no longer will be able to care for the children as she has since their mother died—and "especially little Mary" (346). At the Sanatorium, she meets Stephen Murray, another patient and the role O'Neill modeled upon himself and his own experiences at Gaylord Farm in 1913. Eileen asks if his sisters have any children. "Two squally little brats," he replies, confessing that he doesn't like babies, "I don't get them. They're something I can't seem to get acquainted with" (360).

When in Act two Mary visits Eileen eight months later, she is markedly different from the happy child she was when we first met her: "*The sweetness of her face has disappeared, giving way to a hangdog sullenness, a stubborn silence, with sulky, furtive glances of rebellion*" (394). The change has come about through Eileen's absence and the marriage of their father to the Housekeeper. When Eileen, overjoyed to see her, reaches out for Mary, the girl fidgets nervously and whines, "Let me go!" and breaking away, stammers, "Eileen—you look so—so funny" (396–97). Eileen, stunned and in a dead voice, replies, "You, too! I never thought you—Go away, please," in what is the best dramatic moment in the play, as Eileen recognizes that because of her disease, she has been rejected both by society and her entire family.

More likable perhaps, but certainly no more attractive, is little Mary Mayo, daughter of Ruth and Robert Mayo in *Beyond the Horizon* (1918). Mary is first heard offstage in what her creator calls "*the peevish whining of a child.*"[40] She is two years old, "*a pretty but sickly and anemic-looking child with a tear-stained face*" (116) who begs for her doll, crying, "Dolly, Mama! Dolly!" Her grandmother complains that the child's "racket's enough to split a body's ears" (117). When Robert arrives exhausted from working in the hot fields, Mary runs to him, "(*screeching happily*) Dada! Dada!" (119), and it soon becomes clear as the child clings to her father once Ruth attempts to put her to bed for her nap that mother and father have different views of their daughter.

Ruth wants to whip Mary for her behavior; Robert, to embrace her. Meanwhile, the baby wails until her father gently and lovingly takes her to bed and lulls her to sleep with the result that *"Husband and wife look into each other's eyes with something akin to hatred in their expressions"* (120–21). O'Neill has used the child effectively to arrive at this moment, dramatizing Ruth's feeling that Mary is burdensome while Robert finds joy in taking care of her. Mary and Robert are given a two-page scene alone together in which the child asks her father to play with her. We must see here that Robert's desire to leave the farm no longer carries the strength of his devotion to his child.

Mary dies between Acts two and three in what must be a welcome relief to all performers who have been required to work with a two-year-old actress. What was O'Neill thinking of? There is no such thing as a two-year-old actress! The part is always played by someone older, usually much older, although that makes the necessity to nap and the constant need to hold the child all the more difficult to explain. The role cannot be cut because Mary is essential to the action and it is her death that serves as Robert's final catalyst into depression. Besides, the child has twenty-one speeches in Act two, which O'Neill seems to have thought within the command of a two year old. When he wrote *Beyond the Horizon* in 1918, neither Shane nor Oona had been born, and O'Neill clearly knew little about children except that he didn't like them.

The children who open *All God's Chillun Got Wings* (1923) act as a symbolic chorus consisting of four boys and four girls; two of each set are white, and two are black. Among them, as they play marbles, are eight-year-old Ella Downey, a white girl, and Jim Harris, a black boy whom Ella will someday marry. Even as children, their friendship faces racial prejudice, and Jim must chase both blacks and whites away before he comforts Ella. He confesses that since he has been carrying her books to school, he has been drinking chalk water because the barber told him it would make him white. "Does I look whiter?" he asks. "Yes—maybe—a little bit."[41] Ella asks why he wants to be white, and he says he likes it better, whereas she prefers black. "Let's you and me swap. I'd like to be black. (*Clapping her hands*) Gee, that'd be fun, if we only could!" A long pause follows after which Ella takes Jim's hand shyly, and they both keep looking as far away from each other as possible:

ELLA. I like you.
JIM. I like you.
ELLA. Do you want to be my feller?
JIM. Yes.
ELLA. Then I'm your girl. (304)

Perhaps these are precocious eight year olds, but the moment has its charm, nonetheless. Much has been made by O'Neill biographers and critics that in this play, written when he was thirty-five years old, O'Neill gave these protagonists, a black man and a white woman who grow up and marry, his parents' names.

Gordon Evans first appears in Act seven of *Strange Interlude* (1927) at the age of eleven. O'Neill describes him as *"—a fine boy with, even at this age, the figure of an athlete. He looks older than he is. There is a grave expression to his face. His eyes are full of a quick-tempered sensitiveness. He does not noticeably resemble his mother. He looks nothing at all like his father. He seems to have sprung from a line distinct from any of the people we have seen."*[42] The older he grows, the more like his namesake Gordon Shaw he becomes, even though Ned Darrell is his father and Sam Evans, Nina Leeds's husband, thinks he is.

From this description, it is clear that O'Neill is favorably disposed toward Gordon; his first speech demonstrates his sensitivity, regretting that Ned has appeared on his birthday and wishing he would go away on another trip. "What makes Mother like him so much?" he ponders in the interior monologue that opens the act (138). He quietly defies Darrell: "I'd kick him out if I was big enough!" Sensing that Ned is ridiculing his father, he rushes at his natural father with clenched fists and is sent from the room when he refuses to apologize (142). Darrell comprehends the boy's attitude, "What if he does hate me? I don't blame him! He suspects what I know—that I've acted like a coward and a weakling toward him" (142).

The parallels in this act to O'Neill's own relationship with his eldest son are clear enough in speeches such as this and a subsequent one in which Ned continues to torment himself for abandoning his son to Nina's demands. He shows great insight when he warns Nina that her interest in him is only encouraging Gordon to give his affection to Sam. "Children have sure intuitions. He feels cheated of your love—by me. So he's concentrating his affections on Sam whose love he knows is secure, and withdrawing from you" (144). Ned urges Nina to foster the boy's hatred of him if she wishes to keep his love. But Nina refuses to take Ned's advice, insisting that Gordon doesn't like him because he makes no attempt to be lovable. When she chastises him for failing to bring a birthday present, he reveals that he has left it in the hallway, "to be given to him after I've gone because, after all, he is my son and I'd prefer he didn't smash it before my eyes!" (144). As they kiss a moment later, the boy watches from the doorway and now knows that his intuition is correct.

In the key scene of the act in which O'Neill expands the boy's character with considerable sensitivity, Gordon has found his present, a small scale model of a sloop with the sails set: *"He is in a terrific state of conflicting emotions, on the verge of tears yet stubbornly determined"* (149). The boy clearly adores the gift but asks, "Why did it have to come from him? . . . he kissed Mother . . . she kissed him" (149–50). Ned sees what is coming and braces himself as the boy asks if the boat is for him. Then hearing it is, he trembles in a rage and begins to cry, breaking off the mast and bowsprit, tearing the rigging and throwing the pieces at his father's feet. Ned, at first furious while Gordon stands *"white-faced, defying him,"* then affectionately reasons: "You shouldn't have done that, son. What difference do I make? It was never my boat. But it was your boat. You should consider the boat, not me. Don't you like boats for themselves? It was a beautiful little boat, I thought" (151).

Gordon, sobbing miserably, agrees, "It was awful pretty! I didn't want to do it!" He picks up the pieces and releases the secret he holds: "I saw you kissing Mother!" To Ned's insistence that they were just saying good-bye, the boy replies: "You can't fool me! This was different!" As his father attempts to reason with him, he places his hand on Gordon's shoulder causing the *"terribly torn"* boy to question himself: "Why do I like him now?" (151). But this fleeting second of reversal comes to an end with Sam's arrival. Yet O'Neill has demonstrated the pulls upon the child and made them plausible and his dialogue believable. The scene can be acted effectively, as may be heard in the Columbia recording of the play in which Ben Gazzara plays Ned to the Gordon of Richard Thomas. Gordon is proof that O'Neill understood the frustrations of a young boy toward his parents and his own affection for them, as well as the pain of a tortured father wanting his son's love but knowing he must not reach out for it lest he endanger everyone's happiness.

The Miller brood of *Ah, Wilderness!* (1932) certainly are O'Neill's most famous youngsters. Seventeen-year-old Richard along with Thornton Wilder's George Gibbs of *Our Town* are the best loved and most often performed male adolescents in American dramatic literature. Arthur, at nineteen, is the eldest of the four Miller children, with Richard next, followed by Mildred, fifteen, and Tommy, eleven, all oozing American spunk, good health, and far too much happiness to be believed anywhere except on a television family series, all of which owe as much a debt to this play as television soap opera owes to *Strange Interlude.*

Arthur is everything Richard is not: well adjusted, self-confident, a Yale athlete of good looks whose future is assured. He is *"solemnly collegiate,"* flaunting his pipe and proud of *"his lady-killing activities."*[43] Mildred has beautiful eyes but is not pretty; her vivacity, however, makes everyone think she is attractive. She delights in being the family tease and the town flirt. Tommy, chubby and sunburned, his *"blond hair wetted and plastered down in a part"* is such a good-natured little demon that he actually makes his first appearance with *"a rim of milk visible about his lips"* (186). He cannot wait to set off Fourth-of-July fire crackers, which he will do whenever O'Neill needs a laugh. He suffers from the usual childhood stage diseases such as not being able to keep a secret and not wanting to go to bed. In most productions, he is an insufferable scene stealer, which, up to a point, well serves O'Neill's comic purposes.

But poor frustrated Richard is at the heart of *Ah, Wilderness!* and is clearly in the heart of the playwright as he puts the boy through the worst of growing up. On his first appearance, he characteristically carries a book, with his finger marking the place. Just out of high school, he is neither handsome nor homely, but what O'Neill says "*is a perfect blend of father and mother, so much so that each is convinced he is the image of the other*" (193). As almost always appears in descriptions of characters based in part on himself, Richard is extremely sensitive; there is "*a restless, apprehensive, defiant, shy, dreamy, self-conscious intelligence about him*" (193). In what may be a remembrance of his own past, O'Neill adds, "*He is alternately plain simple boy and a posey actor solemnly playing a role*" (193).

His intellectual development tends toward flamboyant statements about the sham of the Fourth-of-July celebrations by the American slaves of capitalism and quotations from the books he is constantly reading, a mixture of love poetry and socialism that his mother pronounces "awful" when she finds them hidden on the shelf in his wardrobe. His father, while amused, still must investigate the charges made by his mother that he is reading wicked books by Wilde, Shaw, and Swinburne. But it is his infatuation with Muriel McComber that gets him into the most trouble and gives the play its modicum of plot; the girl's father charges that Richard is corrupting the morals of his daughter by giving her suggestive quotations from his favorite authors.

Nat Miller, leaping to his son's defense, calls Richard "a fool kid, who's just at the stage when he's out to rebel against all authority, and so he grabs at everything radical to read and wants to pass it on to his elders and his girl and boy friends to show off what a young hellion he is! Why, at heart you'd find Richard is just as innocent and as big a kid as Muriel is!" (202). McComber is not convinced and forbids Richard ever to see Muriel again, and in storming out the door he cancels his advertising in Miller's newspaper. In the first of two father-and-son scenes, Miller asks the boy about his intentions toward Muriel, and Richard replies with shocked indignation that he loves her and plans to marry her after he finishes college (207). He only gave her the quotations to make her less afraid of life, a fear that when described sounds much like O'Neill's own teenage apprehensions: "Afraid of her Old Man—afraid of people saying this or that about her—afraid of being in love—afraid of everything. She's even afraid to let me kiss her. I thought, maybe, reading those things—they're beautiful, aren't they, Pa?—I thought they would give her the spunk to lead her own life, and not be—always thinking of being afraid" (207). The spunk to lead his own life and to escape his adolescent fears had, for O'Neill, too, come from these same books, which at twenty-five he is still reading in *Long Day's Journey*.

Upon receiving Muriel's forced farewell letter, Richard undergoes depression and melancholia: He "*exudes tragedy*" with statements such as "Life is a joke!" (215). In Act three, he finds out just how funny it is when at a bar in a small hotel to which he's been taken by a Yale friend of his brother's he befriends Belle, "*a typical college 'tart' of the period*" (236). Trying to demonstrate his worldliness, he drinks a man's drink—actually a loaded sloe gin fizz—and smokes his first cigarette. But even when shamed into it, he refuses to take Belle upstairs, saving himself for Muriel. As intoxication advances, he recites verses and lines from Ibsen, much to the amusement of the others. Thoroughly soused, he is finally thrown out by the Bartender.

Embarrassed, physically ill, and more depressed than ever, he is the next morning determined not to say he is sorry, even though he confesses he didn't have any fun: "It only made me sadder—and sick—so I don't see any sense in it" (270). Like Hedda Gabler, he would shoot himself if there were any pistols available because now he is convinced more than ever before that life is a stupid farce, that is, until his sister brings a note from Muriel arranging a secret meeting at nine o'clock.

Act two, scene four, which for those who teach acting to young students is one of the most often performed classroom exercises, takes place on a strip of beach where Richard impatiently waits for Muriel and chastises himself for having been with Belle the night before. Working himself into a romantic ecstasy, he suddenly switches as he sees Muriel approaching to a mood of nonchalance. She is fifteen, beautiful, and thrilled by the adventure of her escape from parental surveillance. The reunion proves rocky at first, neither fully trusting the other until they agree their separation made them both suffer. He can't wait to tell her how much he wanted to kill himself, and she assures him she would have followed his example. But when he describes the events of the previous evening, Muriel is shocked and wants to run away. She bites his hand and dashes off until Richard's assurance that Belle means nothing to him stops her. After she kisses the bite, he says, "You shouldn't—waste that—on my hand" (286). He finally obtains the long-awaited kiss, which is followed by plans for their honeymoon trip—on the road to Mandalay (288)!

By the time he returns home and makes amends with his father who awkwardly instructs him in the difference between good and bad girls, he has made his way out of the wilderness. He kisses his father for the first time in years, and Miller is deeply touched, confirming to his wife, "I don't think we'll ever have to worry about his being safe—from himself—again. And I guess no matter what life will do to him, he can take care of it now" (297). James O'Neill never could have made such a statement about Gene, any more than Gene could have about his sons. But in this comedy of wishful nostalgia he could give his character the independence he never achieved and obviously still longed for.

CONCLUSION

George Jean Nathan, one of O'Neill's oldest and closest friends, noted in 1932 that the playwright had a "boyish quality," which he defined as "an innocent artlessness" that he predicted would remain with him for the rest of his life. In a passage that I have marked in the margin of Nathan's book, "O'Neill as Peter Pan," he describes this innocence:

O'Neill, for all his solemn exterior, gets an unparalleled pleasure from splashing around in a swimming pool and making funny gurgling noises, from putting on the fancily colored dressing gowns he bought several years ago in China, from singing duets with a crony . . . from lying on the ground and letting Blemie, his pet dog, crawl over him, the meanwhile tickling him on the bottom, from watches with bells in them . . . and from drinking enormous glasses of Coca-Cola and making everyone believe it is straight whiskey.[44]

The idea that in some regards O'Neill never grew up also is shared by Louis Sheaffer: "The primary image of Eugene O'Neill that emerges from his writings is that of an eternal son, a man constantly examining and dramatizing his ambivalent feelings toward his mother and father, forever bound to them emotionally, a man never able to mature fully, never free to be a real parent himself. In a basic sense, he was free only to be a writer, a man trying to make peace with himself."[45]

O'Neill's fictional children, for the most part, are the same meddlesome nuisances that got his goat—"stillborn manikins" Sheaffer calls them[46]—but when he created those close to himself, the portrait of the son he had not known in *Strange Interlude* and the adolescent he had never been in *Ah, Wilderness!* come charging to life and must have provided him the momentary satisfaction of knowing that in spite of everything, immaturity and all his other inadequacies, he could be a good father and son, in print.

NOTES

1. Croswell Bowen, "The Black Irishman," in *O'Neill and His Plays: Four Decades of Criticism,* Oscar Cargill, N. Bryllion Fagin, and William J. Fisher, eds. (New York: New York University Press, 1961), 67.

2. Louis Sheaffer, *O'Neill: Son and Playwright* (Boston: Little, Brown and Co., 1968), 126.

3. Ibid., 23–24, 46, 55–56, 63, 71, 83, 85.

4. Ibid., 506.

5. Ibid., 64.

6. Agnes Boulton, *Part of a Long Story* (Garden City, N.Y.: Doubleday and Co., 1958), 67.

7. Sheaffer, *O'Neill: Son and Playwright,* 69.

8. For O'Neill and Jamie, see ibid., 73–74, 94, 99–102, 231, 270, 313.

9. Ibid., 46ff.

10. Arthur Gelb and Barbara Gelb, *O'Neill* (New York: Harper and Row, 1962), 62–63.

11. Sheaffer, *O'Neill: Son and Playwright,* 47.

12. Ibid., 89.

13. Ibid., 87–88.

14. Ibid., 68.

15. Louis Sheaffer, *O'Neill: Son and Artist* (Boston: Little, Brown and Co., 1973), 211.

16. Ibid., 212.

17. For Kathleen Jenkins, see Sheaffer, *O'Neill: Son and Playwright,* 144–50, 152, 156, 158–59, 161, 163, 188–89, 206–7, 214, 223, 231, 234, 263; and idem, *O'Neill: Son and Artist,* 65–66, 67, 147, 175, 631–32. For Eugene O'Neill, Jr., see Sheaffer, *O'Neill: Son and Playwright,* 146, 156, 158–59, 223, 394–95; and idem, *O'Neill: Son and Artist,* 65–67, 98–99, 125, 149, 174–75, 198, 211–212, 213, 230, 246–47, 291, 295, 344–45, 378, 398, 428, 439, 477, 480, 486, 525, 538–39, 561–62, 564, 575, 591, 607, 626–32, 654, 660.

18. Gelb and Gelb, *O'Neill,* 902–4.

19. For Shane O'Neill, see Sheaffer, *O'Neill: Son and Playwright,* 465–67, 473; and idem, *O'Neill: Son and Artist,* 3, 13–14, 26, 48, 49, 56, 58–59, 98, 105, 175, 179, 199, 213, 230, 236, 247–48, 262, 290, 295, 296–97, 303, 311–12, 322, 331, 332, 377–78, 391, 398, 439, 459, 476, 477, 478, 485–86, 488, 507–8, 525, 526, 538, 562, 563–67, 615–16, 620, 624, 626, 628, 658, 660.

20. Boulton, *Part of a Long Story,* 299, 309, 330, 331.

21. Sheaffer, *O'Neill: Son and Artist,* 247–48.

22. Ibid., 459.

23. For Shane's drug addiction and his death, see the *New York Times,* 8 June 1962, p. 20, col. 2; and 7 December 1977, sec. B, p. 14, cols. 3–4.

24. For Oona O'Neill Chaplin, see Sheaffer, *O'Neill: Son and Artist,* 179, 180, 181, 203, 213, 230, 262, 290, 295, 296, 311, 322, 331, 332, 377, 391, 439–40, 486–88, 508, 525–26, 531–32, 533, 537–38, 541–42, 549, 553, 566, 620–21, 623, 626, 641, 651, 654, 655, 658, 660, 662, 666, 672.

25. Ibid., 179.

26. Ibid., 349, 478.

27. Ibid., 487.

28. Ibid., 349, 478.

29. Ibid., 478.

30. Ibid., 518.

31. Eugene O'Neill, "The Last Will and Testament of Silverdene Emblem O'Neill," in *The Unknown O'Neill: Unpublished or Unfamiliar Writings of Eugene O'Neill,* ed. Travis Bogard (New Haven: Yale University Press, 1988), 433.

32. Sheaffer, *O'Neill: Son and Artist,* 296.

33. Elia Kazan, *Elia Kazan: A Life* (New York: Alfred A. Knopf, 1988), 38.

34. Eugene O'Neill, letter to Kenneth Macgowan, 7 August 1926, in *"The Theatre We Worked For" : The Letters of Eugene O'Neill to Kenneth Macgowan,* ed. Jackson R. Bryer with the assistance of Ruth M. Alvarez (New Haven: Yale University Press, 1982), 122.

35. Sheaffer, *O'Neill: Son and Artist,* 508.

36. Eugene O'Neill, *Ten "Lost" Plays of Eugene O'Neill* (New York: Random House, Inc., 1964).

37. Eugene O'Neill, *Servitude,* in *Lost Plays of Eugene O'Neill* (New York: Citadel Press, 1958), 101.

38. Eugene O'Neill, *The Rope,* in *The Plays of Eugene O'Neill,* vol. 3 (New York: Random House, Inc., Modern Library, 1982), 578.

39. Eugene O'Neill, *The Straw,* in *The Plays of Eugene O'Neill,* vol. 1 (New York: Random House, Inc., Modern Library, 1982), 332.

40. Eugene O'Neill, *Beyond The Horizon,* in ibid., 112.

41. Eugene O'Neill, *All God's Chillun Got Wings,* in *The Plays of Eugene O'Neill,* vol. 2 (New York: Random House, Inc., Modern Library, 1982), 304.

42. Eugene O'Neill, *Strange Interlude,* in *The Plays of Eugene O'Neill,* vol. 3, 137 (see n. 38).

43. Eugene O'Neill, *Ah, Wilderness!* in *The Plays of Eugene O'Neill,* vol. 2, 186–

87 (see n. 41).
    44. George Jean Nathan, *The World of George Jean Nathan,* ed. Charles Angoff
(New York: Alfred A. Knopf, 1952), 37.
    45. Sheaffer, *O'Neill: Son and Artist,* 49–50.
    46. Sheaffer, *O'Neill: Son and Playwright,* 68.

10

O'Neill's Psychology of Oppression in Men and Women

Jane Torrey

As a teacher of psychology, I have explored literary ground in search of realistic portrayals of individual personalities to use as a basis for class discussions on personality theory. Characters in works of literature are better material for practice in applying psychology than are people described in psychological case reports. This may be because the information artistic writers provide consists of feelings and actions in concrete situations rather than abstract dimensions or because their descriptions are uncontaminated with the theoretical biases of the reporting psychologist. However that may be, the psychology of personality is largely the creation of clinical practitioners dealing with neurotics, and therefore the most useful fictional "cases" for my purposes are tortured souls. That makes O'Neill's plays a treasure trove of useful materials.

Among the troubled circumstances O'Neill wrote about were many kinds of social-group oppressions. He had many friends who were struggling against the disadvantages of class or race, and he possessed both the interest and the understanding to make them subjects of his work. His intimacy with people on the lower rungs of society made it possible for him not only to sympathize with them but also to see things from their point of view. He knew they had aspirations for their own identity, power, and transcendence like their more fortunate brothers. His men, no matter how degraded, took for granted their right to self-respect and self-determination. Like other men, they had need of women, and they expected their women to help them achieve their goals without necessarily feeling an obligation in return. There are men like this in the real world, and O'Neill's portraits of men, oppressed and otherwise, are apparently drawn from his experience.

O'Neill was exceptional among white Americans in that he understood racial as well as class oppression. He broke ground in the American theater by making clear that the problems of black Americans were caused by whites and by portraying blacks as real men, not unlike white men, rather than in terms of the traditional stereotypes. He even deviated from custom by insisting that black actors portray them instead of the traditional whites in black makeup. Brutus Jones in *The Emperor Jones* enjoys being the boss as much as any man. He doesn't seem to have much trouble with self-esteem, and his conscious motivation is to take care of himself. If he can't be emperor, he can at least be free and financially independent. Nobody else, male or female, figures in his life. Even his unconscious, which pursues and defeats him, doesn't tie him to any particular persons. It is a collective rather than a personal unconscious. In *All God's Chillun Got Wings,* Jim is a black man who dares to marry a white woman because he loves her. He moves to France and then home again to accommodate Ella. He also has ambition to get ahead in the world, but like many other O'Neill men, he has great need of a woman's support and confidence, and it is Ella's unwillingness to believe in him that defeats him. Ella's character shows O'Neill's rare insight into the unconscious and ambivalent racism so often found in white Americans. She loves a black man enough to marry him but is still unable to conquer the ingrained attitudes of her race.

In *The Dreamy Kid,* Abe "Dreamy" Saunders does stay with his dying mother even though the police are after him, but he does it more out of fear that leaving her will bring bad luck than out of any sense of obligation to her. He doesn't seem to care one way or the other about his devoted girl friend who wants to die with him.

O'Neill also understands class oppression well. All the "Icemen" belong to the underclass, but all have ambitions for self-actualization. Some of them have hang-ups about their women, but in no case is it unselfish devotion. Parritt feels guilty about having betrayed his mother, but he does feel she deserved it for not having met his needs. Larry is represented as having been ruined by the same woman, but the implication is that she was at fault for not having been devoted to him. Harry Hope's wife is blamed for his agoraphobia. She was always trying to make him go out. But nothing is said about any obligation he had to her. Hickey is perhaps the most egregious case. He blames Evelyn for his failings because she was *too* devoted to him and then uses her "fault" to justify his killing her in order to effect his own escape from guilt. All of these men seem to have needed their women but not to have considered that their women needed them.

Yank, the seagoing furnace stoker, is oppressed, exploited, and denigrated by society, but, like many women, he accepts his position and glories in it. The event that destroys his self-respect is the discovery that others regard him as disgusting subhuman life, and then, unlike O'Neill's women, he rebels and, furthermore, seeks by his rebellion to gain dignity and meaning for his own existence.

Although men struggling with circumstance is one of O'Neill's more persistent themes, and social-group oppression is one of the oppressive circumstances, it is not so for women. He does not seem to see sex as a *circums*tance but rather as an inner nature. He portrayed many oppressed women, but his idea of an exploited woman's point of view was different.

His women tended to be completely fulfilled by their relationship with men. They were not concerned with any individual achievements. It was their devotion and obligation to their men that dominated their motivation. It is as though they took oppression and exploitation for granted as the destiny of their sex. Thus his women do not struggle against their female role but act as though it were their very essence. Doris Nelson pointed out that in the case of women O'Neill almost never suggests that they have any motivations other than those involved in their relationships with men.[1] There are many women in his plays who might have been but weren't motivated by anything other than their men's needs. For several of them class position suggests a possible career or other motivation for achievement. Nina of *Strange Interlude,* for example, was a professor's daughter and the woman in the lives of a businessman, a physician, and a successful writer. Yet she never discusses anything with any of them except her relationships with her men. She explicitly identifies herself through those connections when she says "My three men! . . . I feel their desires converge in me! . . . to form one complete beautiful male desire which I absorb . . . and am whole . . . they dissolve in me, their life is my life . . . I am pregnant with the three! . . . husband! . . . lover! . . . father! . . . and the fourth man! . . . little man! . . . little Gordon! . . . he is mine too! . . . that makes it perfect!"[2] Deborah and Sara of *More Stately Mansions* are both intelligent women, educated after the manner of women in their time; yet they are as identified with their man, their son and husband, respectively, as is Sara's relatively ignorant mother, Nora, of *A Touch of the Poet.* Lavinia is as capable as her brother Orin in *Mourning Becomes Electra;* yet all her motivations are derived from her relationships with the men in her life.

There are a few possible exceptions. Parritt's mother was devoted to her revolution, and Mary Tyrone still thinks wishfully of her lost career as a nun or a pianist. She yearns even more to be able to fulfill her chosen "career" as a proper lady of a proper family. In some of O'Neill's early work he shows an awareness of the power of conventional relationships between men and women to stifle the woman's potential and subordinate her to the man. Thus the title of the play *Servitude* refers to woman's oppression in marriage, an oppression against which the play protests, though it does not repudiate marriage as an institution. But most of O'Neill's women have nothing and are nothing except through men. Some of the apparent exceptions are in fact part of the very pattern of female dependence from which they seem to diverge. Thus Anna Christie, for example, successfully rejects the condemnation of her father, Chris, and her suitor, Mat, for her experience as a prostitute; yet the result is not autonomy for Anna but her integration into the life of her two men as a conventional daughter and wife. Likewise, Abbie Putnam in *Desire Under the Elms* seeks her own fortune, but she does so through marriage to one man and ultimately gives up everything because of her love for another.

Eleanor Cape, the actress in *Welded,* has her own career, but her most successful roles come from the plays of her husband, John, upon whom she is therefore professionally dependent, and by the end of the play, in spite of the struggles of the two to maintain their individuality in a loving relationship, she has become subordinated to his needs for a wife and mother.

Some of O'Neill's women, furthermore, possess a nearly incredible devotion to their men. Nora, Josie, Evelyn, and the women of *The Dreamy Kid* give more than seems humanly possible. Probably, there are women in the real world who are that selfless without noticeable reciprocation, but none of the real women in O'Neill's life compared with them, though Carlotta Monterey came closer than he had a right to expect. He could not have derived this image of women from his experience in the real world or from his personal relationships. Nor could his fictional women have been based upon the traditional stereotype of the feminine. They are not weak or dependent or even particularly submissive. They are strong and their strength is needed by the men they worship and who are often very dependent on them.

I said that I made use of O'Neill's characters in psychology as though they were examples of real people whose motives and responses could be explained in terms of psychological theories. In this respect I am doing something that literary critics also often do. Another way I might have followed the literary scholars in understanding O'Neill's work would have been to treat it as though his dramas were "thematic apperceptions," that is, products of his imagination that give insight into his own personality. I have come to regard that approach as more useful in understanding his female characters. Perhaps he imprisoned his women in the needs of their men because his own need for women was so great. Trudy Drucker quoted him as saying, "The role a woman should play is that of sacrifice to her man."[3] That may be why his imagination produces so many women who have no other desires than to do just that. It may also be why so many of his men felt threatened and controlled by the women they need so much.

Nora shows the epitome of this sacrificial role in *A Touch of the Poet* when she answers Sara's criticism of her devotion to her "poet": "It's little you know of love. . . . It's when, if all the fires of hell was between you, you'd walk in them gladly to be with him. . . . That's love, and I'm proud I've known the great sorrow and joy of it!"[4] Nora gets little from her husband, but she doesn't seem to expect much. The emotional connection between them is almost entirely one-sided. Josie is another woman who bears the whole burden of her relationship with Jamie. She knows he won't do anything for her except need her, and that is all she wants. Evelyn adopted the same pattern with Hickey, and all she gets in return is resentment and murder. According to him, it is a way of returning the favor.

Another aspect of O'Neill's portrayals of women is his inability to separate the different ways in which they devote themselves to men.

Mother, wife, or whore can be incorporated into one woman. Nora is a mother as much as a wife to Melody. Their daughter Sara becomes a kind of whore in order to secure her mate and much later plays the whore at his request when he gets tired of her as a wife. At the same time he has trouble distinguishing her from his mother: "Sometimes I become so intensely conscious of your unity that you appear as one woman to me. I can't distinguish my wife from . . . [my mother]."[5] Josie consciously impersonates a whoring woman while she offers herself as mother to Jamie in response to his needs. Sara tells Simon in the final line of *More Stately Mansions,* "Yes, I'll be your Mother, too, now, and your peace and happiness and all you'll ever need in life!" (194).[6]

Although O'Neill expects women to be mothers as well as lovers and wives, it is only important that they be mothers to the man, not necessarily to his children. The husband–father role would involve *him* in some obligation to her and the children. O'Neill's women are supposed to be devoted to men, but the men have no reciprocal obligations. It is the women, not the men, who are supposed to be pillars of strength for someone else. Sara's children are sent away to their grandmother or to school. "Ah, the children!" she said to Simon in *More Stately Mansions.* "Not that I don't love them with all my heart. But they're not my lover and husband! You come first!" (81). Abbie of *Desire Under the Elms* carries this priority to the extreme by actually murdering the baby in the hope of holding on to its father. Robert Mayo in *Beyond the Horizon* seems to reverse the pattern of the female sacrificing herself for her man, since he gives up his dream of going to sea to stay on the farm and be a husband to Ruth and a father to their child, but the apparent inversion of the pattern only confirms the pattern it inverts. Because he is a man, Robert's dream is alien to the domesticity for which he sacrifices it. Therefore his sacrifice of his destiny for a woman is unnatural, and it blights his marriage and his life, since as a result the farm fails, Robert and his daughter die, and Ruth's life is ruined. The lesson could hardly be more clear: It is a man's destiny to realize his nature, not to live in service to a woman, and the penalty for defying this "law of nature" is disaster. In O'Neill's moral universe, a woman's destiny is to serve a man, whereas a man's destiny is to fulfill himself.

In this chapter I have attempted to account for the contrast between the realistic and sympathetic portrayal of a wide variety of men in O'Neill's plays and the narrow selection of unrealistically devoted female personalities in his work by showing that his women, unlike his men, are drawn from his need, not from his experience. They are all variations on the mythic mother–wife–whore that haunted O'Neill's own life and that of his brother.[7]

NOTES

1. Doris Nelson, "O'Neill's Women," *Eugene O'Neill Newsletter* 6, no. 2 (Summer–Fall 1982): 3–7.

2. Eugene O'Neill, *Strange Interlude,* in *The Plays of Eugene O'Neill,* vol. 3 (New York: Random House, Inc., Modern Library, 1982), 135.

3. Trudy Drucker, "Sexuality as Destiny: The Shadow Lives of O'Neill's Women," *Eugene O'Neill Newsletter* 6, no. 2 (Summer–Fall 1982): 9.

4. Eugene O'Neill, *A Touch of the Poet* (New Haven: Yale University Press, 1957), 25.

5. Eugene O'Neill, *More Stately Mansions* (New Haven: Yale University Press, 1964), 82.

6. On the autobiographical implications of this theme see Louis Sheaffer, *O'Neill: Son and Artist* (Boston: Little, Brown and Co., 1973), 482–83.

7. For the attitude of the two brothers toward women, see ibid., 500–503.

11

The Author as Oedipus
in *Mourning Becomes Electra*
and *Long Day's Journey*
into *Night*

Richard F. Moorton, Jr.

In describing the genesis of *Mourning Becomes Electra,* Eugene O'Neill once said that of all the Greek tragedies he chose to retell the *Oresteia* because "it has greater possibilities of revealing all the deep hidden relationships in the family than any other."[1] From which family did O'Neill learn about such relationships if not his own? I believe that he was drawn to the *Oresteia* precisely because it provided him with the most potent available dramatic metaphor for bringing the deep hidden relationships of his own inexorably tragic family to the stage in a form so transfigured that they would manifest themselves not as sensational confession but as universal drama. In Clytemnestra's vengeful murder of Agamemnon he saw his own parents' marriage gone wrong, and in the Furies aroused by her curse he saw the hurtful memories, the inexorable ghosts, that comprised his own family's fate.

In *The Haunted* Lavinia exhorts Orin to face his ghosts (142).[2] O'Neill himself did just that in the transparently autobiographical play entitled *Long Day's Journey into Night.* He inscribed that play to his third wife, Carlotta, whose love "enabled [him] to face [his] dead at last and write this play—write it with deep pity and understanding and forgiveness for *all* the four haunted Tyrones."[3] This virtual allusion to the four haunted Mannons of *Mourning Becomes Electra* in the author's inscription to his consummate autobiographical drama is good reason to read the trilogy against *Long Day's Journey into Night* and the text of O'Neill's life itself in an attempt to plumb still more deeply the wellsprings of both works' peculiar power.

The crucial pioneer in the autobiographical interpretation of O'Neill's *Oresteia* is Virginia Floyd, who observes of O'Neill's preliminary notes on the work that "the early concept seemed like an early version of *Long Day's Journey into Night* for a brief period":

> The dramatist clearly identifies the setting of the trilogy as his hometown New London, stating "Christine has always hated the town of N.L. and felt a superior disdain for its inhabitants." This sentiment will be voiced later by Mary Tyrone, who feels similarly

isolated in a hostile New England environment. Similar words are used to describe these two women. Christine's hair is the same color that Mary's was before it turned white. Both women have detached, aloof, sensitive natures. Their husbands are considerably older than they, and the marriages of both are described in the notes as "a romantic mistake." As a consequence, they turn to their younger children, who resemble them, the sons Orin and Edmund, and become obsessively possessive. Christine, like the early Mary Tyrone, pays for her clothes "out of a generous yearly income left by her father," who has spoiled her.[4]

Later Floyd declares that in *Mourning Becomes Electra* O'Neill had presented thinly veiled portraits of the four O'Neills in the four members of Ezra Mannon's family.[5] But nowhere does she attempt to interpret the action of the trilogy autobiographically in a sustained manner. Indeed that is a daunting prospect. What did the family of James O'Neill, Sr., know of infidelity, incest, and murder?[6]

The answer begins precisely where Floyd abandons the hunt. She reports that after O'Neill finished his scenario for *The Homecoming*, he took time off to read Greek plays, particularly the *Oedipus Rex*. Thereupon, Floyd says, in the second part "Orin's attitude to his mother becomes more like a lover's than a son's."[7] Then she abandons, prematurely, a systematic autobiographical interpretation of *Mourning Becomes Electra*. Doris Alexander and Travis Bogard both point out that in 1926, about the time that he formed the plan to write a tragedy on the Greek model, O'Neill underwent psychoanalysis with Dr. Gilbert Hamilton.[8] After six weeks of therapy, Hamilton concluded that O'Neill had an Oedipus Complex. About this diagnosis Louis Sheaffer recorded an anecdote: " 'Gene kidded about it,' Jimmy Light recalls, 'when he told me that after much probing and questioning, Hamilton found he had this complex. "Why, all he had to do," Gene said, "was read my plays." ' "[9] If Floyd is right to see Eugene O'Neill and his mother in Orin and Christine Mannon, as I believe she is, and if we know that both sons were Oedipally attached to their mothers, then it is natural to interpret the drama as a manifestation of the author's sexual psychology.

All his life Eugene O'Neill was obsessed with the quest for the mother. At the conclusion of the play *Welded,* a manifestly autobiographical portrait of O'Neill's marriage to Agnes Boulton written in 1922–1923, Eleanor Cape, the Agnes figure, tenderly addresses her husband, John, as her child.[10] Significantly, the stage couple are childless, whereas Agnes had borne O'Neill one child, Shane, and would soon conceive another, Oona. When Agnes became more concerned with mothering his children than mothering O'Neill, he left her for the actress Carlotta Monterey, who was prepared to devote her whole life to the dramatist. It is Carlotta whom O'Neill was to hail in the private inscription of the manuscript of *Long Day's Journey into Night* as "mother and wife and mistress and friend!"[11] Virginia Floyd has shown, with fascinating implications for my thesis, that O'Neill's first conception of the Mannon trilogy's Clytemnestra figure, then called Clementina, was physically modeled on Carlotta.[12] But as the character evolved, O'Neill worked his way back from his surrogate mother to his real mother, Mary Ella Quinlan O'Neill. Virginia Floyd, in a passage quoted earlier, observed that Christine Mannon has hair the same color as Mary Tyrone's before it turned white. Christine Mannon's hair is thus mentioned in *The Homecoming*: "*The peculiar color of her thick curly hair, partly a copper brown, partly a bronze gold*" (9). Mary Tyrone's hair in her youth was long and beautiful, and reddish brown. One of Ella O'Neill's high school friends described her hair as "burnt gold." In a picture of the young Ella Quinlan O'Neill published by both the Gelbs and Louis Sheaffer, it is possible to see that her hair was indeed thick and curly.[13]

But the physical resemblances between Christine and Ella do not stop there. Christine Mannon is a "*tall striking-looking woman*" (8), with a "*fine, voluptuous figure*" (9). Ella's girlfriend had called her a "tall, superb creature," and Mary Tyrone even in middle age has a "*young, graceful figure*" (12), with which we can compare the "*flowing animal grace*" of Christine Mannon, who can be conceived of more sensually than Ella O'Neill or Mary Tyrone precisely because she is less recognizable as a version of the playwright's mother.

Christine Mannon's face is "*unusual, handsome rather than beautiful . . . a pale mask*" with "*deep-set eyes, of a dark violet blue.*" Mary Tyrone had dark brown eyes, but she and her real life counterpart were pale women, and as a picture of Ella O'Neill taken in the 1880s and published by Sheaffer shows, hers was in fact a strong, handsome face.[14] Compare that image with O'Neill's continuation of the description of Christine Mannon: "*Her black eyebrows meet in a pronounced straight line above her strong nose. Her chin is heavy, her mouth large and sensual, the lower lip full, the upper a thin bow.*" (9) Ella O'Neill as pictured in the two photographs to which I have referred answers to this description quite well: Her lower lip is full, her upper lip a perfect cupid's bow. And Mary Tyrone's eyebrows are described as black in *Long Day's Journey into Night* (12). Eugene O'Neill has created Christine Mannon in his mother's own likeness and image.

Christine Mannon's son Orin is one in a series of self-portraits in O'Neill's plays: As Travis Bogard noted, "Orin Mannon, whose resemblance to his father and to Adam Brant is marked, is tall and thin and has the aquiline nose, dark complexion, black hair and sensitive mouth of the O'Neill portraits."[15] But ultimately, Bogard believed that Orin resembles Jamie Tyrone, Eugene's stage portrait of his elder brother in *Long Day's Journey*, more than he does the Eugene figure in that play, Edmund Tyrone—especially in view of the elder brother's tortured attraction/revulsion for his morphine-addicted mother, which so resembles Orin's growing ambivalence toward Christine. It is true that certain traits of Orin—his sharp hostility to his father and his sharing with his mother of a happy little world in which no Mannons (especially father) are allowed— were also to be found *mutatis mutandis* in Jamie O'Neill, whom Louis

Sheaffer described with words that apply equally well to Orin: "Over and beyond the natural conflict between sons and fathers, the relationship here was sharpened by special conditions. The child viewed the father through his mother's complaints—as so often happens, her sense of grievance was more articulate than her love—and had come to regard himself as her ally against her husband."[16] And no one doubts that Jamie O'Neill had an Oedipus Complex.

But in important ways Orin is much more like Eugene than his brother. Jamie was a wisecracking extrovert, a Broadway rake, whereas Eugene was moody and introverted, like Orin. Moreover, like Edmund, whom Jamie habitually calls "the Kid" in Long Day's Journey (e.g., 22, 26, 30, 55), and like the young Eugene O'Neill himself, Orin is the baby of the family, coddled by a doting mother who blames the father for taking her son away from her.[17] Thus Christine bitterly resents the fact that her jealous husband has insisted on taking Orin, his mother's favorite, off to war, and in Long Day's Journey Mary sees Edmund's prospective hospitalization as just one more attempt by her jealous husband to separate them. Orin, like Eugene and unlike the shorter, stocky Jamie, is tall and slender, all suggesting that Orin Mannon is modeled not on Jamie but Eugene O'Neill.

Oedipus was an only child; to win his mother, he had to kill only one rival, his father. If Oedipus had had a brother with an Oedipus Complex, he would have been compelled to eliminate him too. In Mourning Becomes Electra, O'Neill does just that. In an early version of the trilogy, Orin was a Jamie figure contending for the affections of his mother with a preferred younger brother, Hugh, whose sensitivity marks him as an incarnation of Eugene. In the final draft, O'Neill dropped Hugh and transferred all his qualities to Orin, thus removing a dramatic representation of his rival Jamie from his own Oedipal drama. Similarly, in Long Day's Journey, the first name of the Eugene character was Hugh, and Jamie's first name was Edmund.[18] Here, too, the Eugene character, Hugh, drops his own name and takes over the name of the Jamie character, Edmund. But Jamie, who cannot be excluded from an overt dramatic portrait of the O'Neill family, remains, bearing now his real name.

If O'Neill has introjected his own Oedipus Complex into Mourning Becomes Electra, we can expect Christine Mannon's son Orin to show a strong attraction to the stage mother who so resembles Ella O'Neill and an antipathy for his father. Learning of his father's death, Orin doesn't even pretend to be sorry, and his expressions of affection for his mother appropriate the language of lovers. As he says to Christine in The Hunted: "And I'll never leave you again now. I don't want Hazel or anyone. (With a tender grin) You're my only girl" (90).

It is significant that Orin, like his creator, is fascinated with his mother's hair. As he says to Christine in The Hunted: "And do you remember how you used to let me brush your hair and how I loved to? . . . You've still got the same beautiful hair, Mother" (90). An extraordinary parallel to this fascination occurs in the character Adam Brant. Brant is drawn to both Christine and Lavinia not simply because he sees them as instruments of vengeance against his cousin Ezra Mannon but also because their unusual hair reminds him of his own mother, Marie Brantôme. Brant puts it this way to Lavinia early in *The Homecoming:* "You're so like your mother in some ways. Your face is the dead image of hers. And look at your hair. You won't meet hair like yours and hers again in a month of Sundays. I only know of one other woman who had it. You'll think it strange when I tell you. It was my mother" (22). Then he adds, "Yes, she had beautiful hair like your mother's, that hung down to her knees"—a startling parallel to Mary Tyrone's hair, which she describes in *Long Day's Journey* as being in her youth "so long it came down below my knees" (28). Like O'Neill and his stage avatar Orin, Adam Brant is tall and dark with a mustache. Like both of them he has a fixation on his mother, who bears a striking resemblance to their mothers and to Lavinia, Orin's sister, besides.

Clearly, these facts greatly complicate any Oedipal interpretation of *Mourning Becomes Electra.* Like Orin Mannon, Adam Brant recapitulates O'Neill's Oedipal dilemma but from a different position in the narrative structure of the trilogy. Brant resembles O'Neill physically, and like O'Neill, who in one of the happiest periods of his life served as an able bodied seaman, Brant has a love affair with the sea. His lyrical descriptions to Lavinia of life on the sea and the South Sea Islands (23–24) are prototypes for Edmund's beautiful recounting of his life at sea in *Long Day's Journey* (152–53). Brant's mother, Marie Brantôme, who was the nurse of the Mannon family and whose hair was so like Christine's, seems for several reasons to be modeled, in part, on O'Neill's own governess, Sarah Jane Bucknell Sandy. According to Louis Sheaffer, in real life Sarah Sandy's hair was a reddish gold, the same rare hue that graced the hair of the stage mother Christine Mannon and the nurse Marie Brantôme. Another reason is that O'Neill viewed Sarah Sandy as a second mother in his youth, as can be seen in Sheaffer's reconstruction of an almost illegible diagram of O'Neill's early psychological development the dramatist made while undergoing psychoanalysis. In this diagram the line for nurse love parallels the line for mother love, and when it ends in adolescence O'Neill calls it a mother value. The line of mother love is represented in *Mourning Becomes Electra* by Orin's relationship with Christine, and the line of nurse love as mother love is represented by Adam Brant's love for his mother the nurse Marie Brantôme. Sarah Sandy's influence on O'Neill may have had one other repercussion in the trilogy. She delighted in telling little Eugene macabre tales from real life of murder and scandal, with which motifs *Mourning Becomes Electra* is replete. Interestingly, to judge from Sheaffer's account, Sarah's stories seem to have prominently featured the murder of both kin and spouses.[19]

But in a significant way Ella supersedes Sarah Sandy in O'Neill's portrait of Marie Brantôme. Marie Brantôme's first name is the French equivalent of Mary, Ella O'Neill's true first name and the first name of O'Neill's stage mother, Mary Tyrone, in *Long Day's Journey*. Like Ella O'Neill and Mary Tyrone, Marie Brantôme is married to a man, David Mannon, whose drinking disrupts their marriage and alienates their offspring. As Mary Tyrone and Ella O'Neill suffer from their husbands' stinginess, so Marie Brantôme dies because Ezra Mannon, the trilogy's other representation of James O'Neill, Sr., will not give her money to meet her needs. Louis Sheaffer has pointed out that Ezra Mannon's surname is a pun on Mammon, the biblical word for debasing material wealth, in exchange for which the Mannons have surrendered their souls,[20] and in *Long Day's Journey,* James Tyrone laments the fact that he threw away his great acting talent on the commercial success he found in *Monte Cristo*. By making Orin Mannon a dramatic approximation of himself, O'Neill was able to dramatize his unconsummated Oedipal passion for his mother. But by also projecting himself into the Aegisthus figure Adam Brant, O'Neill was able to portray symbolically the enactment of the Oedipal program, the elimination of the father, and the possession of the mother. It is important to notice the symmetry between Adam Brant and Orin Mannon. Both hate their Mannon fathers and love their mothers. Both unsuccessfully attempt to repudiate the Mannon name and heritage. Brant sees his own hated father in Ezra and his own beloved mother in Christine. By killing Ezra and possessing Christine, he is vicariously eliminating his father and appropriating his mother as he, Orin, and O'Neill wished to do in the reality of their worlds.

If this advances our understanding of the underlying psychological dynamics of the play, it does not explain the position of the Electra figure, Lavinia Mannon, in the center of O'Neill's symbolic schema. Though Lavinia is the fourth Mannon in Ezra's family as Jamie is the fourth O'Neill, and though her interaction with Orin in some ways resembles Jamie's interaction with Eugene—as we shall see—in certain crucial aspects of characterization, she is clearly not Jamie in petticoats. Lavinia is physically modeled on O'Neill's mother figures Christine Mannon and Marie Brantôme, and her erotic alignment in her family is exactly the opposite of Jamie's in his. Jamie hates his father and desires his mother. Lavinia hates her mother and desires her father. That is, she has an Electra Complex.

Geraldine Fitzgerald has argued that Mary Tyrone, just like her real life model Ella O'Neill, had an Electra Complex. "She is what she is because of her sense of guilt. She feels deeply guilty about her relationship with her mother, whom she didn't like, and about her father, whom she adored but who died young."[21] Fitzgerald provides the insight that lets us comprehend Lavinia's position in the symbolic matrix of the drama. O'Neill's Lavinia, like his Christine and his Marie Brantôme, is a covert version of his mother, Ella, but in a different context of relationships. Christine and Marie are both analogues of Ella O'Neill, the mother at odds with her husband and coveted by her rebellious son. Lavinia is a younger version of O'Neill's mother, Ella Quinlan, the girl who adores her father and dislikes her mother. By replacing Jamie with a younger mother figure in this camouflaged version of the O'Neill family, the dramatist exchanged a sibling rival for his mother's affection with a duplicate of the object of his desire, a twofold benefit to the economy of the author's Oedipal psychology.

O'Neill tells us in his notes that when he first contemplated writing a tragedy on a Greek model, he thought of Medea and Electra, but he eventually settled on Electra because, as he wrote in a letter to Robert Sisk, "Electra is to me the most interesting of all women in drama."[22] We are now in a position to speculate about why these heroines came to O'Neill's mind and why he found Electra more intriguing. O'Neill was intent upon recasting the Greek dramatic model. Consciously or not, he was interested in those dramatized myths that most strongly resonated his own familial situation; he was drawn to the myths of the two women, because the person in his family, and in the world, who interested him most was his mother. Medea is a rebellious wife who kills her young sons to spite her husband for turning away from her after bringing her into an alien (in this case, Greek) world. This plot has certain similarities to O'Neill's family history, especially in the light of both Ella's feelings of alienation in her husband's world of theater and the death wishes of both Jamie and Eugene, but Medea's sons are children and therefore their relationship with their mother was too rudimentary to serve O'Neill's purposes. In addition, the story of Medea is not haunted by the sense of a cursed family destiny that hounds both Electra's family and O'Neill's. The fate of the house of Atreus corresponded decisively to the psychological destiny of the O'Neills. As Mary Tyrone puts it in *Long Day's Journey,* when her husband, James, urges her to forget their sorrowful past, including her grievances against him: "Why? How can I? The past is the present, isn't it? It's the future too. We all try to lie out of that but life won't let us" (87). In Electra's story O'Neill found the opportunity to dramatize his own family's hidden relationships and its disastrous collective fate. He chose Aeschylus's version because of its emphasis on destiny, which became the O'Neills' neurotic compulsion to repeat, and the Furies, which he transformed easily into the O'Neill ghosts.

Certain changes were necessary. Appearances to the contrary, Ella O'Neill did not peter out into married banality, and O'Neill's Electra would not either.[23] His mother's emotional barrenness was dramatized as Electra's grim spinsterhood, and O'Neill was led thereby to represent his father and himself in the Atreus plot as the Agamemnon figure Ezra Mannon and the Orestes figure Orin Mannon. But O'Neill, unlike Orestes, desired his mother and resented his father, so O'Neill imposed on Orin and

Ezra the sexual rivalry that existed between Oedipus and his father, Laius, in Freud's interpretation of the myth. To complete the triangle, O'Neill was moved to create an older version of his mother, in one way like Clytemnestra, the hater of her husband, and in another like Jocasta, the beloved of her son. This he was not loathe to do. By projecting himself into the play once again as Adam Brant he was able to recapitulate the whole Oedipal motif as a subplot, an emphasis integral to the effect.

O'Neill's dramatic concept is like a prism, which refracts his image of his mother into three distinct manifestations of the same source whose kinship is marked by their identical hair. This is the ultimate meaning of O'Neill's observation: "Hair of women another recurrent motive—strange, hidden psychic identity of Christine with the dead woman and of Lavinia . . . with her mother."[24] These three women had Ella O'Neill's hair, and by an extension of the playwright's own logic they became identical with his own mother, the woman of anger and sorrows whom mourning indeed becomes.

Louis Sheaffer has pointed out the fundamental contribution that the Freudian dynamics of *Mourning Becomes Electra* makes to the impact of the play: "Its weakness as literature is a prime source of the play's strength as theater, for the schematic Freudian pattern constantly sets the stage for confrontation."[25] Both *Mourning Becomes Electra* and *Long Day's Journey* are incessantly confrontational because both are based on the same enclave of unresolved Freudian conflicts: Both plays depict the same family's desperate internecine warfare for love and power. Thus even distinctions between the two plays often turn out to mask underlying similarities. The Mannon family, for example, is Puritan, whereas the Tyrone family, like the O'Neills, is Irish Catholic. But as Sheaffer has noted, "Of all the national expressions of Catholicism, Irish Catholicism is perhaps the most puritanical."[26] Another illusory difference between the two families is the nature of the capital crisis with which each must contend, the chain of murders and consequent suicides that decimates the Mannon family and the morphine addiction of Mary Tyrone. Yet although these crises seem incommensurable, they soon reveal telling similarities in dramatic function. Both crises arise from the psychological destinies of the families they traumatize, and both constitute terrible secrets that separate the afflicted families from the rest of humanity.

The kinship between the two crises runs even more deeply than this, however, when one seeks the experience in the O'Neill family that might have provided the model for the sexual infidelity of Christine Mannon in *Mourning Becomes Electra*. As far as we know, Ella O'Neill never committed adultery. Nonetheless she was unfaithful to her husband in two significant ways. One was in the hidden desires of her Oedipally fixated sons. Another was in her morphine addiction, by which her husband and children all felt betrayed. It is possible to show that Ella's morphine habit as it worked on Eugene's Oedipal imagination was a psychological model for Christine Mannon's infidelity and the tragic events it inspires.[27]

As a girl, Ella O'Neill, like Christine Mannon, fell in love with her husband-to-be because of his dashing romantic presence. But both women were disillusioned soon after marriage. Christine was repelled by her husband's coldness on their wedding night. Ella was disenchanted by her husband's drinking and the hardships of an actor's life. Consequently, both turned to their young sons, Orin and Eugene, for emotional consolation. After the death in infancy of her second son, Edmund, Ella O'Neill had conceived Eugene only at the insistence of her husband, James. It was a hard birth, and to relieve the chronic pain she experienced afterwards, the family doctor prescribed morphine, to which Ella soon became addicted. For this condition she blamed James O'Neill,[28] as Christine blames Ezra for her unhappy life. Christine responds by taking a lover, Adam Brant. Ella responds by embracing her addiction. In both cases the women act to escape unhappy homes. As Edmund says of Mary Tyrone in *Long Day's Journey* in a statement that probably reflects the author's own judgment of his mother: "You know something inside of her does it deliberately—to get beyond our reach, to be rid of us, to forget we're alive! It's as if, in spite of loving us, she hated us!" (139). In both cases the rest of the family is unanimous in resenting the avenue of escape the woman of the house has chosen.

Like Christine Mannon's sexual infidelity, Ella O'Neill's morphine habit has two aspects, one pleasurable and one destructive. In writing *Mourning Becomes Electra,* O'Neill Oedipally displaced the destructive dimension of Ella's rebellion to the father figure Ezra Mannon. Christine murders her husband with poison, which she pretends is his heart medicine. Horst Frenz and Martin Mueller believed that O'Neill borrowed this incident from the scene in Hamlet in which Claudius pours poison into the ear of Hamlet's father.[29] Whatever influence *Hamlet* had on the poison motif, it has parallels elsewhere in O'Neill's art and life. Her resentful husband often calls Mary Tyrone's morphine "poison" in *Long Day's Journey* (e.g., 78, 123, twice on 139, 142). Mary, Jamie, and Edmund blame the addiction on the stinginess that allegedly led James, Sr., to hire an incompetent doctor to attend Mary, and in *Mourning Becomes Electra,* the Oedipal author turns the poison against the guilty father figure as, in her way, Mary/Ella herself did. As O'Neill significantly remarks in the working notes, poison is a "woman's weapon."[30] Christine uses poison to remove Ezra from her life, as Mary Tyrone uses another poison, morphine, to remove James from her consciousness. In both cases the poison is masquerading as medicine. The seductive pleasure of morphine is displaced by the author with equally Freudian motivation to Christine's experience of her lover, Adam Brant, a projection of the desiring son, Eugene O'Neill.

As Mary Tyrone withdraws psychologically into her morphine haze to experience its raptures, so Christine Mannon withdraws geographically, to

New York, to pursue her affair. In both families the elder sibling learns
first of the mother's secret and informs the younger. As Jamie says to
Edmund in *Long Day's Journey,* "I've known about Mama so much longer
than you. Never forget the first time I got wise. Caught her in the act with
a hypo. Christ, I'd never dreamed before that any women but whores took
dope!" (163). It is important to notice the sexual connotations in this
passage. Jamie caught his mother "in the act"; he associates morphine use
with women engaged in illicit sex, as Christine Mannon had been.

In *Mourning Becomes Electra,* Lavinia catches Christine and Adam in
an adulterous tryst in New York, a parallel to Jamie's walking in on Mary
when she was shooting up. After Christine has poisoned Ezra, she attempts
to negate Lavinia's revelations to Orin by refuting them in advance.
Significantly, she says, "I am no better than a prostitute in your sister's
eyes" (87). When Lavinia confronts Orin with the truth, he is first
disbelieving, then shattered. O'Neill found the truth about his mother no
more easy to take, if we may judge from Edmund's recollection of his
painful discovery in *Long Day's Journey.* He recalls in his response to the
truth about Mary a denial and devastation akin to those in Orin's reaction
to Christine's affair with Brant: "Jamie told me. I called him a liar! I tried
to punch him in the nose. But I knew he wasn't lying. . . . God, it made
everything in life seem rotten!" (118). In both *Mourning Becomes Electra*
and *Long Day's Journey* (when Mary relapses into her habit) the mother
must contend with an accusing elder sibling and a younger sibling who
seeks reassurance that the accusations are false. Her family's suspicions that
she is back on morphine torment Mary Tyrone just as the suspicions of the
other Mannons that she has cheated on Ezra and then killed him torture
Christine. But the analogies do not end there.

When Christine Mannon discovers that Adam Brant is dead, she commits suicide with a pistol because she is unable to live without him. There is
a parallel event in Ella O'Neill's life. In the summer of 1903 she ran out of
morphine, and unable to face life without it, she attempted to drown herself
in the river.[31] The sons of the two women imitate their mothers. Guilty
over the suicide of his mother, Orin too commits suicide with a pistol.
Early in 1912, a few months before the dramatic date of *Long Day's
Journey,* O'Neill attempted suicide in New York. He first planned to drown
himself in the harbor off the Battery (as his mother tried to drown
herself), but he settled instead on an overdose of Veronal, a barbiturate like
morphine.[32] In the autobiographical one-act play that O'Neill wrote on his
suicide attempt in 1919—intriguingly entitled *Exorcism,* perhaps an
allusion to O'Neill's ghosts—the poison *was* morphine. As morphine was
killing his beloved mother, so O'Neill undergoes its effects in his art.
O'Neill eventually destroyed all copies of the play because it was too
autobiographical, an event to which we should compare Orin's retraction
of his gift of the family history in *Mourning Becomes Electra.* But by the
date of the composition of *Exorcism,* Ella's morphine addiction and

O'Neill's Oedipal feelings for her had become associated in his emotional life.

There is an apparent confirmation of such association in an early scenario draft of the trilogy.[33] O'Neill's first name for Adam Brant, whom I have argued to be an O'Neill figure, was Armand, a name curiously similar to Edmund. In an early draft of *The Hunted,* the Lavinia character, still named Elena, decides that *both* Armand and her adulterous mother, still called Clementina, must die for the murder of their father, though Orin thinks that only Armand will be drugged. Both are poisoned with morphine. They go to the bedroom Ezra shared with his wife, a covert dramatic symbol of O'Neill's usurpation of his father. Andre (O'Neill's new name for Armand) lies on the general's bed and sinks into a stupor. Clementina collapses trying to reach the bed as she calls "my lover, my dear lover." Both die reenacting a paradigm of their guilt. Elsewhere, Orin burns with jealousy at the thought of his mother and her lover in bed together but consoles himself with the thought that from the next morning on he will have her all to himself. In this complex fictional transmutation of his own psychological life, O'Neill both punishes himself for his incestuous desires through the death of Andre, his surrogate, and reaffirms them in the hopes of Orin, another surrogate. It is particularly interesting to notice that both Clementina and Andre are poisoned with morphine in the scenario, as Mary Tyrone hoped for an accidental overdose in *Long Day's Journey* and O'Neill's alter ego poisoned himself with morphine in *Exorcism.* The symmetry is not accidental. As symbolic projections of the author and his mother, Armand/Andre and Clementina have consummated O'Neill's hidden desires and must undergo the punishment exacted by his sense of guilt with his mother's own clandestine poison, morphine.

O'Neill gains certain dramatic advantages by having two characters represent the same person in *Mourning Becomes Electra.* By having Christine represent Ella the mother and Lavinia stand for Ella the daughter, O'Neill was able to explore simultaneously quite distinct aspects and phases of his mother in the same dramatic action. Nonetheless, there are implicit logical difficulties in having two characters who stand for the same human being confront one another as rivals in love. O'Neill's kindred rivals resolve this impasse by converging in the end. As his life draws to a close, Orin forgives his mother and Adam Brant and hopes that they find peace together. He is immediately filled with the feeling that his mother has turned back to him, and he rushes off to join her in death. Thus Orin finds happiness with his mother in death by championing his rival, and no wonder, since behind their pointedly similar dramatic masks they are the same Oedipal son. In the same way, Lavinia fills out like her mother and dresses as her mother had dressed. The resemblance strikes everyone who sees them. Orin is so moved that he tries to make love to her. Lavinia struggles to escape her destiny. She repudiates the Mannon name and makes desperate love to Peter Niles, her fiancé. But in the midst of their embrace, she calls him "Adam," the name of her mother's lover. She is after all her mother's daughter, a spiritual and physical duplicate of Christine. In the uncompromising atmosphere of tragedy, such doubles must clash, for they have the same objects of desire. But ultimately their predicament, and that of the O'Neills on whom they are based, is still more profound.

All the Mannon men look alike, as do all the Mannon women. Like James O'Neill the Mannon men are dark, and like Ella O'Neill the Mannon women are fair. Ultimately, the Mannons may be reduced to the same tragic couple. As Orin says to Lavinia in *The Haunted:* "Can't you see I'm now in Father's place and you're Mother? That's the evil destiny out of the past I haven't dared predict! I'm the Mannon you're chained to!" (155). Orin identifies with his father and thus reenacts the family curse. In so doing he exemplifies the tragic fate of both Jamie and Eugene O'Neill. Both rejected their father, the bibulous actor, even as they identified with him. Jamie became a failed actor with a passion for drink, and Eugene, another drinker, wrote plays—in some cases as melodramatic as any his father had ever brought to the stage—which time and again recreated their family dilemma. What is more, in their heart of hearts both boys wanted their father's wife. But in identifying with their father (which paradoxically entailed the desire to displace him), they undertook to reenact a diseased erotic history. The result for both sons was a series of failed relationships and a lasting sadness. This was the psychological destiny on which the modern fate in *Mourning Becomes Electra* was modeled: Because they are what we know, and because we love them, or hate them, or both, we become our parents and relive their lives. In O'Neill's world, the parents do not stand outside the circle of compulsion. Bound to the children they have formed in their own image, the parents share with the children an enduring hell created by mutual wrongs that mutual love will not permit them to escape. From his personal experience of this unbreakable cycle of grief arose O'Neill's dark view of life and his conviction of implacable destiny.

A natural way to pass from the concealed autobiography of the trilogy to the candid autobiography of *Long Day's Journey* is to examine some subtle ways in which *Mourning Becomes Electra* anticipates the later play and to ask what these foreshadowings tell us of the relationship between the two works. In *The Haunted* Orin composes an explicit and damning history of the Mannon family. This he seals in a large envelope and gives for safekeeping to Hazel, so that Lavinia cannot destroy it. Hazel must promise to open it only if Orin dies or Lavinia attempts to marry Peter. When Lavinia agrees to submit to Orin, he reclaims the envelope and the family history remains a secret. I believe that Orin the author represents O'Neill as surely as does Orin the Oedipal son. We know from Louis Sheaffer that O'Neill was extraordinarily secretive about *Mourning Becomes Electra* during its composition.[34] I suggest that this was because he keenly felt that it revealed, in however veiled a fashion, the deepest privileged secrets of his family's psychological life. In its pages are laid bare the incestuous complexes and covert erotic rivalries that tormented the O'Neills. Critics have often remarked that these complexes are too blatantly dramatized and that they do not show the unconsciousness and ambivalence that Freudian theory predicts they would have in real life.[35] But O'Neill was not interested in suppressing or equivocating his family's interior truths in the trilogy. Here he faithfully presents these truths as they had been exposed by his own reflection and his experience of psychoanalysis. What O'Neill does conceal with great effectiveness, however, is the true identity of the family whose transmuted experience is depicted in the work. The passions of the O'Neills are outside of Orin's envelope, but their undisguised story is symbolically sealed within.

In time, O'Neill, like Orin, wrote the explicit story of his house, *Long Day's Journey into Night,* the story prefigured by Orin's sealed manuscript, the truth about the O'Neills to be divulged to the outside world, just as Orin had threatened his dead father with disclosure of the family chronicle.[36] Like Orin, O'Neill chose not to publish his manuscript in his own lifetime. Once Carlotta—who, the director José Quintero tells us, identified with Lavinia—stole O'Neill's text for a few days, as Orin feared that Lavinia would steal his.[37] In an action startlingly like that of his literary counterpart, Eugene O'Neill put the true story of his family in a large envelope, sealed it in the office of his publisher, Bennett Cerf, and his editor, Saxe Commins, and required them to promise not to open it until twenty-five years after his death.[38] In Orin's composition of the undisguised family history of the Mannons, O'Neill had symbolized the task that lay before him, the writing of *Long Day's Journey.* In Orin's concealment of that history in an envelope, O'Neill had expressed the extraordinarily sensitive nature of the family play he would write and his own reluctance to divulge it to the world before all the principals were in the grave. In O'Neill's reenactment of Orin's authorship and concealment he was, according to the logic of his own psychology, both confessional and secretive, fulfilling his own symbolic prophecy, as it may be he had foreseen he would from the start.

When that play was finally unsealed, not twenty-five years after O'Neill's death but two, due to Carlotta's intervention, it became possible to see that *Mourning Becomes Electra* and *Long Day's Journey into Night* are complementary revelations.[39] The trilogy presents with utter candor the most violent and sordid implications of the O'Neills' interior lives but in such a complex and oblique way that the true identity of the protagonists is well protected. *Long Day's Journey* turns *Mourning Becomes Electra* inside out. What was suppressed, the identity of the O'Neills and the outlines of their life, is now transparently extroverted, but what was revealed, the profound sexual dynamics of the family, is now buried and must be inferred from the slight quakes it causes on the surface of the drama. Once we understand that it is appropriate to read the text as a document of sexual jealousy, *Long Day's Journey into Night* appears in a new light.

Early in the play, the father James Tyrone complains that his two sons are always ganging up against him (18). These brothers, Edmund and Jamie, are ostensibly close, as Jamie says (35), but it soon becomes clear that what unites them most intimately is their joint resentment of their father. Allegedly, they object to his parsimonious treatment of their mother, but we may infer that their objection to him is more fundamental than this and that they envy his more intimate possession of a woman who is supremely important to them all. The reason for believing this may be found in the relationship between Edmund and Jamie themselves. Late in the play, Jamie confesses his deep ambivalence, and therefore his deep hatred, for Edmund. He admits that he has tried to destroy his younger brother because of his jealousy over Edmund's preferred position in the family, "Mama's baby, Papa's pet." (165). That his mother is the chief focus for Jamie's jealousy is made clear by the fact that "Mama's baby" comes first in this catalogue of grievances and that the catalogue ends in the charge that the pain of Edmund's birth drove Mary into her morphine addiction. This murderous jealousy of a younger brother over the mother's love is a doublet of the rage that, in Mary's estimation (87), led the young boy Jamie to knowingly expose his infant brother Eugene to his own measles, with fatal results. Jamie resents all rivals for his mother's affection, including his father and his two younger brothers. He is angry with his mother for preferring his rivals to himself and for turning for solace to morphine rather than to him. Edmund, too, resents his mother's morphine addiction, but he turns against Jamie when his elder brother's drunken attacks on Mary grow too bitter. In this his father joins him. Edmund is Mary's baby, and therefore James is jealous of him, but Edmund is younger and less unbridled in his assertion of his erotic instincts than Jamie and thus less threatening to his father's monopoly of the mother. These facts elegantly illustrate that on a fundamental level the basis for contention among the three Tyrone men is the woman of the house.

This erotic rivalry is a key to the fullest understanding of the ending of *Long Day's Journey into Night*. Mary, lost in the morphine world where she has escaped the three demanding and troublesome men in her life, is again a virginal schoolgirl. She has entered the room dragging her old wedding dress, but she allows James to take it without protest and treats him as a stranger, with shy politeness. In so doing she temporarily relinquishes the marriage that unhappily linked her with a hard-drinking actor and produced the two now-grown rivals for her affection. As Edmund tries vainly to bring her back to reality by telling her the truth about his consumption, Mary resists the attempts of her son to touch her with the words: "You must not try to touch me. You must not try to hold me. It isn't right, when I am hoping to become a nun" (174). Mary appears to "misunderstand" the touch of a son as the touch of a would-be lover, but on a deeper level there is no misunderstanding: The two are one. As she stands there, remote from them all, the three fascinated men *"slowly lower their drinks to the table, forgetting them "*(175), for their obsession with this woman is even more compelling than their dependence on whiskey.

In her reverie, Mary tells of her girlhood ambition to become a nun—and thus to avoid the world of adult sexuality. But her confidante, the wise nun Mother Elizabeth, surmised the sensual nature of the naive girl and advised her to put herself to a test by living for a time in the world of a normal young woman, going to parties and dances, that is, exposing herself to the attractions of men. Soon after, Mary recalls, she chose a path different from what she had intended, and in this recollection she returns to the inexorable reality of the family destiny: "That was in the winter of senior year. Then in the spring something happened to me. Yes, I remember. I fell in love with James Tyrone and was so happy for a time. (*She stares before her in a sad dream. Tyrone stirs in his chair. Edmund and Jamie remain motionless*)" (176).

James stirs because he has a share in this part of the dream. He was the man who made love to this beautiful girl in the spring, the season of mating, before their offspring had come into being. Edmund and Jamie had no place in the aboriginal joy of the union, as their stillness signifies. The distinction in the stage directions between action of the father and the inaction of his sons in their response to Mary's monologue points to the dissymmetry of the father and his sons in the Oedipal dilemma of the Tyrones. The father and the sons occupy fundamentally different places in the family structure. Until the sons renounce even the dissembled erotic competition with their father for the sexual possession of the mother, the family will not know peace. The Tyrones' relentless compulsion to repeat, which pulsates like a drumbeat in *Long Day's Journey,* persuades us that ultimately neither Edmund nor Jamie can forgo his impossible yearning and the unquenchable conflict that results is at the very heart of the tragedy of the house.[40]

In both *Mourning Becomes Electra* and *Long Day's Journey into Night,* Eugene O'Neill has thus inserted Oedipal portraits of himself, his father, and his mother.[41] In *Mourning Becomes Electra,* the Oedipal dynamics of the O'Neill family can be forthrightly portrayed because the original identities of the characters are well disguised by being split into multiple personae simultaneously identified with archetypal characters from Greek myth and fictionalized characters set in postbellum New England. In contrast, the characters in *Long Day's Journey into Night* are transparently drawn from members of O'Neill's own family; therefore he feels constrained to represent the sexual tensions between them in a realistic, that is, repressed, manner so subtly executed as to elude detection by those unalerted to their presence. The plays are in fact companion pieces united by common themes and a peculiar reciprocity: Each suppresses what the other reveals and reveals what the other suppresses. Taken together, the two plays form an astonishing and courageous recreation of a family that, through the genius of its youngest member, has become, like the houses of Atreus and Oedipus to which it was assimilated, one of the most important in the history of drama.

NOTES

This essay was first published in *Papers on Language and Literature* 25, no. 3 (Spring 1989). Copyright © 1989 by the Board of Trustees, Southern Illinois University. Reprinted by permission. Minor changes in style and documentation have been made to enable the reprinted text to conform in format with the rest of the volume.

1. Louis Sheaffer, *O'Neill: Son and Artist* (Boston: Little, Brown and Co., 1973), 372.

2. All page references to *Mourning Becomes Electra* are taken from *The Plays of Eugene O'Neill*, vol. 2 (New York: Random House, Inc., Modern Library, 1982).

3. Eugene O'Neill, *Long Day's Journey into Night* (New Haven: Yale University Press, 1955), 7.

4. Virginia Floyd, *The Plays of Eugene O'Neill: A New Assessment* (New York: Frederick Ungar Publishing Co., 1987), 390–91.

5. Ibid., 532–33.

6. In *Eugene O'Neill's New Language of Kinship* (Syracuse: Syracuse University Press, 1982), Michael Manheim underscored the critic's problem in biographically analyzing *Mourning Becomes Electra*: "It [the *Oresteia*] was a ready-made vessel for O'Neill to fill with the various and contradictory facets of his personal agony, but at the same time its precise events were such that it is difficult to recognize O'Neill's own story in them" (77).

7. Floyd, *Plays of Eugene O'Neill,* 392.

8. Doris M. Alexander, "Psychological Fate in *Mourning Becomes Electra,*" *Publications of the Modern Language Association* 68, no. 5 (December 1953): 923–34; Travis Bogard, *Contour in Time: The Plays of Eugene O'Neill* (New York: Oxford University Press, 1972), 344–47.

9. Sheaffer, *O'Neill: Son and Artist,* 190. In his two-part article, "The Psychoanalyzing of Eugene O'Neill," *Modern Drama* 3, no. 3 (December 1960): 242–56; and "The Psychoanalyzing of Eugene O'Neill: Part Two," *Modern Drama* 3, no. 4 (February 1961): 357–72, Arthur H. Nethercot treats with justifiable skepticism O'Neill's well-known reluctance to connect his dramaturgy with Freudian analysis.

10. Eugene O'Neill, *Welded,* in *The Plays of Eugene O'Neill,* vol. 2, 489 (see n. 2).

11. Croswell Bowen, "The Black Irishman," in *O'Neill and His Plays: Four Decades of Criticism,* ed. Oscar Cargill, N. Bryllion Fagin, and William J. Fisher (New York: New York University Press, 1961), 77.

12. Virginia Floyd, ed., *Eugene O'Neill at Work: Newly Released Ideas for Plays* (New York: Frederick Ungar Publishing Co., 1981), 187.

13. Louis Sheaffer, *O'Neill: Son and Playwright* (Boston: Little, Brown and Co., 1968), 15; Arthur Gelb and Barbara Gelb, *O'Neill* (New York: Harper and Row, 1962), plate page facing 266; Sheaffer, *O'Neill: Son and Playwright,* 6 (upper photograph).

14. Sheaffer, *O'Neill: Son and Playwright,* 6 (lower photograph).

15. Bogard, *Contour in Time,* 436.

16. Sheaffer, *O'Neill: Son and Playwright,* 18.

17. For some of the many parallels between *Long Day's Journey* and O'Neill's life, parallels important to this chapter, see Sheaffer, *O'Neill: Son and Playwright,* ix, xiii, 3–4, 16, 20–21, 24, 27, 35, 45, 48–49, 70, 79, 81, 89, 111, 133, 165, 197, 199, 216, 222,

235, 241–42, 245, 280; and idem, *O'Neill: Son and Artist*, ix, 5, 23, 27, 39, 40, 77, 86–87, 169, 191, 209, 250, 309, 357, 411, 482–83, 499, 505–6, 510–17, 528, 530, 673.

18. Pointed out in Floyd, *Plays of Eugene O'Neill*, 391; idem, *Eugene O'Neill at Work*, 285.

19. See Sheaffer, *O'Neill: Son and Playwright*, 23, 55–58, 63, 506.

20. Sheaffer, *O'Neill: Son and Artist*, 338.

21. Geraldine Fitzgerald, "Another Neurotic Electra: A New Look at Mary Tyrone," in *Eugene O'Neill: A World View*, ed. Virginia Floyd (New York: Frederick Ungar Publishing Co., 1979), 291–92.

22. Eugene O'Neill, "Working Notes and Extracts from a Fragmentary Diary," in *The Unknown O'Neill: Unpublished or Unfamiliar Writings of Eugene O'Neill*, ed. Travis Bogard (New Haven: Yale University Press, 1988), 394; letter to Robert Sisk, 28 August 1930, quoted by Floyd, *Eugene O'Neill at Work*, 185.

23. In "Working Notes," 394, O'Neill complained of Electra: "In Greek story she peters out into an undramatic married banality. Such a character contained far too much tragic fate within her soul to permit this—why should Furies have let Electra escape unpunished?"

24. O'Neill, "Working Notes," 398.

25. Sheaffer, *O'Neill: Son and Artist*, 371.

26. Sheaffer, *O'Neill: Son and Playwright*, 101.

27. In *Eugene O'Neill's New Language of Kinship*, Manheim (78–79) has noted in passing the similarity between Christine's adulterous affair and Mary's preoccupation with morphine: "Nor are the attributes of Mary's addiction far removed from those of Christine's desire for Adam."

28. See Sheaffer, *O'Neill: Son and Playwright*, 3–25.

29. Horst Frenz and Martin Mueller, "More Shakespeare and Less Aeschylus in Eugene O'Neill's *Mourning Becomes Electra*," *American Literature* 38, no. 1 (May 1966): 85–100.

30. O'Neill, "Working Notes," 395.

31. Sheaffer, *O'Neill: Son and Playwright*, 89.

32. Ibid., 208.

33. Floyd, *Eugene O'Neill at Work*, 200–202.

34. Sheaffer, *O'Neill: Son and Artist*, 354ff.

35. See especially Alexander, "Psychological Fate in *Mourning Becomes Electra*," 927.

36. Manheim also believed that Orin's manuscript prefigures O'Neill's autobiographical *Long Day's Journey* (*Eugene O'Neill's New Language of Kinship*, 82–88), but he did not discuss the uncanny ways in which Orin's struggle to control his confessional manuscript parallels O'Neill's later struggle to control the manuscript of *Long Day's Journey*.

37. José Quintero, "Carlotta and the Master," *New York Times Magazine*, 1 May 1988, 62, 64.

38. Sheaffer, *O'Neill: Son and Artist*, 560, 634–35; Gelb and Gelb, *O'Neill*, 861–63. In a later note to Bennett Cerf, O'Neill wrote of *Long Day's Journey*, "That, as you know, is to be published twenty-five years after my death—but never produced as a play." (Sheaffer, *O'Neill: Son and Artist*, 635). In seeking by authorial fiat forever to bar *Long Day's Journey* from the stage, O'Neill reaffirmed his keen sense of revealing through the play the sensitive and intimate psychic secrets of his family.

39. Sheaffer (*O'Neill: Son and Artist*, 357) has seen something of the profound kinship between the two plays: "His (O'Neill's) constant allusions in the diary [the working notes for *Mourning Becomes Electra*] to the family or the past as 'fate' indicate that his mind was working along the same lines that eventually would produce *Long Day's Journey into Night*." But Sheaffer did not interpret the trilogy as detailed autobiographical art and called it "one of his less subjective works" (*O'Neill: Son and Artist*, 372).

40. It is not necessarily my intention in advancing a sexual interpretation of *Long Day's Journey* to repudiate non-Oedipal interpretations of the play, and I certainly do not

mean to suggest that the Oedipal meaning of the work is its only meaning. *Long Day's Journey into Night* is a complex masterpiece that can accommodate a host of distinct but complementary interpretations.

41. In "Conscious and Unconscious Autobiographical Dramas of Eugene O'Neill," *Journal of the American Psychoanalytic Association* 5, no. 3 (July 1957): 432–60, a study with obvious affinities to this article, Philip Weissman treated *Long Day's Journey into Night* as a conscious act of autobiography in which O'Neill has, perhaps inadvertently, revealed his Oedipus Complex, but he viewed *Desire Under the Elms* as an unconscious and fictionalized act of autobiography in which Eben's Oedipus Complex is a camouflaged transmutation of the author's own fixation on his mother. Weissman did not analyze the Oedipal matrix of *Long Day's Journey* in any detail, however, and he said virtually nothing about *Mourning Becomes Electra*. Nonetheless, by exploring an example of O'Neill's fictionalized treatment of his own Oedipus Complex in *Desire Under the Elms*, a play written a few years before *Mourning Becomes Electra*, Weissman prepared the way for my autobiographical analysis of the later play.

Part Three
O'Neill Onstage

12

O'Neill's Stage Directions and the Actor

Jeffrey Elliott Sands

Harold Bloom ended a survey of a group of distinguished critical essays on O'Neill's *Long Day's Journey into Night* with "the prophecy that O'Neill, and *Long Day's Journey* in particular, need a different kind of literary criticism of drama than anything we now have, a criticism that might be able to deal more adequately with O'Neill's eloquence of gestures and groupings, which seems to me so much more intense than his more limited rhetorical eloquence."[1] As one grounded more in the theater than literary exegesis, I have reached the same conclusion from a different direction. O'Neill was a man of the theater, and his success must be comprehended in theatrical terms if it is to be really understood at all. This chapter aspires to explore the nature, aims, and methods of a fundamentally dramatic criticism of Eugene O'Neill.

We have available to us a long and detailed account of Eugene O'Neill's relations with actors, directors, and producers, and the story is not always a happy one. From his earliest days with the Provincetown Players on Cape Cod to his final collaboration with the Theatre Guild, America's greatest playwright found reasons to quarrel with those people responsible for placing his work before a live audience. Anecdotal evidence of this conflict abounds in the biographies by Louis Sheaffer and by Arthur Gelb and Barbara Gelb, and additional facts turn up in John Henry Raleigh's *The Plays of Eugene O'Neill*, Helen Deutsch and Stella Hanau's history of the Provincetown, and a variety of other sources.[2] Put in simplest terms, O'Neill never much liked the way actors and others presented his plays.

We can make of this what we choose, and it all holds great interest for us in purely historical terms. Beyond the history itself, however, O'Neill's stormy relations with those who interpreted his plays in the theater may provide the key to a better and more thorough understanding of one of the most fascinating aspects of his plays: the stage directions. It is possible to study the stage directions from a wholly practical and theatrical vantage point. If we accept—and the historical record indicates we must—that

O'Neill never felt satisfied that theater artists, particularly actors, understood his characters and the ways in which he wanted them played, we can use this notion as a model for taking the stage directions seriously. By this I mean approaching the stage directions from the perspective of the stage, as a body of instructions designed to guide the recalcitrant—or merely dense—actor in the "proper" interpretation and presentation of the character.

This is not easy to do. One must confront and reconcile the critical traditions that have long held sway over most discussions on the subject. Throughout the years, a rich and insightful body of commentary has grown up around O'Neill's plays; yet the stage directions have received precious little attention, serious or otherwise. When scholars and critics have taken up the issue, they have tended to do so primarily in terms of thematic or other strictly literary considerations. Because they have had other goals in mind, students of O'Neill have chosen not to examine the stage directions from what seems to me the obvious standpoint: their relevance and importance to the actor. To begin, then, I shall try to establish a perspective on the stage directions that focuses directly and specifically on the actor. Then I shall utilize this critical groundwork for a discussion of one way they may be applied to questions of stage presentation.

Historically, many critics have presumed that the stage directions were intended by O'Neill as a guide to the reader of his plays. In the November 1931 edition of *Theatre Arts Monthly,* for example, we find two articles denigrating the stage directions according to such a criterion. In the first of these articles, John Anderson complained, "Impatient, usually, at trying to express his meaning through actors [O'Neill] has, again and again, reached beyond them to the audience and even to the reader. His plays are strewn with descriptions and opinions which, in the theatre, get no further than the eye of the director or of the cast, but which count full value under the lamp."[3] In the second article, Virgil Geddes—certainly no fan of O'Neill's—more or less echoed Anderson, charging that the playwright used "the methods of the novelist" and repeatedly resorted to "writing which never shows on the stage."[4]

Edmund Wilson had earlier blasted the stage directions, again presuming they had been written for the reader. His comments, though, attacked O'Neill from a different angle: "As a rule, the plays of O'Neill are singularly uninviting on the printed page. The dialogue is raw and prosaic, in texture quite undistinguished, and the author has made no attempt to appeal to the imagination by way of the stage directions, which are not lifted above the baldness of the prompt book."[5]

Anderson and Geddes contended that O'Neill used the stage directions as a means of overcoming an inability to convey his ideas through the traditional conduits of the stage, the actors. If he could not get his characters to say what he meant, they imply, he could "cheat" by explaining things to the reader outside the fictive frame of the plays. Wilson, too, questioned O'Neill's power to express meaning through character. In the process, however, he placed the stage directions on the same level as dialogue. Both are literary components of a published play. In both cases, the idea that the stage directions hold meaning for the actor in terms of *his* art receives no consideration. Hence, according to this view, they must be judged in the context of their appeal to the reader.

Inherent in this "reader's perspective" is the tendency to examine and discuss the plays according to literary criteria. Perhaps the most penetrating and thorough analysis along these lines comes from John Henry Raleigh. In his book he discoursed on various fascinating aspects of O'Neill's dramaturgy, all of which have as their point of departure considerations that have little or no connection to the plays as scripts for performance. Summarizing his work in a very simplified manner, we see that Raleigh's chapters include "Cosmology and Geography," which looks at the plays' statements about the construction of the universe and man's place in it; "History" illustrates the ways in which O'Neill employed the plays' historical settings to comment on philosophy, mores, and social structure at various times in the past; "Mankind" focuses on the human condition according to O'Neill. In the fourth chapter, Raleigh turned to "Form," which at least offers the opportunity to take up matters of the stage, but here again he devoted most of his discussion to literary concerns such as "language" and "structure."

Under "language," though, Raleigh did spend several pages going over some of the salient characteristics of the stage directions and thereby approached a theatrical perspective. He had high praise for most of what O'Neill placed in the parentheses. "In writing stage directions O'Neill was consistently effective, from first to last. . . . Throughout his career O'Neill had no difficulty in describing natural objects, i.e., his settings, with great accuracy and vividness."[6] He went on to assert that O'Neill's "stage directions describing human beings are acute, detailed, and psychologically convincing."[7] Following this, however, Raleigh treated the issues of language in rhetorical terms: word choices, repetitions, dialect, poetic meter, symbolic connotations.

Distinctions between dialogue and stage directions received little acknowledgment. Throughout the study, Raleigh drew upon the two in virtually identical ways to discover the important literary ideas inherent in his choice of chapter titles. In "Mankind," for example, he turned to *All God's Chillun Got Wings* as part of a larger discussion of O'Neill's concerns about racial assimilation in America. This play, Raleigh demonstrated, handles the racial question in the context of the urban black experience:

Even when one is intelligent and educated, there is still no escape from the psychological malaise. Jim's sister Hattie is described as a woman of thirty, intelligent, courageous, even powerful, but high-strung and dressed in a severe and mannish manner. . . . For Hattie the whites must always be "them." All Negroes, no matter how determined, fall under the mother's somber generalization: 'Dey ain't many strong. Dey ain't many happy neider.'[8]

Here stage directions and dialogue serve the common end of elucidating a sociopolitical problem treated in the play. Raleigh believed the character description of Hattie has significance; yet from his perspective this relates to an intellectual issue. He did not examine the possibility that the character description he cited has a practical application for the actress Hattie. Of course he didn't—that is not what he was after here.

None of this is to criticize Raleigh. His book is one of the most important full-length studies of O'Neill that we are fortunate enough to possess. Rather, the point is that scholars have traditionally approached O'Neill from the reader's perspective and, as such, have justifiably treated the stage directions as part of the literary form and content of the plays. That is perfectly reasonable. But it does not help us to take the stage directions seriously in terms of the stage; the plays become literature, and their theatrical qualities, although not necessarily suffering, go unappreciated and unexamined. More than that, this perspective actually sets up a peculiar critical inertia that dwells on the literary and either obscures or precludes consideration of the theatrical.

Indeed, aside from production histories, only two full-length studies demonstrate a heightened awareness of O'Neill's theatrical potentialities: *O'Neill's Scenic Images* by Timo Tiusanen and *A Drama of Souls: Studies in O'Neill's Super-naturalistic Technique* by Egil Törnqvist.[9] The former examines the playwright's construction of "scenic units," which Tiusanen defined as "a specific kind of scenic means of expression, characteristic of the playwright in question and used by him as an element in constructing scenic images."[10] Tiusanen thus gave serious credence to the theatrical impulse behind O'Neill's writing, and he forthrightly acknowledged the importance of the fact that O'Neill created specifically and exclusively for the stage.[11] This is a definite step in the direction of a theatrical perspective: The *basis* for Tiusanen's work derives from the idea of stage presentation. The *aim* of his study, on the other hand, has more in common with the literary perspective: "A *scenic image* is a scene (or, more often, part of a scene) in which several scenic means of expression are used to achieve an effect charged with thematic significance."[12] Like Raleigh, Tiusanen was after something other than the stage directions' relevance to the actor. He shared with Raleigh an ultimate concern for the receiver of the play, although in this case the scholar implied that the receiver may be either the reader or the spectator. At least we are sitting in the auditorium; still, the object is to stand on the stage.

We can see how strongly the literary perspective holds sway over even those who apparently set out to look at O'Neill's theatrical technique. In a curious passage, Tiusanen practically dismissed the stage directions in less than two full pages. He began: "Careful stage directions are a common feature all through the O'Neill canon, so we might just as well deal with them right now."[13] As if to get the stage directions out of the way so that he can proceed with more pressing business, Tiusanen laid out a few of the strong points and flaws that characterize them. His comments are most instructive, however, particularly toward the end of the discussion:

Their language is not polished, and they are full of cliches: the word 'dully' is repeated in almost every play. Yet the directions serve their purpose and give testimony to the fact that the idea of the stage was actively and continuously present in O'Neill's mind during the process of writing. Along with an enjoyment in expressing his feeling about life went an interest in the structure of the play and in the theatre itself. . . .
    . . . They have been appreciated by others, who sense the love and care which motivated them: even if "his written instructions about characters turning pale or sweating . . . seem pointless and impossible to project, they are actually important road signs for the intelligent actor, and many of O'Neill's actors have expressed gratitude for them." Seeing them as "road signs" rather than absolute laws is the most sensible approach, for directors as well as actors. Critics, too, have reason to be grateful for them, because they help to clarify our picture of the dramatist's vision.[14]

The reference to "road signs" comes from the biography by Arthur Gelb and Barbara Gelb.[15] It is a very telling metaphor.

So, here we find the first positive reference to the stage directions as they relate to "O'Neill's actors," and Tiusanen—and the Gelbs—shift the perspective several more degrees toward our new direction. Whereas at first Tiusanen wrote of the reader–spectator range of receivers, he finally came to discuss the spectator–actor dichotomy. These relationships have also been explored by Egil Törnqvist, who managed a neat synthesis of the stage directions' importance to the reader, spectator, and actor. "It would clearly be absurd," he maintained, "to argue that O'Neill wrote solely for the reader." Rather, he continued,

We must assume that he meant the published plays to function not merely as reading matter but also as texts for future productions. And even of the passages that seem directed primarily to the general reader we cannot feel sure that they are not meant as much for the actor and director. Thus . . . he is, I believe, doing two things at the same time. He is explaining the significance of the characters' actions to the *reader* to help him do a better production in his mind. And he is providing "road signs for the intelligent actor" to help him do a better production for the *spectator*. To what extent we consider [these] stage directions . . . [as] primarily meant for the general reader or for the actor and thus, indirectly, for the spectator, depends on to what extent we consider them realizable in the theater.[16]

Törnqvist's triumvirate of reader–spectator–actor identifies the intricate connection amongst the stage directions' several possible functions. It also allows for the final refinement and statement of the actor's perspective. It is my opinion that he did not ask the right question, and I would offer this in its place: Of what value are the stage directions to the actor in the preparation and presentation of his role?

To answer this question we can look at the stage directions' dynamics as they relate to one of the more essential issues of playing O'Neill's characters on the stage: the quality of emotional expression. In the climactic fourth act of *Anna Christie,* Mat Burke returns to the barge to face Anna and her sordid past. He is, the stage direction tells the actor, quite drunk: *"His eyes are bloodshot and heavy-lidded, his face has a bloated look. But beyond these appearances—the results of heavy drinking—there is an expression in his eyes of wild mental turmoil, of impotent animal rage baffled by its own abject misery."*[17] It is not so much a matter of "beyond these appearances" as because of them. The rage goes hand in hand with the alcoholic state. In the action that follows, O'Neill takes advantage of Burke's inebriation to throw the actor one emotionally intense stage direction after another. Confronting directions such as *"his face suddenly convulsed with grief and rage," "raging"*(68), *"then with sudden wild grief"* (69) and *"overcome by rage again"* (71), the actor is faced with an unusually high level of emotional energy and expression. It all comes across as overdone at points, and the actor carrying out O'Neill's instructions might strain the patience and credulity of the audience had he not previously established the context: Burke is drunk.

The real point here, though, is not whether someone would act as Burke does were he not drunk but that the stage directions set the level of emotion intensity in this scene. The quality of emotional expression is at least partly determined by not the dialogue but the stage directions.

Now, O'Neill almost habitually wrote extremely emotional characterizations into his plays, and they often threaten to go overboard even in the absence of some justifying influence such as alcohol. Take the hero of *The First Man*. As his wife endures the child delivery that will soon take her own life, Curtis Jayson engages in a bit of melodramatics:

(There is a pause. Then CURTIS *lifts his head and peers about the room. Seeing he is alone he springs to his feet and begins to pace back and forth, his teeth clenched, his features working convulsively. Then, as if attracted by an irresistible impulse, he goes to the closed door and puts his ear to the crack. He evidently hears his wife's moans for he starts away—in agony.)* CURTIS. Oh, Martha, Martha! Martha, darling! *(He flings himself in the chair by the fireplace—hides his face in his hands and sobs bitterly).*[18]

It would be hard to argue with Tiusanen, who complained that "as a rule, the behavior of the characters in [*The First Man*] consists of that queer mixture of hysterical gestures and conventionality met only in full-blown melodramas."[19] *The First Man* is just that, a melodrama. This disreputable term dogged O'Neill throughout his career, and it is important that we examine the role of melodrama in his writing and in the critical literature about his plays if we are to understand the centrality of the stage directions to the quality of emotional expression in the actor's characterizations.

George Jean Nathan, one of O'Neill's staunchest defenders and a close personal friend, could not help stating his conviction that America's greatest playwright was sometimes unable to distinguish "intensification from mere bald overemphasis and exaggeration."[20] O'Neill himself partly acknowledged this feature of his writing, but he characteristically took elaborate pains to defend himself. In a letter to Nathan he maintained that he applied the emotional traits of melodrama in a manner wholly in keeping with the perspectives of his characters. Regarding *Anna Christie,* for example, he argued that ordinary people in the grip of unusual, overpowering emotions imitate the characters of fiction and the cinema in expressing what they feel, "that is, that in moments of great stress life copies melodrama."[21]

This convenient line of reasoning does not exonerate O'Neill of the repeated charges that a streak of melodrama ran throughout his writing; nor, say some critics, was it simply a matter of style. In reference to his plots, for example, Doris Falk saw melodrama in some of his very best work. *A Moon for the Misbegotten,* she pointed out, has a story line lifted right out of the nineteenth century's popular drama. The dissipated landlord threatens to foreclose on the lease of the poor farmer, who then schemes to offer up his virgin daughter in order to save the family home. Falk rightly branded this "the theatrical cliché of clichés, for which there is no other word but corn."[22]

In his comments about melodramas, Eric Bentley pointed out that such plays are filled with "goodness beset by badness, a hero beset by a villain, heroes and heroines beset by a wicked world."[23] Overall, we should be more hard put to find O'Neill plays that do *not* meet Bentley's criteria than those which do. Evidence abounds; yet we should not hasten to judge O'Neill a melodramatist, nor should we be quick to claim we know the reasons for those melodramatic qualities that we are able to detect. Bernard Beckerman, in *The Dynamics of Drama,* recognized "strong swings of intensity" as one important feature of melodrama, thus suggesting that emotion does play a determining role.[24] Francis Fergusson, who believed there is a melodramatic element to all of O'Neill's plays, also attributed this to a special quality of the playwright's approach to emotion:

I take it that the essence of melodrama is to accept emotions uncritically; which, in the writing, amounts to assuming or suggesting emotions that are never realized either in language or action. Melodrama in this sense is a constant quality in Mr. O'Neill's work. . . . Nevertheless, his naive belief in emotion is related to a priceless quality, which one may call the histrionic sincerity, the essence of mummery. Every dramatist as well as every actor depends for his power over his audience on his own belief in what he is trying to put on the stage, whether it be an emotion, a character, or a situation. An audience is extremely malleable. It may be swayed by suggestion, hypnotized by the concentration of the stage figure. This complete concentration, which would be wrecked by a wakeful critical faculty or a touch of humor at the wrong moment, Mr. O'Neill possesses in a very high degree. It is the secret of his success; and when it is joined to an interest in character, it produces his best scenes.[25]

It distills down, I believe, to a question of "sincerity," the antithesis of calculation (which few have charged O'Neill with possessing to any significant degree). Sincerity presents a constant danger to the artist; it can lead to overstatement and exaggeration. Without it, though, few artists can produce or have produced compelling works of lasting value and meaning. O'Neill, as Fergusson has discovered, possessed an abundance of sincerity, and he expressed this quality predominantly through the uncritical emotions of his characters.

Emotion is the key, and there can be little doubt that it exerts a predominant presence in O'Neill's plays. John Hutchens referred to him simply as "an emotional writer."[26] Virginia Floyd credited the "intensity of his personal emotion" for the effectiveness of his best work.[27] John Mason Brown, as is so often the case, put it most succinctly: "Although poetry may have eluded him, passion and an undeniable grandeur were his."[28] If O'Neill bordered on melodrama, we must concede that melodrama can sometimes, in the right hands, work very well. In turn, we must recognize his emphasis on emotion as one of the most important reasons he found the genre so personally compelling, as in the case of Anna, and so very hard to avoid when expressing his own deep feelings about any of his characters.

We have admitted the presence of an intense emotional quality in O'Neill's plays conducive to melodrama, but exactly how is that emotion created? It would be best to begin with a play—and a certain scene in that play—that I believe most would agree fits the melodramatic label rather well. In Act two, scene two of *The Straw,* written in 1919, Stephen Murray tries to comfort Eileen Carmody. Dying of tuberculosis, Eileen has turned to Stephen for love but finds him unable to return her feelings. To drive home how essential the stage directions in this scene are to its theatrical meaning and expression, I will reproduce first the dialogue alone, without the directions. In those instances in which the stage directions include a blocking instruction, I have substituted for O'Neill's words simple, emotionally neutral, descriptions of the physical actions for which he calls:

MURRAY. . . I'm glad you're free of him [i.e., a former boyfriend, though Stephen is speaking obliquely of himself as well], for your own sake. I knew he wasn't the person. You must get one of the right sort—next time.
EILEEN. (*rises*) Stephen!
MURRAY. He wasn't good enough—to lace your shoes—nor anyone else, either.
EILEEN. Don't be silly. (*Pause*) Well, I've told you—all there is. I might as well go back.
MURRAY. Yes. You mustn't lose too much sleep. I'll come to your cottage in the morning to say good-bye. They'll permit that, I guess.
EILEEN. (*takes a few steps stage right*) Good night, Stephen.
MURRAY. Good night, Eileen.
EILEEN. (*crosses right, stops, turns and crosses left to him*) Stephen!
MURRAY. (*as she puts her arms around him*) Eileen![29]

Here is the scene as O'Neill wrote it, stage directions and all:

MURRAY. . . I'm glad you're free of him, for your own sake. I knew he wasn't the person. (*With an attempt at a joking tone*) You must get one of the right sort—next time.
EILEEN. (*springing to her feet with a cry of pain*) Stephen! (*He avoids her eyes which search his face pleadingly.*)
MURRAY. (*mumbling*) He wasn't good enough—to lace your shoes—nor anyone else, either.

EILEEN. (*with a nervous laugh*) Don't be silly. (*After a pause, during which she waits hungrily for some words from him—with a sigh of despair—faintly*) Well, I've told you—all there is. I might as well go back.

MURRAY. (*not looking at her—indistinctly*) Yes. You mustn't lose too much sleep. I'll come to your cottage in the morning to say good-bye. They'll permit that, I guess.

EILEEN. (*stands looking at him, imploringly, her face convulsed with anguish, but he keeps his eyes fixed on the rocks at his feet. Finally she seems to give up and takes a few uncertain steps up the road toward the right—in an exhausted whisper*) Good night, Stephen.

MURRAY. (*his voice choked and husky*) Good night, Eileen.

EILEEN. (*walks weakly up the road but, as she passes the signpost, she suddenly stops and turns to look again at* MURRAY *who has not moved or lifted his eyes. A great shuddering sob shatters her pent-up emotions. She runs back to* MURRAY, *her arms outstretched, with a choking cry*) Stephen!

MURRAY. (*startled, whirls to face her and finds her arms thrown around his neck—in a terrified tone*) Eileen!

The dialogue tells only a part of the story. Any reasonably competent and intelligent actor could probably infer from the action leading up to this scene the importance of the moment and consequently attempt to inject a relatively high degree of emotional intensity into the dialogue. The dialogue alone, however, simply does not indicate the full level of intensity that O'Neill seems to have intended. The springing to the feet, the cries of pain, the despair, the convulsions, the sobs, the choking—they are not present, or even implied in the dialogue. The way in which the actors speak their lines far outweighs the words themselves in terms of conveying the dramatic and theatrical meaning of the scene. As John Mason Brown said, O'Neill compensates for his lack of poetry with an undeniable passion—a passion that resides within parentheses.

In an article in the *Sewanee Review* in 1935, the critic Edd Winfield Parks wrote that "emotion is language, and the two must be subtly fused into one. Without this fusion, the actor talks about, but never reveals, his emotion. . . . [O'Neill] has consistently refused to put into the mouths of his characters a language which would carry his shades of meaning."[30] Yes, a playwright necessarily relies on language to carry his meaning, but there is more to his craft than that. In the theater, on the stage, the clear delineation and communication of meaning involve, in a wonderful, infinite variety of ratios, a combination of telling and showing. The words themselves that the actors speak—the dialogue—tell, whereas the tone of the actor's voice, the volume at which he speaks, the visual components of his portrayal—facial expression, gestures, posture, movements around the stage—show the audience what is going on in the world of the play. Parks may have been right in that words often failed O'Neill, but he almost never came up short when he set out to show his audiences the lives of his characters, their inner emotions, their reactions to their situation, their relationships with the other characters. We can move away from O'Neill's familiar problems with language, then, and adopt a more reasoned approach: the balancing of this deficiency against his great talent for showing.

Consider this passage from Act three of *A Moon for the Misbegotten*. Jamie Tyrone and Josie Hogan have been slowly and awkwardly working themselves toward the sexual expression of their love for each other. Both steel themselves with a drink. With the dialogue removed and only the stage directions remaining, we can see how brilliantly O'Neill manages to show—rather than tell—the complex interaction that this scene comprises:

TYRONE. (*stares at her—then shrugs his shoulders*) . . . (*He pours a big drink into her tumbler . . .*)
JOSIE. (*ashamed but defiant—stiffly*) . . . (*She raises her glass mockingly*) . . .
(TYRONE *is staring at her, a strange, bitter disgust in his eyes. Suddenly he slaps at her hand, knocking the glass to the ground*)
TYRONE. (*his voice hard with repulsion*) . . .
JOSIE. (*stares at him, too startled and bewildered to be angry. Her voice trembles with surprising meekness*) . . .
TYRONE. (*now looks as bewildered by his action as she does*) . . .(*He picks up her glass*) . . .
JOSIE. (*still meek*) . . . (*She puts the glass on the ground*) . . .[31]

Is it an exaggeration to say that, in this scene, the dialogue supplements the stage directions and not the other way around? Although the words the characters speak are not precisely superfluous, it is the emotional index of the stage directions that, in concert with the actions they describe, shows us what happens. If O'Neill could not always find the words to express emotion, we must allow that he found a way around his "problem."

There is evidence to indicate that his deficiencies vis-à-vis dialogue played an important role in O'Neill's emphasis on the stage directions. He knew he had a problem, and he gives it to his alter ego, Edmund, in *Long Day's Journey into Night,* to confess:

TYRONE. (*stares at him impressed*) Yes, there's the makings of a poet in you all right. . . .
EDMUND. (*sardonically*) The *makings* of a poet. No, I'm afraid I'm like the guy who is always panhandling for a smoke. He hasn't even got the makings. He's only got the habit. I couldn't touch what I tried to tell you just now. I just stammered. That's the best I'll even do, I mean if I live. Well, it will be faithful realism, at least. Stammering is the native eloquence of us fog people.[32]

Writing about emotion on his own behalf, O'Neill once said:

[Emotions] are a better guide than our thoughts. Our emotions are instinctive. They are the result not only of our individual experiences but of the experiences of the whole human race, back through all the ages. They are the deep undercurrent, whereas our thoughts are often only the small individual surface reactions. Truth usually goes deep. So it reaches you only through your emotions.[33]

The expression of thought implies telling. Emotions, while also amenable to telling, must also be shown. In many of his plays, O'Neill almost totally foregoes thought and embarks on the expression of pure emotion, via the stage directions. This is particularly true at the climax, as in the final scene of *Beyond the Horizon*. Andrew and Ruth grieve over the body of Robert:

ANDREW. (*facing* RUTH, *the body between them—in a dead voice*) He's dead. (*With a sudden burst of fury*) God damn you, you never told him!

RUTH. (*piteously*) He was so happy without my lying to him.

ANDREW (*pointing to the body—trembling with the violence of his rage*) This is your doing, you damn woman, you coward, you murderess!

RUTH. (*sobbing*) Don't, Andy! I couldn't help it—and he knew how I'd suffered, too. He told you—to remember.

ANDREW. (*stares at her for a moment, his rage ebbing away, an expression of deep pity gradually coming over his face. Then he glances down at his brother and speaks brokenly in a compassionate voice*) Forgive me, Ruth—for his sake—and I'll remember— (RUTH *lets her hands fall from her face and looks at him uncomprehendingly. He lifts his eyes to hers and forces out falteringly*) I—you—we've both made a mess of things! We must try to help each other—and—in time—we'll come to know what's right— (*Desperately*) And perhaps we— (*But* RUTH, *if she is aware of his words, gives no sign. She remains silent, gazing at him dully with the sad humility of exhaustion, her mind already sinking back into that spent calm beyond the further troubling of any hope*).[34]

Homer E. Woodbridge observed that melodramatics of "the more distinctive O'Neill sort" turn up when the emotion of the scene overtakes the logic of the situation.[35] The words in this passage do express strong emotions—there is just no way to deny that they hold a certain intensity—but it is more the power of emotion as described in the stage directions, emotion that the actors must show the audience, that defines this final moment in which there is little if anything left to say. Andrew becomes virtually incoherent in his last, long speech, and his attempt to get through to Ruth cannot really be conveyed through the dialogue. O'Neill takes a situation already charged with melodramatic potential energy and heightens the effect significantly by devising an emotional subtext to express the pathos of the play's ending.

Turning to *Mourning Becomes Electra,* we have a very different—and brilliant—example of how O'Neill turned his problems with dialogue to his best advantage through the creative use of stage directions. Discussing the various phases he had gone through in seeking the right theatrical form for the trilogy, he explained how he ultimately arrived at the "masklike faces" of the Mannon family: "With *Mourning Becomes Electra,* masks were called for in one draft of the three plays. But the Classical connotation was too insistent. Masks in that connection demand great language to speak— which let me out of it with a sickening bump! . . . So it evolved ultimately into the 'masklike faces,' which expressed my intention tempered by the circumstances."[36] Each of the Mannons is introduced with a variation on the same stage direction: "*One is struck at once by the strange impression* [the character's face] *gives in repose of being not living flesh but a wonderfully life-like pale mask.*"

The general aim was to remove the highly emotional framework of theatrical expression that had characterized so much of his work up to that point. He strove, he noted in his work diary, to create "straight dialogue—as simple and direct and dynamic as possible—with as few words—stop doing things to these characters—let them reveal themselves."[37] Searching for a means of emphasizing the suppressed emotionality of the characters, O'Neill hit upon the idea of the masklike faces, and explained it to himself thus:

Keep mask connotation—but as Mannon *background,* not foreground!—what I want from this mask concept is a dramatic, arresting visual symbol of the separateness, the fated isolation of this family, the mark of their fate which makes them dramatically distinct from the rest of the world—I see now how to retain this effect without the use of built-in masks—by make-up—in *repose* (that is, background) the Mannon faces are like life-like death masks. . . . I can visualize the death-mask-like expression of characters' faces in repose suddenly being torn open by passion as extraordinarily effective—moreover, it's exact visual representation of what I want expressed. . . . [38]

Feeling incapable of providing a "great language" to complement the property masks of the Greek classical theater, O'Neill compromised with makeup and a very important reliance upon the actors to maintain the type of deathlike facial expressions described in the stage directions. Moreover, earlier in his notes he agreed with his original decision to "stick to modern tempo of dialogue without attempt at pretense of Civil War-time lingo. That part of 1st draft is right."[39]

What is really interesting about this motif of repressed emotions and deathlike mask–faces is that it allowed O'Neill to reduce to a minimum the stage directions that, in other plays, guide the actors' approach to the emotional subtext of their characters in action. Instead, the mask–faces determine the quality of emotional expression very effectively, stated all at once at the beginning of the play.

The following exchange between Christine and Lavinia Mannon in *The Homecoming* typifies the operation of the prevailing emotional framework:

CHRISTINE. You wanted Adam Brant yourself!
LAVINIA. That's a lie!
CHRISTINE. And now you know you can't have him, you're determined that at least you'll take him from me!
LAVINIA. No!
CHRISTINE. But if you told your father, I'd have to go away with Adam. He'd be mine still. You can't bear that thought, even at the price of my disgrace, can you?
LAVINIA. It's your evil mind!
CHRISTINE. I know you, Vinnie! I've watched you ever since you were little, trying to do exactly what you're doing now! You've tried to become the wife of your father and the mother of Orin! You've always schemed to steal my place!
LAVINIA. (*wildly*) No! It's you who have stolen all love from me since the time I was born! (*Then her manner becomes threatening*) But I don't want to listen to any more of your lies and excuses! I want to know right now whether you're going to do what I told you or not![40]

The scene is certainly filled with potential violence, as the repeated exclamation points indicate. But the exclamation points themselves do not represent the outer expression of emotion. O'Neill was most fond of this manner of punctuation, but nowhere else in the canon does it substitute for stage directions. Lavinia's last speech, with four exclamation points, is nonetheless the only one to carry a stage direction and really shows how O'Neill pursued his vision of the performance.

Had he not specified the prevailing mode of masklike faces, O'Neill would probably not have ever achieved the desired results. Most actresses playing Lavinia would interpret this passage as a continuous ascending emotional curve, finally reaching the crescendo that O'Neill labels "*wildly.*" His own stated conception of the performance calls for something very different. When Lavinia becomes "*wild*" her face, masklike in repose, is "suddenly . . . torn open by passion." It is, as O'Neill believed it would be, extraordinarily effective.

The issue here, then, is not whether this or any other scene of O'Neill's falls over into the realm of what we call melodrama or whether he relies so heavily on emotion as to damage the credibility of his characters. Instead, we should recognize that, from whatever artistic angle he approaches a scene or play, the quality of emotional expression depends to a very high degree upon the actors' use of the stage directions that influence the theatrical effect of the characters' words and actions. His dependence on the stage directions to ensure that actors carried out—or at least understood—his intentions gives further evidence for the idea that O'Neill, perhaps more than any other modern playwright, could not separate the act of writing from the idea of performance. This connection between what the characters say and do, and the ways in which they go about it, renders the stage directions indispensable to grasping O'Neill's conception of emotional expression. Without the stage directions, the plays remain open to a broad range of interpretations on the stage. To ignore them is to ignore much of his meaning—to change them is to change the play.

In a like manner, every stage direction can yield some useful information to the actor. To analyze them as merely "realizable in the theater" or not does a disservice to the actor, his talent, his training, and his artistic integrity. Looking at each individual stage direction and asking, "Can the actor really do that?" and "Can he really show that to the audience?" lead to an atomistic view of stage presentation and reveal little of true interest. A broader means of examining the stage directions has the potential for drawing back the curtain that has until now obscured a vital element of O'Neill's endeavor. He wrote for the stage. He created characters that he intended to be presented by actors.

His preoccupation with the actor's performance, as implicit and explicitly demonstrated in the stage directions, suggests a serious interest in how these artists do what they do. We know that O'Neill had received a lifetime of experience in watching actors practice their art long before he ever took up a pen. His early forays into the professional theater must have deepened and expanded the knowledge he brought to playwrighting. The remarkable actors who played his characters—Charles S. Gilpin, Walter Huston, Mary Blair, Pauline Lord, Louis Wolheim, Paul Robeson—offered him an education in the mysteries of acting that few playwrights have enjoyed. Rightly or wrongly, O'Neill felt certain he knew what actors were all about.

What is needed, then, is a study of O'Neill's work with the actor. The stage directions can reveal his central concerns regarding the stage presentation of his characters, the ways in which he expressed his intentions to the actor, and the means by which he hoped they would attack and resolve a variety of artistic problems. Ultimately, this line of inquiry will attain its true relevance by demonstrating that a thorough understanding of the operation of O'Neill's stage directions goes beyond the actor to the theatrical fabric of the plays themselves. Adopting the actor's perspective gives *us* a new perspective. We stand at the epicenter of the action and gain a deeper appreciation of O'Neill as a playwright, which is to say a man of the stage.

NOTES

1. Harold Bloom, ed., *Eugene O'Neill's "Long Day's Journey into Night,"* Modern Critical Interpretations (New York: Chelsea House Publishers, 1987), vii–viii.

2. See, for example, Louis Sheaffer, *O'Neill: Son and Artist* (Boston: Little, Brown and Co., 1973), 568–89; Helen Deutsch and Stella Hanau, *The Provincetown: A Story of the Theatre* (New York: Farrar and Rinehart, 1931; reprint, New York: Russell and Russell, 1972), 96; Arthur Gelb and Barbara Gelb, *O'Neill* (New York: Harper and Row, 1962), 524–28, 650–51; John McCabe, *George M. Cohan: The Man Who Owned Broadway* (Garden City, N.Y.: Doubleday and Co., 1973), 226, 227, 228.

3. John Anderson, "Eugene O'Neill," *Theatre Arts Monthly* 15, no. 11 (November 1931): 939.

4. Virgil Geddes, "Eugene O'Neill," *Theatre Arts Monthly* 15, no. 11 (November 1931): 944.

5. Edmund Wilson, "Eugene O'Neill as a Prose Writer," in *O'Neill and His Plays: Four Decades of Criticism,* ed. Oscar Cargill, N. Bryllion Fagin, and William J. Fisher (New York: New York University Press, 1961), 464.

6. John Henry Raleigh, *The Plays of Eugene O'Neill* (Carbondale: Southern Illinois University Press, 1965), 210–11.

7. Ibid., 211.

8. Ibid., 113.

9. Timo Tiusanen, *O'Neill's Scenic Images* (Princeton, N.J.: Princeton University Press, 1968); Egil Törnqvist, *A Drama of Souls: Studies in O'Neill's Super-naturalistic Technique* (New Haven: Yale University Press, 1969). For histories of productions of O'Neill plays, see Mary H. Arbenz, "The Plays of Eugene O'Neill as Presented by the Theatre Guild" (Ph.D. diss., University of Illinois, 1961); David Byron Cook, "José Quintero: The Circle in the Square Years, 1950–1963" (Ph.D. diss., University of Kansas, 1981); Doris Hart, "An Historical Analysis of Three New York Productions of Eugene O'Neill's *Long Day's Journey into Night*" (Ph.D. diss., New York University, 1982).

10. Tiusanen, *O'Neill's Scenic Images,* 16.

11. Ibid., 3–4.

12. Ibid., 12.

13. Ibid., 39.

14. Ibid., 39–41.

15. Gelb and Gelb, *O'Neill*, 325.

16. Egil Törnqvist, *A Drama of Souls*, 25, 27.

17. Eugene O'Neill, *Anna Christie*, in *The Plays of Eugene O'Neill*, vol. 1 (New York: Random House, Inc., Modern Library, 1982), 68.

18. Eugene O'Neill, *The First Man*, in *The Plays of Eugene O'Neill*, vol. 2 (New York: Random House, Inc., Modern Library, 1982), 594.

19. Tiusanen, *O'Neill's Scenic Images*, 91.

20. George Jean Nathan, *The House of Satan* (New York: Alfred A. Knopf, 1926), 201.

21. Eugene O'Neill, letter to George Jean Nathan, 1 February 1921, in *"As Ever, Gene": The Letters of Eugene O'Neill to George Jean Nathan*, ed. Nancy L. Roberts and Arthur W. Roberts (Rutherford, N.J.: Fairleigh Dickinson University Press, 1987), 44.

22. Doris V. Falk, *Eugene O'Neill and the Tragic Tension: An Interpretive Study of the Plays* (New Brunswick, N.J.: Rutgers University Press, 1958), 172.

23. Eric Bentley, *The Life of the Drama* (New York: Atheneum, 1964), 200.

24. Bernard Beckerman, *Dynamics of Drama: Theory and Method of Analysis* (New York: Alfred A. Knopf, 1970), 100.

25. Francis Fergusson, "Melodramatist," in *O'Neill and His Plays*, 272–73 (see n. 5).

26. John Hutchens, "*Mourning Becomes Electra*," in Cargill et al., *O'Neill and His Plays*, 190 (see n. 5).

27. Virginia Floyd, "The Enduring O'Neill: Which Plays Will Survive?—A Panel Discussion," *Eugene O'Neill Newsletter*, Preview Issue (January 1977): 12.

28. John Mason Brown, *Dramatis Personae* (London: Hamish Hamilton, 1929), 13.

29. Eugene O'Neill, *The Straw* in *The Plays of Eugene O'Neill*, vol. 1, 389 (see n. 17).

30. Edd Winfield Parks, "Eugene O'Neill's Symbolism," *Sewanee Review* 43, no. 4 (October–December 1935): 442–43.

31. Eugene O'Neill, *A Moon for the Misbegotten* (New York: Random House, Inc., 1952), 121–22.

32. Eugene O'Neill, *Long Day's Journey into Night* (New Haven: Yale University Press, 1955), 154.

33. Törnqvist, *A Drama of Souls*, 40.

34. Eugene O'Neill, *Beyond the Horizon*, in *The Plays of Eugene O'Neill*, vol. 1, 168–69 (see n. 17).

35. Homer E. Woodbridge, "Beyond Melodrama," in *O'Neill and His Plays*, 314 (see n. 5 above).

36. Eugene O'Neill, "Memoranda on Masks," *The Unknown O'Neill: Unpublished or Unfamiliar Writings of Eugene O'Neill*, ed. Travis Bogard (New Haven: Yale University Press, 1988), 409.

37. Eugene O'Neill, "Working Notes and Extracts from a Fragmentary Work Diary," in *The Unknown O'Neill*, 400 (see n. 36).

38. Ibid., 400.

39. Ibid., 397.

40. Eugene O'Neill, *The Homecoming* from *Mourning Becomes Electra*, in *The Plays of Eugene O'Neill*, vol. 2, 33 (see n. 18).

13

Theater and the Critics

Linda Herr

While surveying the critical landscape in a pungent essay entitled "The Humanist and the Artist," Robert Brustein—the current artistic director of the American Repertory Theater at Harvard's Loeb Drama Center and former dean of the Yale School of Drama—found the humanist and artist behaving toward "each other like two mutually hostile and antagonistic carnivores."[1] When they are not hurling bloody epithets at their adversaries, they tend "to ignore each other." This extreme oscillation of humanists and artists between all-out war and frosty disregard is in no small part due to the intellectual snobbery of academics. University scholars in today's academe, said Brustein, wrinkle their nose at the working theater artist and generally view theater as an alien and lesser form, one that great writers would have avoided had a better form been available to them.[2] In fact, few critics, and I am speaking now of the opening night reviewer as well as the scholarly critic, have specifically set out to nurture or inspire a playwright or theater artist. Some exceptions do come to mind: Brandes and Ibsen, Jan Kott and Peter Brook, and perhaps we might also include Kenneth Macgowan and Eugene O'Neill. But in general, critics and theater artists treat one another with hostility or less than benign neglect.

Why does this state of affairs prevail, and prevail so dramatically, between the critic and the theater artist? Surely, it has to do with the process of their pursuits. The critic works in solitude at a desk or carrel, finding truth and meaning by analyzing words and syntax. The theater artist finds truth and meaning in the moment-to-moment work of the rehearsal hall. It is in the spontaneous gesture, the verbal pause, the shift of movement, or the cadence of an important monologue that the theater artist notes and shapes the meaning of the text. Furthermore, Brustein, Kott, Brook, and a host of theater artists believe that a play has not found its life until what was discovered in the rehearsal hall is played on the boards in front of an audience. A play only becomes a play, then, in the act of performance. The mere text is embryonic.

Certainly, Eugene O'Neill was a consummate man of the theater who deeply understood the importance of the rehearsal process. We know that he spent hours in rehearsal and many more hours preparing for the rehearsal procedure through his close attention to the casting choices and design details of most of his productions. Yet although scholars customarily mention his ferocious attention to this area of his art, they usually focus their critical attention not on the preparations for performance or its results but on the script. Perhaps the rehearsal process is too ephemeral and imprecise to yield comprehensive analysis, but it is clear that O'Neill knew the importance of casting and rehearsal to his art. It is in the realm of the preludes to performance that a play lives or dies, takes wing or expires. The arid or leaden moment is found in the studio where, if anywhere, rewriting and restructuring can keep the play alive.

Another man of the theater, the playwright J. B. Priestley, has complained of the exhausting rehearsal process, the "cases of whiskey and pounds and pounds of tobacco," the endless and lengthy changes, rewrites, conversations, and more rewrites that constitute the typical round of rehearsals.[3] Yet Priestley conceded that theater cannot exist on a page. "If there is no Theatre, then there is no drama, only something else to read. . . . A man who writes to be read and not to be performed is not a dramatist. The dramatist keeps in mind not the printer but a company of actors, not readers but playgoers. He is as closely tied to the Theatre as a chef is to the kitchen."[4] For all of his well-documented frustration with casting and rehearsing, O'Neill was firmly grounded in the theatrical process, knew its importance, knew its rules, and knew that his presence at rehearsals was necessary if the play he intended was to be realized in performance.

Yet when the successful runs end, and all of the actors and actresses, technicians, crew, and ushers have gone home, when the lights have dimmed for the last time and the stage and house are dark and empty, what remains of the performance is the text itself.[5] It is in this silent space between performances, when the script has been returned to the shelf, that the solitary critic begins to explore the text in ways not possible within the noisy complexity of rehearsal and performances. If, as in O'Neill's case, the years also yield a cache of letters, journals, work diaries, and reminiscences of those who worked closely with him in and out of production, the researcher can shed even more light on issues with important implications for future performances.

It certainly matters a great deal to theatrical practitioners that a generation of scholars have traced both the symbolic structure of O'Neill's plays and their autobiographical backbone while documenting the fact that his characters and their relationships are fashioned not only from their ostensible fictive or mythic starting points but also from O'Neill's life and family. The critical insights concerning the autobiographical nature of his work have surely changed the way in which directors, actors, and designers currently conceptualize O'Neill, in contrast to the interpretations of the first productions, particularly the works of his early and middle periods, when the study of the playwright's life was in its infancy and autobiographical issues were therefore not a consideration.

I speak from experience. As the director of a staging of *Desire Under the Elms* mounted at Connecticut College during the centennial year, I can attest that the production was deeply influenced by the critical insights of scholars such as Arthur Gelb and Barbara Gelb and Louis Sheaffer concerning the influence of O'Neill's life, especially his memories of grief and loss, on the crafting of the play. Everyone involved in the production was guided by the awareness of the presence of O'Neill's life in the play not because we had all been seduced by some mutation of the intentional fallacy but because an understanding of the relationship between biography and art in *Desire Under the Elms* enabled us to see more clearly and deeply the dramatic lines of force that were *in the play*. Resonances of O'Neill's life echoing in the mouths of the actors created an acute and particular richness in their approaches to the roles. Innumerable aspects of the play—Abbie speaking of the importance of home to Eben, Ephraim's need for Abbie to understand how he wrestled with the stones and God himself to create the farm, the tension between father and sons, the murder of the baby, the awkwardness of parentage, the painful confusion between maternal and sexual love, and many more—became for us even more poignant and powerful through our understanding of their roots in O'Neill's own knowledge and sorrow. So it was that the situations and relationships in *Desire Under the Elms* were interpreted afresh and the music of the dialogue heard anew by the players because of the historical and analytical work of scholars and critics.

As auditions of both student and professional performers were being held for this production of *Desire Under the Elms,* I cast a young black actress from New York, Vicki Tanner, in the role of Abbie. This was an interpretive act. Although the racial aspect of this casting decision caused controversy, the choice underscored the importance to Abbie of finding a place to belong, a real home. Moreover, it clarified the struggle of Eben to break his obsessive ties to his dead mother and find a mature sexuality with a woman not of his blood. Both themes are as vital to the play as they were vital to the life of its author, a fact that scholarly studies of O'Neill helped me to understand.

Thus although the artist and the critic may be frequently at loggerheads, may too often come together only to quarrel, the artist can heed and assimilate the critic's work by using nuances in voice, movement, and gesture and other conditions of performance to create interpretive patterns that embody current critical insights. The play is then played and seen in its appropriate context, the theater, where the intellectual and practical dimensions of drama can find a balancing point.

But does this coin have another side? Can the critic learn from performance? Probably not if he believes with André Bazin that "one would never deny that the essential thing in the theater is the text."6 But this is a problematic conclusion, as our very language tells us. The English word *theater* comes from the Greek *theatron,* which means "place for seeing" and therefore emphasizes the spectacle of performance. *Drama* in Greek means "action," and at the dawn of criticism Aristotle described tragedy as the "representation [i.e., imitation] of an action." He did not scant what we would call the text, for he realized that language is vital to tragedy and that the soul of tragedy is its plot, but he insisted that a play is language in motion (*Poetics* 1449b). Aristotle also warned that in constructing dramas the writer should picture the action in his mind's eye to find the truth of the play and avoid absurdity: "In constructing plots and *completing the effect by the help of dialogue* [emphasis mine] the poet should, as far as possible, keep the scene before his eyes. Only thus by getting the picture as clear as if he were present at the actual event, will he find what is fitting and detect contradictions."7 Kenneth Reckford, an Aristophanic scholar as familiar with modern drama as he is with Aristotle's thoughts on tragedy, gives us reason to believe that, whether the critic knows it or not, he needs a dynamic visual conception of a play—"as if he were present at the actual event"—as much as the playwright does:

It was my experience of directing Aristophanes' *Clouds* at Harvard in 1959 that, more than anything, convinced me that most criticism of that play was ridiculously off base. Reading in depth is hard, and takes training, but it need not be very complicated: indeed even a slight sense of performance brings out many simple and obvious things about a comic (or tragic) performance that the sophisticated critic so often ignores. When Tom Stoppard lectures on the "event and the text [i.e., performance and the script]," he prefaces his remarks by telling of an experience in California, when he told an audience of university professors that he did not write his plays to be studied. The professors looked absolutely appalled, and he realized that what was unimportant to him—studying the plays—was in fact their justification for existing.8

Enactment is the perfection of a dramatic text, and the critic should never forget it.9 If he does, he simply cannot do the job of truly comprehending drama.

In the end theater artists and critics share common ground, for by the very nature of what they do both are dedicated in their different but kindred ways to the interpretation of drama, the loving labor of striving to reveal what it means and how it works. They are respectively the practitioners and theoreticians of the same ancient, living art. The world-wide O'Neill centennial has brought the contemplators and the doers of drama together to celebrate one of the artists who constitute their raison d'être. In testimony to that common ground the lectures in this volume offer the performer, the director, and other theater artists a surer sense of where to stand in a creative approach to staging O'Neill.

NOTES

This chapter was improved by the suggestions of Richard F. Moorton, Jr.

1. Robert Brustein, "The Humanist and the Artist," *Who Needs Theater? Dramatic Opinions* (New York: Atlantic Monthly Press, 1987), 313.

2. Ibid. (with special reference to Lionel Trilling), 314.

3. J. B. Priestley, *The Art of the Dramatist: A Lecture Together with Appendices and Discursive Notes* (London: Heineman Educational Books, 1973), 66.

4. Ibid., 3, 66.

5. As Brustein ("The Humanist and the Artist," 311) noted, "It is a paradox of the theatre that a text has no real life until it is acted, yet the text is the one thing about the performance that manages to survive."

6. André Bazin, *What Is Cinema?,* vol. 1, trans. Hugh Gray (Berkeley: University of California Press, 1967), 111.

7. *Poetics* 1455b; translation from W. Hamilton Fyfe's rendering of the *Poetics* in *Aristotle: "The Poetics" ; "Longinus" : "On the Sublime" ; Demetrius: "On Style,"* trans. W. Hamilton Fyfe and W. Rhys Roberts, Loeb Classical Library, rev. ed. (Cambridge, Mass.: Harvard University Press, 1932), 65.

8. Kenneth Reckford, *Aristophanes' Old-and-New Comedy,* vol. 1 (Chapel Hill, N.C.: University of North Carolina Press, 1987), 141.

9. As the dramatist Priestley puts it in the first sentence of *The Art of the Dramatist* (3): "A dramatist writes for the Theatre."

Works Cited

This list includes virtually all of the reference sources in this book, excluding newspapers, encyclopedias, and literary works not by O'Neill quoted from a second source or only in passing.

Adkins, Arthur W. H. *Merit and Responsibility: A Study in Greek Values.* Oxford: Clarendon Press, 1960.

Ahuja, Chaman. *Tragedy, Modern Temper, and O'Neill.* Atlantic Highlands, N.J.: Humanities Press, 1984.

Alexander, Doris M. "Psychological Fate in *Mourning Becomes Electra.*" *Publications of the Modern Language Association* 68, no. 5 (December 1953): 923–34.

Anderson, John. "Eugene O'Neill." *Theatre Arts Monthly* 15, no. 11 (November 1931): 938–42.

Andrew, Dudley. *Concepts in Film Theory.* Oxford: Oxford University Press, 1984.

Arbenz, Mary H. "The Plays of Eugene O'Neill as Presented by the Theatre Guild." Ph.D. diss., University of Illinois, 1961.

Aristotle: "The Poetics"; "Longinus": "On the Sublime"; Demetrius: "On Style." Translated by W. Hamilton Fyfe and R. Rhys Roberts. Loeb Classical Library. Revised edition. Cambridge, Mass.: Harvard University Press, 1932.

Barlow, Judith E. *Final Acts: The Creation of Three Late O'Neill Plays.* Athens, Ga.: University of Georgia Press, 1985.

Bazin, André. *What Is Cinema?* Vol. 1. Translated by Hugh Gray. Berkeley: University of California Press, 1967.

Beckerman, Bernard. *Dynamics of Drama: Theory and Method of Analysis.* New York: Alfred A. Knopf, 1970.

Benedict, Ruth. *The Chrysanthemum and the Sword: Patterns of Japanese Culture.* Cambridge, Mass.: Riverside Press for Houghton Mifflin, 1946.

Bentley, Eric. *The Life of the Drama.* New York: Atheneum, 1964.

———. *In Search of Theater.* New York: Alfred A. Knopf, 1953.

Blau, Herbert. *Take Up the Bodies: Theater at the Vanishing Point.* Urbana: University of Illinois Press, 1982.

Bloom, Harold, ed. *Eugene O'Neill.* Modern Critical Views. New York: Chelsea House Publishers, 1987.

———. *Eugene O'Neill's "Long Day's Journey into Night."* Modern Critical Interpretations. New York: Chelsea House Publishers, 1987.

Blum, H. "On the Concept and Consequences of the Primal Scene." *Psychoanalytical Quarterly* 48 (1979): 27–47.

Bogard, Travis. *Contour in Time: The Plays of Eugene O'Neill.* New York: Oxford University Press, 1972.

Boulton, Agnes. *Part of a Long Story*. Garden City, N.Y.: Doubleday and Co., 1958.
Braudy, Leo. *The World in a Frame: What We See in Films*. Garden City, N.Y.: Doubleday and Co., Anchor Press, 1976.
Brooks, Van Wyck. *The Confident Years, 1885–1915*. New York: E. P. Dutton and Co., 1952.
Brown, John Mason. *Dramatis Personae*. London: Hamish Hamilton, 1929.
Brustein, Robert. *Who Needs Theater? Dramatic Opinions*. New York: Atlantic Monthly Press, 1987.
Cargill, Oscar; Fagin, N. Bryllion; and Fisher, William J., eds. *O'Neill and His Plays: Four Decades of Criticism*. New York: New York University Press, 1961.
Carlson, Marvin. *Theories of the Theatre: A Historical and Critical Survey, from the Greeks to the Present*. Ithaca, N.Y.: Cornell University Press, 1984.
Chabrowe, Leonard. *Ritual and Pathos: The Theater of O'Neill*. Lewisburg, Pa.: Bucknell University Press, 1976.
Chasseguet-Smirgel, Janine. *Sexuality and Mind: The Role of the Father and the Mother in the Psyche*. New York: New York University Press, 1986.
Chothia, Jean. *Forging a Language: A Study of the Plays of Eugene O'Neill*. Cambridge: Cambridge University Press, 1979.
Clark, Barrett H. "Aeschylus and O'Neill." *English Journal* 21, no. 9 (November 1932): 699–710.
————. *European Theories of the Drama with a Supplement on the American Drama*. Revised edition. New York: Crown Publishing Co., 1947.
Clurman, Harold. "The O'Neills." *Nation* 182, no. 9 (3 March 1956): 182–83.
Commins, Saxe. *"Love and Admiration and Respect": The O'Neill-Commins Correspondence*. Edited by Dorothy Commins. Durham, N.C.: Duke University Press, 1986.
Conrad, Joseph. *The Nigger of the "Narcissus."* Concord Edition. Garden City, N.Y.: Doubleday and Co., 1914.
Cook, David Byron. "José Quintero: The Circle in the Square Years, 1950–1963." Ph.D. diss., University of Kansas, 1981.
De Unamuno, Miguel. *The Tragic Sense of Life in Men and Peoples*. Translated by J. E. Crawford Flitch. London: Macmillan and Co., 1921.
Deutsch, Helen, and Hanau, Stella. *The Provincetown: A Story of the Theatre*. New York: Farrar and Rinehart, 1931. Reprint. New York: Russell and Russell, 1972..
Dodds, E. R. *The Greeks and the Irrational*. Sather Classical Lectures, vol. 25. Berkeley: University of California Press, 1951.
Drucker, Trudy. "Sexuality as Destiny: The Shadow Lives of O'Neill's Women." *Eugene O'Neill Newsletter* 6, no. 2 (Summer–Fall 1982): 7–10.
Eaton, Walter Prichard. "O'Neill—'New Risen Attic Stream'?" *American Scholar* 6, no. 3 (Summer 1937): 304–12.
Eco, Umberto. *A Theory of Semiotics*. Bloomington: Indiana University Press, 1976.
Elam, Keir. *The Semiotics of Theatre and Drama*. London: Methuen, 1980.
Ellman, Richard. *The Consciousness of Joyce*. New York: Oxford University Press, 1977.
Emerson, Caryl. *Boris Godunov: Transpositions of a Russian Theme*. Bloomington: Indiana University Press, 1986.
Engel, Edwin A. *The Haunted Heroes of Eugene O'Neill*. Cambridge, Mass.: Harvard University Press, 1953.
Esman, A. "The Primal Scene: A Review and Reconsideration." *Psychoanalytic Study of the Child* 28 (1973): 49–81.
Falk, Doris V. *Eugene O'Neill and the Tragic Tension: An Interpretive Study of the Plays*. New Brunswick, N.J.: Rutgers University Press, 1958.
Floyd, Virginia. *Eugene O'Neill: A World View*. New York: Frederick Ungar Publishing Co., 1979.
————. *Eugene O'Neill at Work: Newly Released Ideas for Plays*. New York: Frederick Ungar Publishing Co., 1981.

———. *Eugene O'Neill: A World View*. New York: Frederick Ungar Publishing Co., 1979.

———. *The Plays of Eugene O'Neill: A New Assessment*. New York: Frederick Ungar Publishing Co., 1987.

Floyd, Virginia, et al. " 'The Enduring O'Neill: Which Plays Will Survive?'—A Panel Discussion." *Eugene O'Neill Newsletter* Preview Issue (January 1977): 2–15.

Foley, Helene, ed. "The 'Female Intruder' Reconsidered: Women in Aristophanes' *Lysistrata* and *Ecclesiazusae*." *Classical Philology* 77, no. 1 (January 1982): 1–21.

———. *Reflections of Women in Antiquity*. New York: Gordon and Breach, Science Publishers, 1981.

Frank, Joseph. *The Widening Gyre: Crisis and Mastery in Modern Literature*. New Brunswick, N.J.: Rutgers University Press, 1963.

Frenz, Horst. *Eugene O'Neill*. Berlin: Colloquium Verlag, 1965.

Frenz, Horst, and Mueller, Martin. "More Shakespeare and Less Aeschylus in Eugene O'Neill's *Mourning Becomes Electra*." *American Literature* 38, no. 1 (May 1966): 85–100.

Frenz, Horst, and Tuck, Susan, eds. *Eugene O'Neill's Critics: Voices from Abroad*. Carbondale, Ill.: Southern Illinois University Press, 1984.

Freud, Sigmund. *The Standard Edition of the Complete Psychological Works of Sigmund Freud*. Translated from the German under the general editorship of James Strachey in collaboration with Anna Freud and assisted by Alix Strachey and Alan Tyson. Vol. 16 (1916–1917), *Introductory Lectures on Psycho-Analysis (Part III)*. London: Hogarth Press and the Institute of Psycho-Analysis, 1963; Vol. 17 (1917–1919), *"An Infantile Neurosis" and Other Works*. London: Hogarth Press and the Institute of Psycho-Analysis, 1955; Vol. 18 (1920–1922), *"Beyond the Pleasure Principle," "Group Psychology," and Other Works*. London: Hogarth Press and the Institute of Psycho-Analysis, 1955; Vol. 19 (1923–1925), *"The Ego and the Id" and Other Works*. London: Hogarth Press and the Institute of Psycho-Analysis, 1961; Vol. 21 (1927–1931), *"The Future of an Illusion," "Civilization and Its Discontents," and Other Works*. London: Hogarth Press and the Institute of Psycho-Analysis, 1961.

Gagarin, Michael. *Aeschylean Drama*. Berkeley: University of California Press, 1976.

———. "Morality in Homer." *Classical Philology* 82, no. 4 (October 1987): 285–306.

Geddes, Virgil. "Eugene O'Neill." *Theatre Arts Monthly* 15, no. 11 (November 1931): 943–46.

Gelb, Arthur, and Gelb, Barbara. *O'Neill*. New York: Harper and Row, 1962.

Genet, Jean. *The Balcony*. Translated by Bernard Frechtman. Revised edition. New York: Grove Press, 1966.

Gill, Brendan. "Unhappy Tyrones." *New Yorker,* 12 May 1986, 93–95.

Goldberg, Isaac. *The Theatre of George Jean Nathan*. New York: Simon and Schuster, 1926.

Goldman, Michael. *The Actor's Freedom: Toward a Theory of Drama*. New York: Vintage Press, 1975.

Gorchakov, Nikolai. *The Theater in Soviet Russia*. Translated by Edgar Lehrman. New York: Columbia University Press, 1957.

Grene, David, and Lattimore, Richmond, eds. *The Complete Greek Tragedies*. Vol. 1, *Aeschylus*. Chicago: University of Chicago Press, 1959.

Halfmann, Ulrich. *Unreal Realism: O'Neills dramatisches Werk im Spiegel seiner szenischen Kunst* (Francke Verlag: Bern, 1969).

Harrington, John, ed. *Film and/as Literature*. Englewood Cliffs, N.J.: Prentice-Hall Press, 1977.

Hart, Doris. "An Historical Analysis of Three New York Productions of Eugene O'Neill's *Long Day's Journey into Night*." Ph.D. diss., New York University, 1982.

Havelock, Eric A. *"DIKAIOSUNE:* An Essay in Greek Intellectual History." *Phoenix* 23, no. 1 (Spring 1969): 49–70.

Hayman, Ronald. *Nietzsche: A Critical Life*. New York: Oxford University Press, 1980.

Heilman, Robert B. *The Iceman, the Arsonist, and the Troubled Agent: Tragedy and Melodrama on the Modern Stage*. Seattle: University of Washington Press, 1973.

Heller, Erich. *The Disinherited Mind*. Cambridge, Eng.: Bowes and Bowes, 1952.
Husserl, Edmund. *The Phenomenology of Internal Time-Consciousness*. Translated by James S. Churchill and edited by Martin Heidegger. Bloomington: Indiana University Press, 1964.
James, William. *The Principles of Psychology*. Vol. 1. New York: Henry Holt and Co., 1890.
Kael, Pauline. *5001 Nights at the Movies: A Guide from A to Z*. New York: Holt, Rinehart and Winston, 1982.
Kalbouss, George. *The Plays of the Russian Symbolists*. East Lansing, Mich.: Russian Language Journal, 1982.
Kanzer, Mark, and Glenn, Jules, eds. *Freud and His Patients*. New York: Jason Aronson, 1980.
Kardiner, Abram (with the collaboration of Ralph Linton, Cora Du Bois, and James West [pseud.]). *The Psychological Frontiers of Society*. New York: Columbia University Press, 1945.
Karl, Frederick R. *Modern and Modernism: The Sovereignty of the Artist, 1885–1925*. New York: Atheneum, 1985.
Kazan, Elia. *Elia Kazan: A Life*. New York: Alfred A. Knopf, 1988.
Kern, Stephen. *The Culture of Time and Space, 1880–1918*. Cambridge, Mass.: Harvard University Press, 1983.
Kierkegaard, Søren. *"Fear and Trembling" and "The Sickness unto Death."* Translated and edited by Walter Lowrie. Garden City, N.Y.: Doubleday and Co., Anchor Press, 1954.
Kracauer, Siegfried. *Theory of Film: The Redemption of Physical Reality*. New York: Oxford University Press, 1960.
Kubler, George. *The Shape of Time: Remarks on the History of Things*. New Haven: Yale University Press, 1962.
Lemon, Lee T., and Reis, Marion J., trans. *Russian Formalist Criticism: Four Essays*. Lincoln: University of Nebraska Press, 1965.
Lesky, Albin. *Greek Tragic Poetry*. Translated by Matthew Dillon. New Haven. Yale University Press, 1983.
Lloyd-Jones, Hugh. *The Justice of Zeus*. Sather Classical Lectures, vol. 41. Berkeley: University of California Press, 1971.
Mahony, Patrick J. *Cries of the Wolf Man*. History of Psychoanalysis, no. 1. New York: International Universities Press, 1984.
Manheim, Michael. *Eugene O'Neill's New Language of Kinship*. Syracuse: Syracuse University Press, 1982.
Mast, G., and Cohen, M., eds. *Film Theory and Criticism*. 3d ed. New York: Oxford University Press, 1985.
McCabe, John. *George M. Cohan: The Man Who Owned Broadway*. Garden City, N.Y.: Doubleday and Co., 1973.
Meredith, George. *An Essay on Comedy and the Uses of the Comic Spirit*. Edited by Lane Cooper. Ithaca, N.Y.: Cornell University Press, 1956.
Miller, Arthur. *The Theater Essays of Arthur Miller*. Edited by Robert A. Martin. New York: Viking Press, 1978.
Milner, John. *Vladimir Tatlin and the Russian Avant-Garde*. New Haven: Yale University Press, 1983.
Mitchell, Juliet. *Psychoanalysis and Feminism*. New York: Pantheon Books, 1974.
Mitchell, Juliet, and Rose, Jacqueline, eds. *Feminine Sexuality*. New York: Pantheon Books, 1982.
Nathan, George Jean. *The House of Satan*. New York: Alfred A. Knopf, 1926.
———. *The Intimate Notebooks of George Jean Nathan*. New York: Alfred A. Knopf, 1932.
———. *The World of George Jean Nathan*. Edited by Charles Angoff. New York: Alfred A. Knopf, 1952.
Nelson, Doris. "O'Neill's Women." *Eugene O'Neill Newsletter* 6, no. 2 (Summer–Fall 1982): 3–7.

Nethercot, Arthur H. "The Psychoanalyzing of Eugene O'Neill." *Modern Drama* 3, no. 3 (December 1960): 242–56.
———. "The Psychoanalyzing of Eugene O'Neill: Part Two." *Modern Drama* 3, no. 4 (February 1961): 357–72.
———. "The Psychoanalyzing of Eugene O'Neill: Postscript." *Modern Drama* 8, no. 2 (September 1965): 150–55.
Nietzsche, Friedrich. *Nietzsche: Werke. Kritische Gesamtausgabe.* Pt. 3, vol. 2. Edited by Giorgio Colli and Mazzino Montinari. Berlin: Walter de Gruyter, 1973.
O'Neill, Eugene. *"As Ever, Gene": The Letters of Eugene O'Neill to George Jean Nathan.* Edited by Nancy L. Roberts and Arthur W. Roberts. Rutherford, N.J.: Fairleigh Dickinson University Press, 1987.
———. *Eugene O'Neill: Meisterdramen.* Frankfort: S. Fischer Verlag, 1963.
———. *Long Day's Journey into Night.* New Haven: Yale University Press, 1955.
———. *Lost Plays of Eugene O'Neill.* New York: Citadel Press, 1958.
———. *A Moon for the Misbegotten.* New York: Random House, Inc., 1952.
———. *More Stately Mansions.* New Haven: Yale University Press, 1964.
———. *Nine Plays by Eugene O'Neill.* Edited by Joseph Wood Krutch. New York: Random House, Inc., Modern Library, 1932.
———. *The Plays of Eugene O'Neill.* 3 vols. New York: Random House, Inc., Modern Library, 1982.
———. *Selected Letters of Eugene O'Neill.* Edited by Travis Bogard and Jackson R. Bryer. New Haven: Yale University Press, 1988.
———. *Seltsames Zwischenspiel.* Translated by Marianne Wentzel. Dramen der Zeit. Emsdetten:
Verlag Lechte, 1957.
———. *Ten "Lost" Plays of Eugene O'Neill.* New York: Random House, Inc., 1964.
———. *"The Theatre We Worked For": The Letters of Eugene O'Neill to Kenneth Macgowan.* Edited by Jackson R. Bryer with the assistance of Ruth M. Alvarez. New Haven: Yale University Press, 1982.
———. *A Touch of the Poet.* New Haven: Yale University Press, 1957.
———. *The Unknown O'Neill: Unpublished or Unfamiliar Writings of Eugene O'Neill.* Edited by Travis Bogard. New Haven: Yale University Press, 1988.
O'Neill, Joseph P. "The Tragic Theory of Eugene O'Neill." *Texas Studies in Literature and Language* 4, no. 4 (Winter 1963): 481–98.
Orlandello, John J.. *O'Neill on Film.* Rutherford, N.J.: Fairleigh Dickinson University Press, 1982.
Parks, Edd Winfield. "Eugene O'Neill's Symbolism." *Sewanee Review* 43, no. 4 (October–December 1935): 436–51.
Peradotto, John. "The Omen of the Eagles and the *ETHOS* of Agamemnon." *Phoenix* 23, no. 3 (Autumn 1969): 237–63.
Peristiany, J. G., ed. *Honour and Shame: The Values of Mediterranean Society.* London: Weidenfeld and Nicolson for the University of Chicago Press, 1966.
Priestley, John Boynton. *The Art of the Dramatist: A Lecture Together with Appendices and Discursive Notes.* London: Heineman Educational Books, 1973.
Quinn, Arthur Hobson. *A History of the American Drama from the Civil War to the Present Day.* Vol. 2. Revised Edition. New York: F. S. Crofts and Co., 1936.
Quintero, José. *If You Don't Dance They Beat You.* Boston: Little, Brown and Co., 1974.
Raleigh, John Henry. "O'Neill's *Long Day's Journey into Night* and New England Irish-Catholicism." *Partisan Review* 26, no. 4 (Fall 1959): 573–92.
———. *The Plays of Eugene O'Neill.* Carbondale: Southern Illinois University Press, 1965.
Reaver, J. Russell. *An O'Neill Concordance.* Vol. 2. Detroit: Gale Research Co., 1969.
Reckford, Kenneth. *Aristophanes' Old-and-New Comedy.* Vol. 1. Chapel Hill: University of North Carolina Press, 1987.
Rowell, George. *Theatre in the Age of Irving.* Totowa, N.J.: Rowman and Littlefield, 1981.

Schickel, Richard. *D. W. Griffith: An American Life.* New York: Simon and Schuster, 1984.

Seligson, M. E.; Abramson, L. V.; Semmel, A.; and von Baeyer, C. "Depressive Attributional Style." *Journal of Abnormal Psychology* 88 (1979): 242–47.

Sewall, Richard B. *The Vision of Tragedy.* New edition, enlarged. New Haven: Yale University Press, 1980.

Shaw, M. "The Female Intruder: Women in Fifth-Century Drama." *Classical Philology* 70, no. 4 (October 1975): 255–66.

Sheaffer, Louis. *O'Neill: Son and Artist.* Boston: Little, Brown and Co., 1973.

———. *O'Neill: Son and Playwright.* Boston: Little, Brown and Co., 1968.

Shelley, Mary, ed. *The Poetical Works of Percy Bysshe Shelley.* Vol. 1. Boston: Houghton, Mifflin and Co., 1865.

Slonim, Marc. *The Russian Theater from the Empire to the Soviets.* Cleveland and New York: World Publishing Co., 1961.

Smyth, Herbert Weir, trans. *Aeschylus.* Vol. 2. Loeb Classical Library. New York: G. P. Putnam's Sons, 1926.

States, Bert O. *Great Reckonings in Little Rooms: On the Phenomenology of Theater.* Berkeley: University of California Press, 1985.

Steiner, George. *Language and Silence: Essays on Language, Literature, and the Inhuman.* New York: Atheneum, 1977.

Steiner, Peter. *Russian Formalism: A Metapoetics.* Ithaca, N.Y.: Cornell University Press, 1984.

Taplin, Oliver. *The Stagecraft of Aeschylus: The Dramatic Use of Exits and Entrances in Greek Tragedy.* Oxford: Clarendon Press, 1977.

Terras, Victor, ed. *Handbook of Russian Literature.* New Haven: Yale University Press, 1985.

Tiusanen, Timo. *O'Neill's Scenic Images.* Princeton, N.J.: Princeton University Press, 1968.

Törnqvist, Egil. *A Drama of Souls: Studies in O'Neill's Super-naturalistic Technique.* New Haven: Yale University Press, 1969.

The Ursuline Manual, or a Collection of Prayers, Spiritual Exercises, etc., Interspersed with the Various Instructions Necessary for Forming Youth to the Practice of Solid Piety; Originally Arranged for the Young Ladies Educated at the Ursuline Convent, Cork. Revised by the Very Rev. John Power, D.D., and Approved by the Most Rev. John Hughes, D.D., Archbishop of New York. New York: Edward Dunigan and Brother, (James B. Kirker), No. 371 Broadway, 1859.

Valgemae, Mardi. *Accelerated Grimace: Expressionism in the American Drama of the 1920s.* Carbondale: Southern Illinois University Press, 1972.

Vellacott, Philip. "Has Good Prevailed? A Further Study of the *Oresteia.*" *Harvard Studies in Classical Philology* 81 (1977): 113–22.

Weissman, Philip. "Conscious and Unconscious Autobiographical Dramas of Eugene O'Neill." *Journal of the American Psychoanalytic Association* 5, no. 3 (July 1957): 432–60.

Wellman, Mac. "The Theatre of Good Intentions." *Performing Arts Journal* 24, vol. 8, no. 3 (1984): 59–70.

Williams, Tennessee. *The Theatre of Tennessee Williams.* Vol. 4. New York: New Directions, 1972.

Wilson, Elizabeth. *Adorned in Dreams: Fashion and Modernity.* Berkeley: University of California Press, 1987.

Winnington-Ingram, R. P. *Studies in Aeschylus.* Oxford: Alden Press for Cambridge University Press, 1983.

Zeitlin, Froma I. "The Dynamics of Misogyny: Myth and Myth-Making in the *Oresteia.*" *Arethusa* 2 (1978): 149–84.

Index

About the Contributors

ROGER BROWN is John Lindsley Professor of Psychology in Memory of William James at Harvard University and a member of the National Academy of Sciences. He has received many awards and honors, including an honorary doctorate of science at Northwestern University (1983) and the Fyssen International Prize in Cognitive Sciences (1984). Brown's numerous publications include the books *Words and Things, Psycholinguistics: Selected Papers* and *Social Psychology: The Second Edition* and chapters and articles on cognition, the psychology of music and language, and the psychological implications of literature.

BURTON L. COOPER is professor of English and associate dean of student affairs at Boston University, where he has taught a wide range of courses in literature, theater, and film and has served in many administrative capacities. He is the editor of *Twelve Prose Writers* and the coeditor of *Achievements in Fiction*. Cooper is also the translator of Roger Asselineau, *The Evolution of Walt Whitman*.

SPENCER GOLUB is associate professor of theatre and comparative literature at Brown University. He is the author of *Evreinov: The Theatre of Paradox and Transformation* and the Russian theater and drama entries for *The Cambridge Guide to World Theatre*. In addition, Golub has published many book reviews and articles on drama and film in journals including *Soviet Drama, Theatre and Film, Slavic and East European Drama and Theatre, Theatre Research International*, and *Theatre Quarterly*. His most recent articles relate *Hamlet*, Charlie Chaplin, gender, and socialist realism to Soviet theatrical iconography.

LINDA HERR is professor of theater at Connecticut College. She has directed widely in the modern idiom and has been a literary advisor for projects including the American Place Theater's production of James de Jongh's *Do Lord Remember Me* (1985) and *The Sea Mother's Son*, a television documentary on Eugene O'Neill. She is the author of the article "Dickens' Jaggers and Shaw's Bohun: A Study in Character Lifting!" in *Shaw Review* and is writing a monograph on the motif of dead babies in O'Neill's plays.

RICHARD F. MOORTON, JR., is associate professor of classics at Connecticut College. His book reviews, translations, and articles on Aristophanes, Virgil, and O'Neill have appeared in various journals, including *Eugene O'Neill Newsletter; Greek, Roman, and Byzantine Studies; Transactions of the American Philological Association; Classical Journal; Classical World; Classical and Modern Literature;* and *Papers on Language and Literature.* He is currently at work on a book on the political interpretation of Aristophanes.

S. GEORGIA NUGENT has taught at Swarthmore College and Princeton University and is now assistant professor of classics at Brown University. A past Fulbright and National Endowment for the Humanities research fellow, she is currently writing a book on the poetics of exile while on leave as a Howard Foundation fellow. Nugent has published book reviews and articles on the theory of comedy in antiquity and on O'Neill. Her forthcoming articles include studies on Ovid and Ausonius, and she is the author of *Allegory and Poetics: Structure and Imagery in Prudentius' "Psychomachia."*

KRISTIN PFEFFERKORN is associate professor of philosophy at Connecticut College. She is the author of *Novalis: A Romantic's Theory of Language and Poetry.* Pfefferkorn is presently at work on studies on two topics, the question of home from a phenomenological perspective and the role played by aesthetics as a medium for philosophical intuition in Japanese film.

JEFFREY ELLIOTT SANDS holds a doctorate in theater history and criticism from the University of Illinois at Urbana-Champaign. He is currently an arts administrator at the Krannert Center for the Performing Arts at that university. Sands conducts research into O'Neill's plays in production. His articles on O'Neill and theater have appeared in the *Eugene O'Neill Newsletter* and the *Bulletin of the Association of Performing Arts Presenters.*

RICHARD B. SEWALL is professor emeritus of English at Yale University. He has received honorary degrees from Williams College and Albertus Magnus College. Sewall co-edited the book *Tragedy: Modern Essays in Criticism.* He is the author of the acclaimed study *The Vision of Tragedy* and a distinguished biography in two volumes, *The Life of Emily Dickinson,* which won the National Book Award for biography that year.

He has also written many articles on topics including Jean-Jacques Rousseau, Dostoevski, Stephen Crane, and Emily Dickinson.

LOWELL SWORTZELL is professor of educational theater at New York University. He has written articles and reviews in the *New York Times Book Review, Theatre Journal, Children's Theatre Review, Eugene O'Neill Newsletter,* and *English Teacher,* among others. He is the editor of *All the World's a Stage: Modern Plays for Young People,* selected by the *New York Times Book Review* as an outstanding book of the year. He is also the author of *Here Come the Clowns: A Cavalcade of Comedy: From Antiquity to the Present* and the editor of *An International Guide to Children's Theatre and Educational Theatre* (Greenwood Press, 1989). Swortzell is also the coeditor of an O'Neill centennial edition of the *Recorder* and coeditor (with Liu Haiping) of a selection of the proceedings of the O'Neill centennial conference in Nanjing, China, *Eugene O'Neill in China* (Greenwood Press, 1991).

RITA TERRAS is professor emerita of German at Connecticut College. She is the author of more than fifty book reviews; among her books and articles are "Friedrich Justus Riedel. A German Sensualist," in *Lessing Yearbook IV,* "The Development of the Doctrine of the Three Faculties in German Aesthetics," in *Monatshefte,* "Juvenal und die satirische Struktur der *Nachtwachen* von Bonaventura," *German Quarterly,* and *Wilhelm Heinses Aesthetik.* Terras has also written articles on Günter Grass, Christa Wolf, Thomas Bernhard, and Simone de Beauvoir. She is also a translator and poet whose verse publications include *Unterwegs* and *Informative Definitionen.*

JANE TORREY is professor of psychology at Connecticut College. She is the author of "Phases of Feminist Re-vision in the Psychology of Personality," in *Teaching of Psychology* and "Teaching Standard English to Speakers of Other Dialects," in *Applications of Linguistics.* In addition, Torrey has published book reviews and articles in *Contemporary Psychology, Elementary English, Journal of Verbal Learning and Verbal Behavior, Harvard Educational Review, Journal of Contemporary Business,* and *Reading Research.*